CELEBRITIES
Series Editor: Anthony Elliott

Published
Ellis Cashmore, *Beckham*
Charles Lemert, *Muhammad Ali*
Chris Rojek, *Frank Sinatra*

Forthcoming
Dennis Altman, *Gore Vidal*
Cynthia Fuchs, *Eminem*
Richard Middleton, *John Lennon*
Daphne Read, *Oprah Winfrey*
Nick Stevenson, *David Bowie*
Jason Toynbee, *Bob Marley*

TYSON
Nurture of the Beast

ELLIS CASHMORE

polity

First published in 2005 by Polity Press

Polity Press
65 Bridge Street
Cambridge CB2 1UR, UK.

Polity Press
350 Main Street
Malden, MA 02148, USA

ISBN: 0-7456-3069-3
ISBN: 0-7456-3070-7 (paperback)

A catalogue record for this book is available from the British Library.

Typeset in 11 on 13 pt Palatino
by SNP Best-set Typesetter Ltd., Hong Kong
Printed and bound in Great Britain by MPG Books, Bodmin, Cornwall

For further information on Polity, visit our website: www.polity.co.uk

261503

CONTENTS

Contents

ACKNOWLEDGMENTS

My friend Mickey Wells, at the University of Tampa, has been absolutely indispensable. He's introduced me to sources I didn't know existed and steered me in directions I didn't know were there. I couldn't have written this book without his support.

I wrote portions of the book while a visiting scholar at the University of South Florida. Maralee Mayberry, the chair of USF's sociology department, invited me and offered me abundant facilities. I thank her for making me so welcome.

The initial idea for this book came from Marcus Ryder, of BBC Television, who read my earlier work *The Black Culture Industry* and suggested I adapt the approach I used for understanding black music to Mike Tyson. This is it.

James Jennings, of Tufts University, Massachusetts, is my friend, colleague and fellow boxing aficionado with whom I have regularly corresponded and exchanged views on Tyson throughout the writing of this book and beyond.

Michele Froman, of ESPN, has kept a vigilant Tysonwatch for me, keeping me updated, especially on Tyson's misadventures.

I'm 36 years old, going on 37. I never dreamed of living this long. I never dreamed of fornicating with as many beautiful women as I did and having as much money as I did. And having as beautiful and intelligent kids as I did. So, if I was to die tomorrow, I've won. I've won. *I've won.*

CNN *People in the news*, June, 2002

I expect that one day somebody, probably black, will blow my fucking brains out over some fucking bullshit, that his fucking wife or girlfriend might like me, and I don't even know she exists.

Playboy, November, 1998

I'm not supposed to have a mind. I'm a monster.

Esquire, April, 1996

I understand these people. They want to crush me, they want me to cry, to get on my knees. And evidently, it is not in my nature to do that. And that is what people respect most. Not the fact that I'm knocking out everybody, not the fact that I contributed money. That's what people respect, the fact that I wasn't a chump that laid on his back and gave up.

Ebony, September, 1995

When you see me smash somebody's skull, you enjoy it.

Albany Times, January, 1986

one

INTRODUCTION: I WILL KILL YOU.
DO YOU UNDERSTAND THIS?

Imagine this. It's 1982. Catskill, New York. Here, a rough-hewn training camp for boxers is presided over by Cus D'Amato, a white trainer who, in the 1950s, guided Floyd Patterson to the world heavyweight title. D'Amato senses that he doesn't have too long to live and craves for another heavyweight champion before he dies. He believes one of his young charges has the raw material. All he needs to do is shape it. The boy with the untutored talent arrived at the camp as a squat 12-year-old, weighing 186 lbs. Like many other African American youths from the Brownsville district of New York, he already has an ample rap sheet.

The trainer with the responsibility for refining the coarse ability is a young white man with a reputation for being a perfectionist, a demanding taskmaster and an all-round disciplinarian. He listens to D'Amato, but is independent-minded enough to know what's what. Like the others at the camp, he sees the potential of D'Amato's protégé who has the swaggering manner of many black kids reared on the streets. He has a physical strength that belies his years and a willingness to learn that bodes well for a career in boxing. Yet the trainer senses a waywardness: the boy isn't rebellious, not even openly disobedient; but he has a defiant streak that surfaces every so often.

He suspects that D'Amato, in his quest to turn the boy into a world champion, allows him indulgences that he wouldn't extend to other members of the camp. On some occasions, he's suspended the youth from the gym as a punishment for threatening a schoolteacher or pestering girls, only to find himself overruled by D'Amato. For instance, the old man once allowed him to train in private after all the others had gone, despite the fact that he had been temporarily banned by the trainer. He thinks D'Amato is cutting the young man too much slack. While living in Catskill, the trainer marries a local woman and moves away from D'Amato's big house to an apartment.

One day, after the session, the trainer gets home to find his wife and her 11-year-old sister sitting at the kitchen table, both of them in tears. The sister-in-law reveals to him that D'Amato's charge, by then 16, has made unwelcome sexual advances toward her. The trainer flies from the apartment in a rage, heads to a friend's to pick up a .38 revolver, checks it's loaded, then speeds back to camp to wait for the boxer. On finding him in the empty gym, he pins him against a wall, jams the gun into the boxer's ear and delivers this message: "You piece of shit! Don't you ever put your hands on my family. *I will kill you.* Do you understand this?"

There is a pause, then a click as the trainer cocks the gun, a sound that usually means the gunman isn't bluffing. The young man seems strangely composed, unmoved. He glowers, his eyes never moving from his adversary's, never blinking in the face of danger. Then, he smiles derisively and answers: "No, mother-fucker." The trainer squeezes the trigger.

TRAINER KILLS BOXER IN COLD BLOOD reads one of the headlines in the local *Poughkeepsie Journal*. It doesn't rate a mention elsewhere. The trainer is found guilty of murder in the first degree and is sentenced to life. That was back in 1982. He's now eligible for parole.

This is a true story in all but one respect. "If he would have smiled, if he would have said no, I would have killed him," reflected the trainer, whose name is Teddy Atlas, in an interview with David Remnick in 2000. "I pulled the gun away from his ear and pulled the trigger. I fired. At that moment, he knew. He got very weak, I could see that in his eyes" (p. 36).

Atlas was looking into the eyes of Mike Tyson. If he'd have kept the barrel of the gun at his head when he fired, you would not be reading this book. Another African American male with a criminal record would have met his death at the hands of a gunman. It wouldn't have been recorded outside the local paper. It would have been just another statistic.

How much that incident affected Tyson, we'll never know. Atlas had been continually frustrated at the way D'Amato vetoed his attempts to discipline the teenage Tyson and D'Amato was concerned that Atlas would ruin his prize asset before it had time to ripen. D'Amato's priorities became clear after the incident: Atlas left and D'Amato assigned Tyson a new trainer, Kevin Rooney.

Atlas remains aware of his role in history. In 1992, with Tyson imprisoned for rape, he was quoted by Montieth Illingworth in the book *Mike Tyson: Money, myth and betrayal*: "Maybe Cus was right. If we did it my way, Tyson might never have become champion" (p. 54).

What would have happened if Atlas had been allowed to exercise more control over Tyson, or even killed him back in 1982? It's difficult to picture the late twentieth century, and perhaps even the early twenty-first, without Tyson. He has been such a prominent feature of our cultural landscape. At one point, he vied with Nelson Mandela as the most famous man in the world. His recognition rating was globally high. His name and image were inescapable. If you weren't aware of Tyson, you must have been a recluse.

But it wasn't just his name, or his face, or even his body that made Tyson universally famous and, later, infamous. It wasn't even anything Tyson did in the ring. Of course, he knocked people out and he did so in a fashion that sent shudders through his audiences. There seemed a primal force at work when Tyson attacked an opponent. This was not an ordinary boxer dispatching his opponents. It was more a natural predator descending on its prey, its instinct determining its actions. No conscious control was necessary.

There was something else. Perhaps it was his behavior away from the ring. Not just the lavish indulgences, the multiple homes, several dozen cars, pet tigers, traffic-stopping shopping blitzes and other extravagances that made the lifestyles of other rich and famous look gray and uninteresting. Maybe it was the live-by-the-sword philosophy, acting fast and often perilously, never far from a scrape with the law, always poised to crash into the headlines, whether for wrecking a car, knocking someone out in a nightclub or groping an unwilling woman. Or, worse. It could have been the elliptical path he cut, like a comet soaring upwards only to return on itself. Having earned hundreds of millions of dollars over nineteen years in professional boxing, he filed for bankruptcy, listing among his main creditors the Internal Revenue Service. Or it could have been all these things, plus one other.

The other reason is that Tyson was, in the eyes of the world, resistant to the most basic civilizing influences. The popular view of Tyson was captured by Jake Tapper, of the *Washington City Paper*, who, in 1998, observed that Tyson "has become the saddest, most frightening, most damning evidence of man's capability for bestiality" (December 11).

The adage that "you can take the man from the ghetto but never the ghetto from the man" never seemed truer than when applied to Tyson. He was a living fulfillment of age-old images of African Americans, images that had their sources in the brute nigger archetype of yore. Blessed with a superabundance of brawn, Tyson was a fearsome figure; his apparent lack of intellect and self-control made him more frightening. Yet, as his ex-wife Robin Givens acknowledged when talking of her own fascination with Tyson, that was "part of the attraction."

Following the misadventures of Tyson made the follower party to something primitive and uninhibited. It also provided crucial evidence that was to comfort and soothe white American consciences: that, given the opportunity, even the most spectacularly successful blacks are prone to self-destruction. In this respect, Tyson was the perfect cipher for a culture eager to rid itself of the legacy of pre-civil rights segregation yet uneasy with the prospect of accepting African Americans as fully fledged equals. Without realizing it, Tyson performed in what the scholar Jan Nedeerven Pieterse once called a racial psychodrama.

Tyson wasn't just a symbol in the eyes of white America, he was a theatrical enactment of what all African Americans were like once the patina of civilization, the thin crust of culture had been scratched away. He might have more money than he knew how to spend, wear designer clothes, have three or four mansions, countless Ferraris and a personal zoo, but, lurking not too far beneath the surface, was the beast. It was the same beast that slaveowners once sought to tame.

———

On December 3, 2002, Tyson walked into a Las Vegas jewelry store and picked up a diamond-encrusted gold chain. Price: $173,706. He didn't pay for the item; it was simply added to the $23 million of debt specified in the Chapter 11 petitions he filed just over eight months later.

Tyson was well known at Jewelers Inc., where his credit rating was good. "He had open credit with me," confirmed the store's owner, Mordechai Yerushalmi. "He's been through his ups and downs. He will make good on it."

For sure, Tyson had been through his ups and downs. At his nadir, he spent three years in an Indiana prison – three of what might have been his peak boxing years, in which he could have earned as much as $300 million and remained champion of the world. At his zenith, he was among the best-known and best-paid figures in the world, respected as the best heavyweight since Muhammad Ali and envied for his opulent lifestyle.

And it *was* opulent. In the 1995–7 period, Tyson had six fights and netted $112 million. He blew just under $5 million on cars and motorcycles, plus a further $1.7 million on maintenance and insurance. The lawn care alone for his three estates totaled $750,000. His monthly clothes and accessories bill came to $95,000. His love of pigeons dates back to his childhood, but he would never have dreamed that he'd eventually spend over $400,000 on them. The monthly bill for his pagers and cellphones was about $7,300. Personal security was $385,000. Per diem expenses, or loose change, came to about $236,000 per month (read it again: $236,000 per month). His thirtieth birthday party in 1996 cost nearly $411,000. Then, of course, there were hidden costs, like the $229,000 for child support, the accountant's fee of just over a million dollars and the Internal Revenue Service's slice, $32.4 million. Even then, he still managed to fall behind on his taxes. Among the debts specified in August, 2003, was $13.4

million owing to the IRS and a further $4 million payable to Britain's tax authority, the Inland Revenue.

Sports Illustrated writer Richard Hoffer, in trying to fathom how such a big earner landed in debt, quoted Tyson's reply to his inquisitive accountant: "I can't have it and not spend it." That was Tyson's elementary but revealing explanation, leading Hoffer to a Micawber-like conclusion: "Here's how to go broke on $112 million: Spend $115 million" (May 20, 2002).

Tyson's list of creditors was formidable. Seven law firms were owed $600,000. One financial manager alone was due $500,000. A music producer was owed $450,000 (Tyson had a brief foray into the music business). He owed $23 million in total, despite a professional boxing career that, since 1986, had brought him $400–500 million.

In March 2004, Tyson, then in his thirty-eighth year and completely broke, announced that he had no thoughts of retirement and would continue his quest for a world title. It surprised nobody. Tyson had died a thousand deaths and had resurrected himself every time. He had rarely shown much respect for the conventions of boxing and was not about to start.

Tyson's is an epic story indeed, one of abundance and prodigality, growth and decay, trust and treachery, defilement and castigation. But these are elements not only of Tyson's life, but of the world he lived in and the times he lived through.

Popularly depicted as a monster, a psycho, a reprobate, and, most repeatedly, an animal, Tyson demanded our attention. Not because he wanted it: for the most part, he hated the persistent intrusions into his life, despised the caricatures drawn of him, resented the way in which he was used as fodder with which the media could feed their gluttonous, celebrity-fixated consumers.

Still, it could be argued that he turned himself into coarse feed. After all, interest in him might easily have waned after he'd lost his world title in February 1990. Tyson's unexpected descent to the ranks of mere mortals was greeted with surprise spiced with some satisfaction, the satisfaction that comes of watching the world's most intimidating man's public humiliation.

Interest didn't subside so easily. Residual thoughts of the Tyson menace remained. None of his contemporaries could excite imaginations as Tyson did. Not even the likes of Michael Jordan, a towering, iconic presence, though too pure and wholesome to stir the passions like Tyson. The rape allegation, the trial, the imprisonment, the comeback, the upset defeat, the ear-biting, the assault, the press conference brawl, the divorce and, of course, the barely believable declaration of bankruptcy: these were all parts of the grand Tyson narrative. It was a narrative in which we were all involved and it took place in a context in which tranquillity and change seemed to vie.

Tyson's life doesn't reflect its context. Rather, it's an integral part of that context. It seems an audacious claim, but no account of late twentieth- and early twenty-first century Western culture can exclude the presence of Tyson. Like him or, as is more likely the case, loathe him, he has been right there, occupying headlines and commanding our thoughts. He has precipitated all manner of moral dispute, moving people to march in the streets either in protest or exultation. And, of course, he has made us watch him. Even in the twilight of his career, having edged past his best and at an age when many men think of walking the dog as exertion, Tyson remained the most precious metal when it came to boxoffice. What other athlete in history has exerted such magnetic power?

Tyson has made his presence felt in three separate decades. He has appalled and enthralled us in roughly equal proportions. Breaking through the 1980s like some terrifying fiend from another age, he slid perfectly into the emerging celebrity culture, his globally publicized relationship with Robin Givens the most prominent athlete/actor liaison since Di Maggio and Monroe. He continued to engage us throughout the 1990s, mainly with his well-known transgressions, but also with his preternatural ability to bring mayhem to the most predictable of situations. The buzz was that anything could happen where Tyson was concerned. He wasn't subject to the same mechanisms of control as the rest of us.

Exceptional figure that he is, Tyson deserves something other than the conventional sports biography. This book situates Tyson in his social context. It might have been called "The Life and Times of Mike Tyson," the times being as important as the life.

7

Tyson is neither consistent nor coherent, nor is his life and nor is the story of his life. I have written a book that conveys the fragmentation of Tyson. His life began in a commotion of disorder and will probably end that way. I've tried to impart a sense of the confusion without collecting all the crises into a single plot pattern. Many sports biographies bring together the lives of their subjects with the cozy ordinariness of a tv soap. Tyson's life, like his times, is extraordinary. In an effort to reflect this, I have ditched a linear format and written of a fragmented life in a fragmented way.

The story begins in the present and proceeds back to the mid-1960s, occasionally transferring the reader to unusual destinations. There are frequent segues out of Tyson's life, some deep into history, others into the lives of figures who shaped Tyson, still others into episodes that affected the culture of which Tyson is both a product and producer. I have arranged events in a way that displays a narrative constantly interrupted by events over which Tyson had no control, but which influenced the course of his life. And our lives.

The thing about Tyson's life is: we know what happened next. Looking back, there are no surprises. We probably all suspect we know how it will end too. Tyson himself certainly does. What we don't necessarily know is why everything happened. The hidden causal links in Tyson's life become visible when we work backwards through the drama. Not that I'm suggesting everything in Tyson's life has a material cause. His life was no more predetermined than anyone else's. He is, after all, a willful and frequently wild spirit, one that moves in mysterious though not unfathomable ways. There may appear to be a reasonless inconsistency in his thought and behavior. But there has often been logic in Tyson's apparent lunacy, as I hope to reveal.

In the interests of clarity, I'll provide an outline of the method I use to slice up Tyson's life. Even though the chapters cover periods of time, there are shuttles back and forth. As I stated before, the book begins in the present. Chapter two takes us back to June 2002, when Tyson and we were finally disabused of any notions that he was still the best heavyweight boxer in the world. It was 17 years and three months after Tyson's first professional fight. His humbling defeat at the hands of Lennox Lewis and his demureness in the wake of the fight suggested a passage from one era to another.

Chapter three takes us further back, to early 2002, prior to the press conference to announce the Lewis fight, a press conference that culminated in typical Tyson mayhem. In this chapter, there is a detour into the life of Monica Turner, whom Tyson befriended while in prison, married shortly after his release in 1995 and was divorced from in 2003. But, the main period covered is winter 2001/2 to summer 2002.

An incident in March 1998 serves as an emblem for countless other similar incidents in Tyson's life. Allegations of boorish behavior are often leveled at prominent athletes, though Tyson seems to have attracted much more than his fair share. Maybe it was because Tyson was, as he once described himself, "penis-centered." Whatever: women seemed to line up to accuse him of misconduct of some kind. Chapter four opens with the 1998 incident and examines the spiral of allegations that have affected Tyson. It closes at the end of 2001, briefly deviating away from Tyson to take account of the murder of Amadou Diallo, someone whom Tyson didn't know, but to whom he was unknowingly connected. Span: spring 1998 to winter 2001/2.

Chapter five covers the period from October 1996 to early 1998, a period that includes the Grand Guignol of the two fights against Evander Holyfield, the second of which featured the infamous ear-biting. Earlier, Tyson had expressed an affinity with Sonny Liston, the late heavyweight champion to whom he has been compared. It's a justifiable comparison, as the chapter suggests.

Two crucial events bookend chapter six: the O. J. Simpson case of 1994/5 and the killing of Tupac Shakur in September 1996. The chapter deals with Tyson's release from prison and the subsequent passage back into active competition under the guidance of Don King. Tyson may not have known Simpson, but he certainly knew Tupac Shakur and, indeed, shared many of the experiences of growing up in the ghettos and finding fame and fortune thanks to a talent for which others were prepared to pay. The main phase of the chapter is fall 1995 to fall 1996.

Chapter seven concentrates on the events leading up to the rape of Desiree Washington in July 1991 and the ensuing trial, which resulted in Tyson's imprisonment. During the trial, Tyson's own defense resorted to dehumanizing him in a way that made him seem a lower order of being. It was an unsuccessful strategy and one that left its impress on Tyson for years after. While the chapter dwells on the trial, the whole period covered in this chapter stretches from summer 1991 to summer 1995.

Between March 1990 and June 1991, Tyson was a man searching for a way back: his world title gone and his reputation damaged, though not irreparably, he was showing glimpses of his best form. In March 1991, Rodney King was stopped for speeding by Los Angeles police officers. Four white officers administered a brutal beating, setting in motion a chain of events which would culminate in rioting across the USA. Chapter eight examines Tyson's attempted rehabilitation against the fiery background of the King case.

Chapter nine explores the period between December 1988 and February 1990. For most of this time, Tyson was regarded as invincible. There was nothing to suggest that any fighter in the world could pose a threat. In February 1989 he brushed aside the challenge of Frank Bruno, then ended the hopes of Carl Williams. Then an ordinary fight became extraordinary. In perhaps the biggest upset in sports history, James "Buster" Douglas pounded Tyson to his first ever professional defeat. It was an astonishing fight that threw up many more questions than it answered. There was a sense almost of relief when Tyson was finally dispatched, the reasons for which probably lie in events far removed from the fight itself, in particular the events surrounding the cases of the Central Park jogger and Charles Stuart.

In the 22 months that separated January 1988 and November 1989, Tyson's life was transformed by two people, both of whom sought a measure of control over him, neither of whom appeared to serve his best interests. Tyson first announced his relationship with Robin Givens in spring 1987 and they married in February 1988; a month before Givens had announced she was pregnant. They were divorced a year and a week after the wedding. On

March 23, 1988, Tyson's co-manager Jim Jacobs died. Sensing a vacuum, Don King rushed in. He didn't expect to meet with resistance from, of all sources, Tyson's new mother-in-law. Chapter ten explores the conflicting interests of Givens and King and how both massively affected not only Tyson himself, but our perception of him.

In November 1987, Tawana Brawley's disappearance shocked many almost into disbelief. This was a scandalous case toward which Tyson was drawn. It brought him into contact with the Reverend Al Sharpton, who was to become a prominent figure on the political scene, not least because of his support for Tyson. Chapter eleven opens with this case, concentrating on the period between fall 1986 and the end of 1987 when Tyson unified a heavyweight title which had hitherto been divided among the various boxing organizations, each of which recognized its own champion. Tyson's campaign was designed to ensure his un-disputed right to call himself the champion. The campaign was conducted while the USA was in racial turmoil.

Chapter twelve is concerned with the term spring 1980–fall 1986. Cus D'Amato took custody of Tyson from June 30, 1980, the date of Tyson's fourteenth birthday. Tyson had been training at his camp in Catskill for a while before, but the adoption con-stituted the start of a new period in his life. Six-and-a-half years later, Tyson was approaching his first world title challenge. The poverty of his early years had long since been left behind and Tyson was already contemplating the millions he would earn as heavyweight champion. The chapter also segues into the life of D'Amato, who was a formative influence on Tyson, though not without his critics.

Almost a year before Tyson was born, an incident on August 11, 1965, contributed to a climate which transfigured the USA's cultural landscape and so affected not only Tyson, but perhaps every child born after that date. Chapter thirteen takes account of the event, which sparked the "race riots" of the mid-1960s, and then moves through Tyson's first fourteen years as a member of what some writers called the black underclass. Looked at one way, Tyson was utterly unexceptional: just one of hundreds of thousands of ghetto-born children virtually condemned to a life of petty larceny, imprisonment and/or early death. In another, he was truly exceptional: one of the few that managed to escape. Of course, many have suggested, he merely exchanged one type of confinement for another.

The fourteenth and final chapter asks: how will Tyson be remembered? The whole of this book suggests one way, of course. But, I consider the perspectives already on offer from a number of writers who have analyzed, examined and evaluated a man whose unmistakable presence will be felt long after he's finished boxing. In concluding, I return to the scenario with which I opened this chapter: what would life have been like without Tyson?

two

IF YOU'D BE KIND ENOUGH,
I'D LOVE TO DO IT AGAIN

On the night of June 8, 2002, a conspicuously defeated Mike Tyson shuffled meekly to the center of the ring at the Pyramid Arena, Memphis, his face grotesquely distended, blood seeping from a cut over his right eye. Comprehensively beaten and, in the eyes of many, humiliated, Tyson had failed in his attempt to regain the heavyweight championship of the world, his bid subsiding in the eighth round, with Tyson lying helplessly on the canvas. He looked and sounded pitiful as he praised his conqueror Lennox Lewis as "splendid . . . a masterful boxer." There was an almost contrite quality in Tyson's voice as he admitted his gratitude to Lewis. "The payday was wonderful," he feebly acknowledged. "I really appreciate it."

Who or what was speaking? A voice that had the tone, cadence, even the lisp of Mike Tyson; not the words, though. Surely an imposter had snatched his body. Then, as if to confirm that this was not Tyson at all, the voice humbly submitted a proposal: "If you'd be kind enough, I'd love to do it again. I think I could beat you if we tried one more time."

If this didn't astonish enough, the imposter, after hugging Lewis, moved away. As he did, he must have seen a smear of his own blood that he'd rubbed onto Lewis. He reached across and, with an almost caress-like movement, wiped the smudge away.

This was not Mike Tyson. Mike Tyson had gone, replaced by a simulacrum, a replicant maybe, like those in *Blade Runner*, but without the dissidence. Maybe someone had given him the *Stepford Wives* treatment, stripping away every characteristic that made him an individual and leaving just a hard outer covering.

This simply could not have been Tyson, the man who had earlier promised to eat Lewis' children (if he had any – he didn't), who, following a routine demolition of Jesse Ferguson in 1986, revealed that: "I tried to punch him and drive the bone of his nose back into his brain." The man who once proclaimed about opponent Razor Ruddock, "If he didn't die, it didn't count. If he's not dead, then we'll have to do it all over again." Who confessed to his sometime confidant José Torres that: "I like to hurt women when I make love to them . . . I like to hear them scream with pain, to see them bleed. It gives me pleasure." And who once boasted that the best punch he ever threw was the one that sent his ex-wife rebounding off every wall in the apartment.

What had happened to the terrifying, primeval creature, that minatory fiend which wrung its diabolical deeds, cruelly and abominably, leaving a pitiful trail of victims hurt and helpless? "If you'd be kind enough . . ." What kind of words were these from the fiend that seemed to close in from the outer reaches of the imagination, one so offensive, so repugnant, so sickening, so nauseating?

"I'd really appreciate it." *I'd really appreciate it.* There was a time when to acknowledge appreciation would have been a confession of moral, if not physical weakness. The words wouldn't have formed in his mouth. Surely, this was not Mike Tyson. A pod maybe from *Invasion of the Bodysnatchers.*

"You wanted to ask Tyson for ID," wrote Rick Reilly, of *Sports Illustrated.* "Where was the madness, the rage? Why wasn't he in the locker room swinging at cops, smashing watercoolers, demanding a rematch?" he asked in his article "Unlike Mike" (June 17, 2002).

An hour after the Lewis fight, Tyson sat in his dressing room, bruised and bloodied, his eyes hideously swollen, but surprisingly content. In his arms he held his two-month-old son, Miguel. Looking at the baby, he explained: "I didn't quit. I nearly got murdered in there, so maybe I should've."

The precautions before the Lewis fight were reminiscent of the scene in *Silence of the Lambs* when Hannibal Lecter is wheeled off the plane and onto the runway strapped in the kind of conveyance that porters use for heavy luggage. A leather mask covers his face. Even the breathing space across the mouth is barred. Tyson had been likened to Hannibal the Cannibal before, of course. In Memphis, he wasn't physically secured, though he was contractually bound to stick to procedures that ensured no physical contact with Lewis prior to the fight.

A decoy in disguise was sent ahead of the real Tyson, who landed in a small private jet in a remote Arkansas airfield. Tyson eventually emerged, sporting a tribal tattoo on the left side of his face. Such was the fascination with Tyson that an expert on the significance of tattoos was brought in to explain that it signified a warrior spirit.

Tyson wasn't even allowed to approach his opponent when receiving the referee's instructions, as is customary in boxing. Instead, the referee visited each boxer in his dressing room and delivered his directives. Only after the first bell was Tyson permitted to get within punching distance of his foe. Even then, he didn't get too near after the first three minutes.

He didn't do any of the things people had half hoped for; any of the things ringsiders had coughed up $2,400 a seat for: he didn't bite, or headbutt; but he didn't cause his opponent to crumble either. In fact, he didn't do much at all, save for taking a beating like a stalwart. "There was something seriously wrong with the whole scenario," wrote Duke Eatmon, of *Community Contact*. "Tyson at no time threw any punches with 'bad intentions.' No combinations, no hooks. He offered no defense, no bobbing, no weaving; only a stationary target for Lewis to hit at will . . . he didn't hit low, break arms or bite ears" (June 20, 2002).

Perhaps most disappointing of all was the measured reflection that came after. "I got this reputation of being a dirty fighter," said Tyson. "But, it's not me that's a dirty fighter. I just had to fight [Orlin] Norris and [Evander] Holyfield. They fought me dirty. But, Lewis? I knew he wasn't dirty." All the same, both boxers had a clause in their contracts stipulating that an "onerous foul" disqualification would mean a $3 million forfeit. To the disappointment of fans, they kept their money. Tyson never seemed so stable, so restrained, so humdrum.

"Tyson is a despicable character," declared Reilly. "A rapist, a thug you would not want within an area code of your daughter.

But it's going to be just a little harder to despise him now." Only a little harder.

"I'd be crazy to ask for a rematch," said Tyson once his head had cleared. "He's too big and too strong." He still owed the IRS as well as sundry other creditors, of course. While he may not have wanted a rematch, he was forced into considering one. Still, there are always other ways of earning money for a figure like Tyson, if indeed there has ever been a figure quite like Tyson. Fox Sports signed him for an advertising campaign for its show *Best Damn Sports Show Period*, which ran in fall, 2002.

In the slyly humorous advertising spot, Tyson, himself the father of five children, babysits the infant of one of the show's hosts and sings a sweet lullaby. The ad was pulled after a week of protests. The *New York Times* and *Advertising Age* were among the several publications that condemned the commercial as offensive. As Brian Mulhern, of Clifford Freeman & Partners, Fox's advertising agents, explained with a hint of disingenu-ousness: "We knew that Mike Tyson would be very, very con-troversial. We didn't know that he would be very, very, *very, very* controversial." The gigantic coverage that followed Tyson's promise to devour Lewis' progeny was surely enough to alert him.

The episode secreted a little more information about the attitude of middle America than perhaps Fox or its ad agency recognized. The directors of the commercial were the Hughes Brothers, best known for their mainstream feature films like *Menace II Society* and *From Hell*. "We've hated him enough," Allen Hughes said of Tyson, acknowledging to *Advertising Age* that "half the problem with Mike Tyson is himself and what he's done and the other half is the way he looks; it scares people" (September 30, 2002). Actually, there was another problem and a deeper one that Hughes himself realized without giving it the weight it deserved: "The baby is white. If there was a little black baby in his hands no one would have a problem with that."

His title gone, his once-formidable skills conspicuously eroded and his fearsome reputation perhaps unsalvageable,

Tyson could still cut an image to horrify. Even in self-mocking mode, he represented a quality of terrifying *Otherness* that mainstream culture could not accommodate. The black man's access to mainstream culture is conditional: a servant, or entertainer who doesn't dare threaten the status quo, an anodyne, sexless character, like a scholar, minister or color-free politician, or a beast that's capable of being tamed. Tyson, having been locked up, punished, disciplined and castigated, was still not completely crushed. Sheepish in defeat, contrite in expressing remorse, Tyson could still conjure images that chilled the soul of white America. He remained beyond the pale, a black male incapable or perhaps unwilling to assimilate – an Other, whose unchangeable difference made him something of a metaphor, a mirror. In the mirror, whites could see not just an image of what blacks were really like once the pretense of culture and civilization was effaced, but a reflection of what they *were not*.

For a time in the 1980s, every move, every little move he made, every word he uttered was framed in notions of savagery, fear, peril, even death. Verging on a fantasy character, Tyson necessitated distance. This was something in our midst, but not in our universe – neither in real nor psychological terms. Intriguing, perhaps: you wanted to read about him, see him on television, look at him fight. He was there as delectation. But you wouldn't want to think of him as part of the same species as yourself. Or, if you did, you'd want to add incontestable qualifications. He may be a member of *Homo sapiens*, but he was only distantly related to the particular branch of humanity of which you liked to think you were a part. You wouldn't want to have a drink with him, less still invite him round for dinner. If you did, you'd be careful to alert the police first.

The attraction and the repulsion were twinned. Seeing Tyson was a little like watching a slasher movie: this was fright made flesh. An accessible monster who would, given the chance, devour both you and your family. Yes, accessible. You could experience the Tyson terror without actually leaving your home. Pay-per-view and bigscreen tvs made it possible to look this menace in the eyes, sense his power, almost feel his breath, yet never actually come into contact. The dread that Tyson brought was experienced vicariously from a position of absolute safety.

Eight months after his humiliation, Tyson began to sound more like his normal self. "To do what I do you have to have heart and character and discipline," he reminded reporters, following his 49-second knockout of Clifford Etienne. "There's so much more to fighting, but who cares if a nigga dies in the ring?" he asked rhetorically. "Nobody."

Gathered to collect a few quotes on the fight (far from Tyson's fastest: he'd finished off five other fighters more quickly), reporters were treated to a diatribe. "You reporters, you white doctors. You never stole a loaf of bread in your life. So, what do they care about me? They hope I go to prison and die there."

However Tyson thought white America regarded him, he could be in no doubt about one thing: white America paid handsomely to see him perform. For returning to the same Memphis arena where he had been discredited, Tyson received a million dollars up front and a percentage of the profits, which probably came to around $4.5 million. For a 36-year-old fighter who had lost his previous fight so abjectly and who was fighting a mediocre opponent, this was very good money. Even the most generous of observers couldn't have believed that Tyson was anywhere close to being the fighter of the eighties and early nineties. Yet, he could fill the Memphis Pyramid and move the pay-per-view buys like no other entertainer in history.

Tyson knew it; which is probably why he equivocated so much in the lead-up to the fight, certain that, wherever he went, people would follow, whatever he did they would report, whatever he said they would listen to. Stories of Tyson's absence from the gym circulated two weeks before the Etienne fight. This was excused by the fight's promoters as owing to sickness, though trainer Jeff Fenech threw up his hands in disgust and flew home to Australia after Tyson's umpteenth missed training session. Tyson decided to pull out of the fight, then changed his mind, whereupon Etienne pulled out, only to change *his* mind.

There was no abatement of intrigue. As the CNN news reporter put it, in June 2002: "Even just walking from the car into a building, he makes news" (*CNN Live Today*, June 4). This was sixteen years after he'd first won the world title. Sixteen years. He had no title, had been humbled in his last fight and, at 36, was slipping into middle age. Yet, his power to engage people was undiminished.

Even his conqueror tacitly affirmed this when he issued a $20 million lawsuit against Tyson. Lewis was furious when Tyson pulled out of a promotion scheduled for Los Angeles in June 2003. Lewis was due to defend his title, while Tyson was to meet Oleg Maskaev on the same bill. Tyson's withdrawal persuaded television network HBO that even a world title defense by Lewis was not worthy of pay-per-view. Tyson was the real attraction. Even the site fee paid by the Staples Center dropped by $4 million purely because of Tyson's absence.

In a gesture hardly befitting a champion, Lewis offered to give Tyson more time to prepare, but Tyson was unmoved. $8 million, it seems, was not enough to get Tyson into the ring. That was what Tyson stood to earn for his labors. Incensed, Lewis also filed a $100 million lawsuit against King, alleging that the promoter was trying to pry Tyson from a projected rematch.

Instead, Lewis suffered the ignominy of a pay cut and a troublesome defense against Vitali Klitschko, while Tyson, almost without trying, kept creating big news. The day before Lewis raised his leaden arm of triumph over Klitschko, Tyson was arrested following a brawl outside the Brooklyn Marriott, New York, and charged with third-degree assault and disorderly conduct. The other two men involved in the incident were charged with menacing behavior. Tyson was pondering whether he'd face yet another jail sentence.

"Mike is a branded man," Tyson's spiritual advisor, Muhammad Siddeeq, told CNN's *People in the News* in 2002 (June 1). He wasn't referring to the Maori facial tattoo that Tyson affected around that time. The stigma was as much ascribed as earned. Tyson was reminded of its indelibility probably every day of his life.

———

Tyson deserves his place in history. He offered a form of entertainment and an ideology with special appeal to all those who lived in the afterglow of civil rights: those who felt a sense of

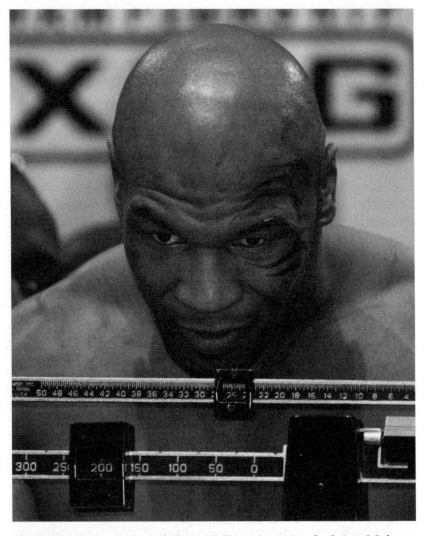

Figure 1 "Mike is a branded man," Tyson's spiritual advisor Muhammad Siddeeq declared in 2002. The facial tattoo that enhanced his glowering menace served as a reminder of the indelible stigma.

accomplishment following the dissolution of segregation and those who felt betrayed. The legislation of 1964 and 1965 was meant to make a mockery of America's virtual caste system. It was a common complaint in the 1930s that the US population was being fed a lie – that America was a democracy. Puritan ethics that included sound education, hard work, diligence and practical common sense were all encouraged by a culture based on the idea of merit. Merit, which was supposed to mean talent allied to application, would be rewarded with scant regard for background, class, or anything else. There was good reason to keep quiet about "anything else": if it included "race" or "color," then merit and the virtuous democracy that was thought to promote it fell flat.

By 1944, when Gunnar Myrdal and his team of researchers published their 1,300-page, two-volume, 45-chapter *An American Dilemma*, the game was up. The nation had long lived with a painful dilemma caused by the discrepancy between its democratic and libertarian ideals of freedom and equality for all and its accursed treatment of African Americans, first as disenfranchised chattels and, later, as segregated outcasts. Myrdal supplied proof that this so-called dilemma was far from being solved. The Swedish scholar, who was a Nobel laureate (Economics) in 1974, predicted that there would be a gradual realignment.

Actually, "dilemma" is, on reflection, an improper word: it suggests a choice between two alternatives, neither of which is entirely satisfactory. In the 1940s, there was no real decision to be made. The segregated system that had followed the dissolution of slavery was sturdy enough to withstand any challenges. America's mind was made up. "Paradox" would have been more accurate. America was living in self-contradiction. Its ideals of unrestricted opportunity and freedom of expression were grotesquely undermined by the reality of racism. African Americans were not even allowed to vote. If this was democracy, it was a demented democracy. Consider the case of *Brown vs. Board of Education of Topeka, Kansas*, which was decided on May 17, 1954.

The eponymous Brown was Oliver Brown, whose daughter had been forced to travel by bus to an all-black school even though she lived close to an all-white institution. The National Association for the Advancement of Colored People (NAACP) threw its weight behind Brown and eventually secured the agreement of the presiding Chief Justice Warren, who concluded: "In the field of public education, the doctrine of 'separate but equal' has no place." In ruling segregation unconstitutional, the Brown decision overturned the conclusions of *Plessy vs. Ferguson*, 1896, which gave rise to the period known as the Jim Crow era. The segregation of "races" was absolute.

After the Brown decision, states were instructed to proceed with "all deliberate speed" to abolish segregation in public schools. While five of the southern states, encouraged by governors, senators, representatives, and white Citizens' Councils, resisted the decision, twelve states and the District of Columbia (DC) immediately began to desegregate. The Supreme Court declared the fundamental principle that racial discrimination in public education was a violation of the 14th amendment. All provisions of federal, state or local law that either permitted or required such discrimination were made to cease.

Eighteen months after the decision, Rosa Parks, a black seamstress, refused to give up her seat on a public bus in Montgomery, Alabama. Her refusal to surrender her seat to a white passenger resulted in her arrest. Protest from black organizations in the South was so swift and substantial that an alliance known as the Southern Christian Leadership Conference and led by the Reverend Dr Martin Luther King was soon formed. This became the central vehicle for the civil rights movement and its momentum gathered over the following years.

Between 1957 and 1960, civil rights legislation introduced enforcement powers through a Civil Rights Division of the US Department of Justice. But the crucial period came over the next four years. Pressure from King's movement resulted in the strengthening of voting rights for blacks in 1960 and the banning of discrimination in work and labor unions, as well as in access to hotels, restaurants, and theaters. Education was progressively desegregated.

The watershed piece of legislation was the Civil Rights Act of 1964 – twenty years after the publication of Myrdal's research –

which extended federal powers to eliminate discrimination in public places. Discrimination in employment on the grounds of "race, color, sex, or national origin" was outlawed. The denial of black rights was effectively over, but, while this was clear under law, the practice was more obscure.

While parts of America rejoiced at the end of discrimination, other parts quaked at the instability threatened by the end of an institution that had held sway since the sixteenth century, in the beginning with slavery, then with *de jure* segregation. Whether it was just anxiety or a mixture of anxiety, fury, contempt, malice, and sheer hatred, we don't know for sure. But, study after study revealed that, while civil rights might have appeared as a blessing to many, it was regarded as an affront to many others.

The story of the epic effort of whites to resist the consequences of civil rights has been told many times. Between 1886 and 1968, 4,709 racially motivated murders remained unsolved. In most civil rights slayings, the killers walked free, often despite overwhelming evidence and often after only minutes of deliberation by all-white juries. Its landmarks of the civil rights struggle include the case of Medgar Evers, an officer of the National Association for the Advancement of Colored People who went to Money, Mississippi, to investigate the murder of Emmett Till, a fourteen-year-old African American from Chicago, whose "offense" was to say "bye, baby" to a young white woman working in a store in Money in 1955. He was tortured, mutilated, shot through the head and dumped in the Tallahachie River. Ignoring compelling evidence, an all-white jury needed less than 75 minutes before returning a "not guilty" verdict in favor of the accused, two whites. Evers had found witnesses and evidence for the prosecution and was in the courtroom in Sumner, Mississippi, during the trial. As such, he was at the forefront of the case.

Evers withstood threats to his life and carried on his work for the NAACP, organizing rallies, marches, and other forms of demonstration. But, in 1963, he too met his death. History repeated itself: two trials and no convictions for the slaying of Evers.

By the time Tyson was born on June 30, 1966, "the bridge to freedom," as Juan Williams calls it in his book *Eyes on the Prize: America's civil rights years, 1954–1965*, was in the final throes of construction. Two years earlier, a bill had been passed to end segregation. The 1964 Civil Rights Act proposed changes that were to transfigure America, though perhaps not in the way intended. The following year's Voting Rights Act ensured that African Americans had gained access to the USA's political system. While America had prided itself on being a democracy, it was a democracy in a genuine sense only after it had widened the franchise to include all sections of its population. In the year of Tyson's birth, Edward W. Brooke of Massachusetts became the first black politician elected to the United States Senate.

The decade spanning the Brown decision and the Voting Rights Act saw more protest, more court cases, more legislation and more cultural change than any decade in America's history. The struggle for civil rights continued, but, after 1965, the focus shifted from issues of moral absoluteness, such as racial segregation, the denial of educational opportunity and the right to vote, toward more uncertain issues. These included relief from poverty, access to housing, and admittance to all employment sectors. Declaring racism and discrimination to be wrong and unlawful in a legal sense was one thing. Removing them or their vestiges from every recess of American society was quite another. But the process had begun.

The rise and fall of Tyson has to be set against this background. Was there ever a better emblem of black achievement in post-civil rights America? A powerful athletic body, not beautiful but pullulating with animal power. Quiet and, at times, seemingly serene; but given to volcanic bursts of uncontrollable anger that terrified any sane human within striking distance. He coursed through American society, from a multiple-pathological family to petty larceny, then to serious felony and then onto a fast track to fortune. The very thing that was his savior as a boy became the source of his benediction. Blessed with an ability to fight, Tyson discovered a way of making this pay. Fighting offered him a way to earn delirious amounts of money, the kinds of riches he wouldn't have dreamed possible, even in his early boxing days.

He was on his way to his first million by the age of 21 and, two years after that, had more money than he knew how to spend. His profligacy made this seem literally true. Famed throughout the world, he commanded the quality much sought after but often denied black people: respect. Respect born out of fear? Maybe. But Tyson's pose, his attitude, his demeanor earned him respect from all sources. He was honored, admired and perhaps even approved of. At first.

There weren't many clearer proofs of how effective America was in the 1980s. Less than two decades after the passing of civil rights, here was a new society, a meritocracy in which an African American from an impoverished single-parent family in the Bronx could become rich and globally famous. Boxing had always been one of the few routes out of the ghetto, but no one had taken it quite like Tyson. He was a proper celebrity, someone who could eclipse Hollywood stars. Everyone knew about Mike Tyson.

Yet there was ambiguity. It was ambiguity that served a purpose. What happens when a black man gets everything he, and probably everybody else, wants? Wealth, respect, admiration, fame. What happens when he earns so much that the burdens of paying bills, mortgages, car payments are for ever lifted? What happens when his unruly soul is relieved of the kind of ordeal that faces so many other black people?

Tyson obliged with answers. He disclosed aspects of himself that confirmed what many had suspected and helped explain why the American dilemma had – and would – never be wholly resolved.

The first glimpse of this came on February 16, 1986, less than a year after he had turned professional. Already attracting the interest of the national media, he talked to the press following his sixth-round win over Jesse Ferguson and declared that "I tried to punch him and drive the bone of his nose back into his brain." He laughed as he said it; so did the surrounding media crews.

Boxers are usually full of bravado before a fight, forecasting their own glory and their opponent's demise. But, after a win, as Phil Berger pointed out in his *Blood Season: Tyson and the world of boxing*, fighters are typically civil. They often credit an opponent for giving them a good fight or showing resolve. "That Tyson was not given to such clichés was, for the writers at least, a refreshing change," Berger affirms. "Nor had Tyson's brutal imagery been a slip of the tongue" (p. 126).

At the time, it might have been interpreted as exactly that: a careless remark voiced by an immature young man, elated by his 18th straight knockout victory and harboring no ill will toward a luckless victim. Yet it was a hint that Tyson may not have been posturing: maybe his intentions were as savage as he said. From then, the signs began to appear.

A brush with a parking attendant, rumors of a suicide attempt, claims of beating his wife, a nightclub altercation, a psychiatric examination following a car wreck, a tantrum at a photoshoot, in which he smashed a camera to pieces. No single incident amounted to much, but, cumulatively, they contributed to an image of a man either veering out of control or never quite in control in the first place. When, in 1991, it emerged that Tyson had been charged with rape, there was less surprise than might be expected. The remarkable and scary fighter, it seemed, was hellbent on destruction of some sort: if not of himself, then of whoever happened to be in his way.

In 1992, he was convicted of rape and spent three years in prison. The conviction coincided with several lawsuits, most filed by women who alleged some form of sexual misconduct. In 1997, in a world title fight with Evander Holyfield, he bit a chunk out of his opponent's ear, an offense for which he was disqualified and banned from boxing. In the lead-up to his fight in 2002 with Lennox Lewis, Tyson threatened to eat his opponent's babies and attacked him at a press conference.

He was abominable, a repulsive presence fit for only savagery. Boxing has often been seen as a sport of savages, of course. Many see it as a direct descendant of gladiatorial contests in which humans fought each other and sometimes beasts to the death.

And yet, for almost twenty years, Tyson was the biggest box-office draw in sports, drawing sell-out crowds wherever he fought and even when he did not (he once refereed a wrestling contest). The sources of the fascination with Tyson may lie in the conflict that tormented the West in the decades following civil rights. Unburdened of *de jure* segregation and enabled by anti-discrimination legislation, the USA in particular sought to shed its racist past and stride toward an inclusive culture of equal opportunity. Yet evidence presented a different picture of reality, one in which minority groups, especially African Americans, continued to struggle. Tyson, in his own unwitting way, provided tangible evidence of why this was so.

"I feel like Norman Bates, surrounded by all these doctors," Tyson said when undergoing tests to determine his suitability to fight. Tyson may actually have been seen like the fictional motel owner of *Psycho*. Disturbed, dangerous, and incapable of the kind of self-reflection that might incline more rational persons to modify their behavior. Punishment seemed to have little effect on Tyson, who, at times, sounded penitent, but acted as if he wished to be anathematized.

As Jay Larkin, Showtime cable television's head of boxing, said of Tyson after his defeat by Lewis: "Love him or hate him, you know *he's there*." That was the thing about Tyson: he could have wandered off after the fight, found himself some remote island in the North Pacific and spent the rest of his life as a recluse. We would have still felt his presence.

"The defining moment of my legacy." That's how Lewis described his win over Tyson. He'd beaten a worn-out 30-something, at least ten years removed from his electrifying prime who was trading only on persona. Lewis himself was 37, though he hadn't dissipated himself like Tyson. And yet, it was a defining moment. Beating Tyson, even a pathetically depleted Tyson, was an achievement that guaranteed Lewis a distinction along with Buster Douglas and Evander Holyfield, the other men who had beaten Tyson. We might also add other names: Don King, Desiree Washington, Robin Givens, Monica Turner. Tyson didn't go down without a fight against any of them; but they beat him, if only because they ended up with money, a measure of stability in their lives, soundness of body and mind and a sense of wholeness. As he approached 40, Tyson had none of these.

three

ARE YOU AN ANIMAL?
IT DEPENDS

Even at 35, and with little evidence in his recent fights of a resurgence, Tyson was considered by many as the best heavyweight in the world. He'd lost his World Boxing Association title over five years before and had since been suspended and imprisoned, got married and was being sued for divorce. He'd also split acrimoniously with his erstwhile advisor Don King and, despite his considerable earnings over the previous seventeen years, owed millions in back taxes. Many suspected he was completely broke. Whenever a boxer in his mid-thirties chooses to ignore evidence of his own physical decline and extend his active career, the motive is either insolent pride, misguided sureness, or money.

Tyson had never been a haughty or imperious type. Everything he'd done or said indicated that, while he had long since left the ghetto streets of Brownsville, much of those streets had traveled with him. For all his cockiness, there was a humility about his demeanor. Nor would he have been kidded by anyone who told him he was as good a boxer as he was fifteen years before, when he was on his way to becoming the undisputed champion of the world, or ten years before, when he was ailing in a prison cell, or even five years before, when he was being disqualified for biting Evander Holyfield in the midst of a savage battle for the heavyweight title. Which left money. Tyson had earned much of the stuff; and he'd blown most of it, probably all of it.

So, when the world champion, Lennox Lewis, reversed the protocol and issued a challenge to a challenger, it was an odd, though not unexpected, development. Having beaten Holyfield, Lewis might, in any other circumstance, be regarded as the best heavyweight in the world. But, that recognition just didn't come. And he *was* a haughty type: it must have been a source of torment to him. There was Tyson, barely ticking over, beating nonentities, yet still drawing all the interest. Worse still: a wide constituency of opinion held that Tyson, even without a title, was the real world champion.

Lewis got his way: Tyson agreed to challenge for his title at the MGM Grand, Las Vegas, in April, 2002. The fight was contingent on the Nevada State Athletic Commission's reinstatement of Tyson's license to box, which it had revoked in 1997. A press conference to announce the details of the fight was scheduled for the Hudson Theater in New York. Pedestals were set up twenty feet apart, so that the rivals could enter from either side of the stage and stare at each other from a distance.

Some, like Tyson's former trainer Kevin Rooney, were convinced that Tyson had genuinely misunderstood the rules of engagement, thinking that a phony face-off and a brief scuffle for the sake of the cameras was all set. Faux fights are commonplace at boxing press conferences. "Mike threw the left hook at the bodyguard. He completely missed him," Rooney observed on *CNN Live Today* (June 4, 2002). If Tyson had really wanted to hit Lewis' minder, he would have done so. "That was staged, they were supposed to do that," concluded Rooney.

Dramatically, perhaps over-dramatically, Tyson brushed aside the chaperon and proceeded to Lewis, who, it seems, didn't expect the confrontation. A rumpus broke out, with Tyson exercising dramatic license to ironic effect in biting Lewis' ankle. Tyson put it down to "miscommunication between our camps with regard to the face-off," which seemed a credible explanation, though Lewis saw fit to arrange a further press conference without Tyson at which he complained about his rival's behavior. "I wasn't going to be intimidated."

An image such as Tyson's might weigh like a millstone around the neck of many. There was a time when it seemed to drag Tyson ever nearer the ground. Yet, he arrived at the theater in Manhattan pumped, primed and, it seemed, ready for the cue "action!" "Tyson was out of control," said the *Pittsburgh Courier*, echoing the sentiments of the media (January 23, 2002). But, was he? Tyson "stood on stage and stared in the direction of Lewis," the paper reported. "One of Lewis' handlers got between the fighters and Tyson greeted him with a left-handed punch. Lewis then swung at Tyson, both entourages began pushing and shoving and a mêlée ensued."

When two of the most dangerous unarmed men in the world and their well-trained teams of bodyguards get involved in a no-holds-barred brawl, chances are that serious injuries will result. Apart from minor abrasions, no one was hurt. The affair bore the hallmarks of a stage-managed means of generating publicity for a fight that, in truth, needed no extra exposure.

As if to acknowledge that this was Tyson playing *Tyson* again, the ex-champion, having extricated himself, swore at members of the press corps, then clutched his groin in the manner of Michael Jackson circa '88 while he shouted at Lewis. His hand gestures were like those of rap artists who flail their arms like pincers as they stare at the camera. Overacting, Tyson mouthed crude dialogue that might have been retrieved from Snoop Dogg's wastebasket. The Hudson Theater turned out to be an appropriate setting for what was surely one of Tyson's more transparently dramatic scenes. And a global tv audience looked on in dazed fascination.

Show business or not, the mock-violent affair elicited a bout of tut-tutting among boxing authorities and the Vegas date was thrown into doubt when the Nevada State Athletic Commission convened a meeting to determine whether to reinstate Tyson. Writing in the *New York Amsterdam News*, Howie Evans asked: "Why is Tyson being punished for something that didn't happen in the ring? Since when is it legal or justified to hand down an indictment against Tyson for a boxing tradition: hyping a championship fight?" No crime was committed, noted Evans: "No one was arrested. And the promoters quietly were smiling to themselves" (February 6, 2002).

"Easier to find a clock in a casino," wrote Bernie Lincicome about the chances of the commission's not approving Tyson's fight against Lewis. Clocks are never seen in Vegas casinos: gamblers are encouraged to lose track of time in their quest for life-altering riches. Why remind them that it's past their bedtime?

Writing in his paper *Rocky Mountain News*, Lincicome figured that "Assorted boxing commissions, Tyson's parole boards more or less, seem to enjoy putting Tyson through his mea culpas" (January 23, 2002). He speculated in his story "Tyson is profitably out of control again" that Tyson would soon be "back amongst us, a better man for our censure but, hopefully, not too much."

Lincicome would have been better advised to search for a clock. Tyson's application to fight was rejected by a vote of 4–1 by the state-appointed commission. The lone dissenting member of the commission was Dr Luther Mack, its chair and sole African American. Mack had been an outspoken critic of Tyson and blamed him for the brawl at the press conference to announce the proposed April 6 fight. It was this incident, among others, that inclined the commission to nix the fight.

Evans reasoned that: "The scars of Tyson's history continued to be exposed and exploited by the Nevada Athletic Commission and the media – even while the hearing was in process, Internet sites around the country were taking polls as to whether Tyson should be granted a license. Newspapers were taking polls and sports journalists also weighed in with their mostly negative opinions."

While many endorsed Nevada's stance, others detected hypocrisy. The *New York Voice*, for example, reminded its readers that "boxing is not a gentlemen's game. It's brutal and at times it is not pleasant to see two people fighting each other like animals," before asking Nevada to inspect itself. "The whole strip in Las Vegas is filled with illicit activities such as prostitution" (February 6, 2002).

While Lewis had arrogantly – and rather patronizingly – announced that "Tyson must get some psychiatric help before we go forward," he may have regretted adding fuel to the Nevada commission's fire: the proposed fight vanquished, he stood to lose more than $17.5 million. The buzz was that, while Lewis was desperate to fight Tyson, he was shocked when the fight was thrown into doubt. A payday of monumental proportions seemed to have slipped by.

According to Evans, in another *New York Amsterdam News* article, Tyson was "shafted" by the Nevada committee and by a procession of other states, such as Colorado, New York, and Texas, which followed Nevada's lead and denounced attempts by other states to stage the fight. "Mass murderers and crooked politicians are treated with more respect than Mike Tyson," wrote Evans (March 28, 2002). "Tyson is being treated as if he's Public Enemy No. 1. Who has he killed?"

The answer, of course, was no one, though Tyson, by this time, understood the value of perpetuating the belief that he was at least capable of doing so. When approached by a woman interviewer for CNN/*SI* tv, he reminded her: "I normally don't do interviews with women unless I fornicate with them, so you shouldn't talk any more unless you want to." When reporting this for *Sports Illustrated*, Richard Hoffer added, in case his readers hadn't quite caught on to Tyson's whimsical artifice: "He is not serious. Of course" (May 20, 2002). At times, though, the whimsy was just not in evidence at all.

"I prefer to kill someone else than to kill myself," he told Rita Cosby on Fox News' *The O'Reilly Factor*. The interview took place in May. By then, the Lewis fight was back on and Tyson was in Hawaii preparing (May 7, 2002).

"You've just heard him say that he could kill somebody, all right? I mean he could. He *could*," the show's host Bill O'Reilly responded to the clip, directing his comment to George Getz, of the National Libertarian Party, an organization that supported Tyson's right to fight and upheld the decision of the state of Tennessee to allow Tyson a license to box. "You know he's already bitten off half the ear of an opponent. He's attacked other people. He has done all kinds of irrational things. This is, in my opinion, a gross dereliction for the state of Tennessee to license this psychopath to do anything, anything and you're sticking up for it."

O'Reilly echoed the views of many. Then again, so did Getz: "I am as appalled by everything Mike Tyson has said and done as you are, but I don't think I should have the right to prevent him from getting into the ring . . . in a free market, people should be able to watch whatever sports events they want . . . no one is going to be forced to watch Mike Tyson box."

After Nevada's refusal to let him fight, there had been interest from other states, including the District of Columbia, whose mayor, Anthony A. Williams, an African American, had unreservedly welcomed Tyson and wanted the fight in the nation's capital city. But, it was Tennessee that captured the fight. Criticism of the Tennessee decision centered on the state's responsibility for permitting a "psychopath" to ply his dark trade. Defense of it centered on the public's right to watch him do exactly that. Abominate him as they may, they still had the right to take pleasure from his abominations.

The Tyson interview for O'Reilly's show was both confessional and accusatory. "Are you an animal?" asked Cosby, to which Tyson replied: "If necessary. It depends on what situation am I in to be an animal . . . If I'm fighting, constantly from being assailed against your cohorts or people in the street because they feel that they have the right to assail me because of what people write in the papers, because of the courts, [then you're] correct and you're right."

Pledging his love for his five children, Tyson announced that he would advise them, "you're a nigga and the society will treat you like a second-class citizen for the rest of your life, so there are certain things that you must not get upset for. But, you must fight."

Asked if he was "evil," Tyson divulged: "I think I'm capable of evil," before adding "like everyone else." "Are you mentally sick?" "I don't know if I'm mentally sick, but I have episodes sometimes. I'm a depressant kind of dude. I have episodes and I'm human . . . sometimes I'm in episodes when I'm at work."

This was Tyson outside the cocoon of torment that had been both liberating and stifling. Liberating because he had earned and blown several fortunes and luxuriated in the kind of lifestyle he could, on his own admission, never have imagined; stifling because it meant he must maintain the image of the depraved psycho even though he believed his frailties were no more exceptional than anyone else's. His, however, were exaggerated by a media that "assailed" him and which in turn slaked the thirst of "people in the street."

"People respect force," Tyson believed. "People respect being assertive and that's what I am because they won't respect me for what I truly am." He talked in terms of his "essence," which interested no one and of love, which his reputation denied him. And of money: "I do need the money. That's why it's called 'money' – because we all need it. It's our god. It's what we worship and, if anybody tells me anything different, they're a liar." If anyone doubted him, they should follow his instructions: "Stop working, just live on the street and show me how much God's going to take care of you."

Despite the parental warnings that preceded the interview ("The language and subject matter of this interview are not appropriate for children"), the Tyson on view was repulsive, but knowingly so. "Where does the rage come from?" asked Cosby. Tyson's reply condensed a question that has occupied scholars for a century or more: "You're so white. Where does *that* rage come from?"

———

Long before she met Tyson, Monica Teresa Turner had been attracted to a dangerous man. Not dangerous in the way of the most dangerous man in the world in a boxing ring. But dangerous in the way of a high-end drugs baron responsible for up to half the coke and heroin that flows into DC. Dealing in that kind of quantity of illicit drugs brings its own dangers. Far from being fearful of this, Turner appears to have been a moth to danger's flame.

Born in the DC's middle-class neighborhood of Petworth, Turner attended the Regina High School in Hyattsville, Maryland, an all-girl Catholic school. Her father earned a modest living working for the city and her mother, Maebell Steele, raised her with her half-brother Michael. Turner majored in psychology at the University of Virginia with grades good enough to gain her a place at Georgetown University's School of Medicine, where she specialized in pediatrics. She took advantage of a program designed to assist minority groups in medical studies. The pride of her family, Turner worked assiduously in her efforts to qualify, yet there was something of the Jekyll and Hyde about her.

"Turner conducted an improbably high-octane social life, keeping company with students who drove fast cars," wrote Patrick Rogers in *People Weekly* (August 21, 1995). "She began dating Eugene Byrd, manager of the Les Nieces nightclub."

Twenty-eight years her senior and married, Byrd, according to Rogers, "cut a charismatic figure but was also deeply involved in the drug underworld." In 1963, Byrd, then age 26, was arrested for carrying a deadly weapon, though he became known to the Federal Bureau of Narcotics and Dangerous Drugs in the late 1960s, when he was identified as a drugs dealer. He was indicted in Florida in 1973 for his part in a narcotics ring.

Shortly before Turner began at Georgetown, Byrd was sentenced to ten years in a federal prison in Lewisburg, Pennsylvania, for conspiracy to distribute cocaine. At the time of his arrest in 1989, he was described by law enforcement officials as one of a dozen men involved in a cocaine and heroin business. Some idea of the scale of their operation can be gained from the fact that one of the partners borrowed $80 million from a loan corporation to finance Byrd's operations. He pled guilty to possession with intent to distribute more than eleven pounds of cocaine. Co-operating with prosecutors helped get Byrd's sentence reduced to three years. At the time of his arrest, Turner accompanied Byrd to his lawyer's offices, though she wasn't asked to testify in the case. "Monica seemed entranced by him," said the assistant US attorney who prosecuted Byrd.

"It's hard to know whether she learned it from the nuns or Byrd, but Turner clearly developed a head for finance," wrote Roxanne Roberts, of the *Washington Post*, when profiling Turner in 1995 for her article "In Mike Tyson's ring Georgetown medical student Monica Turner is something of a fighter herself" (April 25). "She purchased a $124,500 town house off Georgia Avenue near the Maryland border, and has an interest in a four-unit building near Catholic University." Her daughter by Byrd, Gena, was enrolled in a private preschool. The program in which she entered medical school provided for a waiver of tuition fees for twelve months only. After that, they ran to $22,500 per year. So Turner was hardly down-at-heel when she met Tyson. Though she was considerably better off when they split.

Turner met Tyson at a party at the New Jersey home of Eddie Murphy in the late 1980s. Quite how Turner got on the list of invitees is not clear. She wasn't a singer, actor, or involved in show business. Tyson and she struck up a friendship and one that lasted.

The rules of Indiana Youth Center are very strict: a person was allowed to visit only once every fourteen days, for two hours on a weekday, or one hour on a weekend. Every six months, Tyson could submit a list of the people who wanted to visit him. Tyson's list included celebs such as Spike Lee, James Brown, Shaq O'Neill, and Maya Angelou. And Monica Turner. Between 1992 and 1995, she became a regular invited guest, flying to Indianapolis every two weeks and checking into a hotel near the correctional institution. It's not clear who financed the visits. Sometimes, Turner would have Tyson's daughter Mikey with her.

She was waiting for him when he was released after three years in 1995. He was there when she graduated from Georgetown in May 1995. Tyson incongruously carried a pair of opera glasses. It was one of Turner's rare appearances in public and she denied all interview requests. Tyson spoke only rarely of her. In a 1995 interview for *Ebony*, he was studiously evasive, acknowledging only that: "She [Monica] is very strong and fortunate. You know what I mean, to have a child and go to school for ten years and everything. I respect women like that, because I know how hard it is to be a woman, especially a black woman" (vol. 50, issue 11, September).

Gossip about a possible marriage started the moment Tyson bought her a diamond ring, which Turner often wore on her left hand. Tyson's previous marriage had been brief and ill-starred. But, Turner appeared to be cut from a different cloth to Robin Givens, Tyson's first wife, who was an actor with a flair for self-publicity and a habit of discussing family business on national television. Turner's academic background and commitment to working with children gave her a patina of respectability and down-to-earthness that was, of course, belied by her former relationship with a cocaine baron.

Tyson and Turner were wed by Tyson's confidant, advisor, and spiritual guide, Muhammad Siddeeq, in an Islamic ceremony in

April, 1997. Turner shuttled between a Bethesda home Tyson bought for her, Tyson's own gated estate in Southington, Ohio, and his home in Vegas. She extended her intern year over 24 months to allow her more time with her family. On one of the rare occasions she spoke about Tyson, Turner called him "the most complicated of men, the most desirable too. He is beautiful on the outside and the inside. I can't help but love him." Writing for *The Advertiser*, Malcolm Folley in his headline called her "The Tyson Tamer" (June 28, 1997). "He is the most compassionate and gentle man I have ever been with," Turner told Folley.

It was not an evaluation shared by many others, though Muhammad Siddeeq was one of them. Around the time of the wedding, he spoke to Roberts and told her: "Mike's belief in God has brought out in him the latent respect for women that was always there." It was interesting that a confidant believed Turner had somehow tapped into the respect for women that had hitherto been concealed. Deeply concealed, we might add: Tyson had for years seemed the all-purpose misogynist and had often spoken out as if proud of the fact. "I never dreamed of fornicating with as many beautiful women as I did," he reflected.

Muhammad Siddeeq told Roberts that Turner would change Tyson radically: "I see Monica as one who will continue to help stabilize Mike and help to keep him directed and focused towards the positive goals that he has set for himself." Within two years, Tyson was back in court accused of assault and being described by the prosecution as a "timebomb."

Turner remained publicly supportive of Tyson throughout the period of his imprisonment in 1999 for an assault in Maryland. But, in January, 2002, she filed for divorce, claiming that Tyson had moved from their home to one of his other estates in Las Vegas and spent little time with his family. By this time, the couple had a daughter, Rayna, age six, and a five-year-old son, Amir.

Somehow, everyone knew it would end like this. The words "happily ever after" were never going to close a Tyson story. Even the torments of the damned are made more sufferable with a loved one to share them. For a short while, it seemed Tyson had found one. Turner appeared to be an alkali to Tyson's acid: someone who could neutralize the effects of life's cruel, capricious corrosion. Her perceptiveness, sensitivity and sheer stoicism appeared to be just what Tyson needed. Yet she became a kind of emblem for put-upon womanhood, despairing at Tyson's seeming inability to change, claiming to have tired of being an unloved mother of his children. When she filed for divorce after five years of marriage, she claimed that Tyson, then 35, was a profligate spender and an adulterer.

A year later, when the settlement was reached, Tyson agreed to pay Turner $6.5 million from future earnings and hand over the deed to the couple's home in Farmington, Connecticut. The 61-room home (38 bathrooms), which had an indoor pool, movie theater, working elevator and 3,500-square-foot nightclub, was put on the market at $4.75 million. Turner's payout would include the proceeds of the sale. Turner was also awarded the $4 million Potomac house where she lived with their children, of whom she was granted custody. She received an undisclosed sum plus a percentage of Tyson's ring purses. If he failed to pay on time, the total amount would increase to $9 million. The couple reached what was initially described by Turner's attorney, Sanford K. Ain, as a "quiet, respectful and dignified settlement." Quiet, respectful and dignified are not adjectives readily associated with Tyson.

The settlement appeared anything but that. Earlier, in October, 2002, Tyson, still smarting from the Lewis defeat, contested a $10 million divorce settlement that had been reached. He had earned more than $20 million from the Lewis fight, but much of that had been absorbed in outstanding debts. Turner filed to require her husband not to spend his fight earnings. The next month, Tyson called Turner and reportedly asked whether she would be willing to settle their differences privately. The couple drafted a settlement document that stated Tyson should pay Turner an additional $10 million from the Lewis fight purse and two subsequent fight purses. She could remain at the couple's home in Bethesda, Maryland, and would raise their two children.

Tyson predictably missed paying the first installment in full and Turner moved to enforce the schedule. In reply, Tyson's lawyers answered that the settlement was invalid: part of it was drawn by Turner's half-brother, Michael Steele, a lawyer and

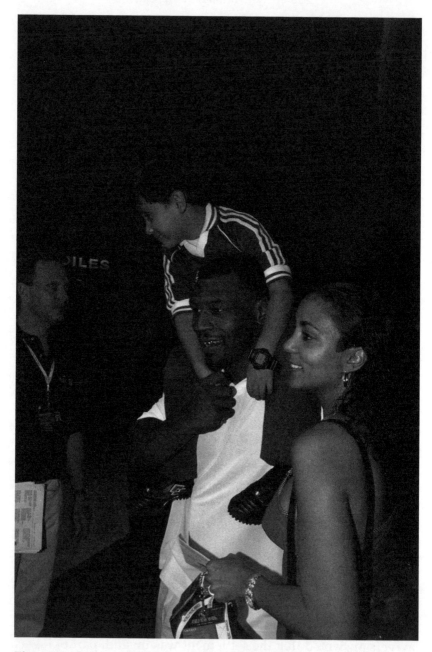

Figure 2 Prior to marrying Tyson, Monica Turner described him as "beautiful on the outside and the inside." After filing for divorce in 2002, she complained that he had squandered millions on "clothes, jewelry and other women."

Republican candidate for lieutenant governor of Maryland. A resulting affidavit provided an insight into the prodigal lifestyle of Tyson. "Mike had spent and against my wishes wasted millions on clothes, jewelry, cars and other women," according to Turner. "He has spent most of this amount primarily on waste and people, other than for the benefit of the children and myself. He saves nothing."

As well as the homes in Connecticut and Maryland, Tyson also had a luxury estate in Las Vegas. The court documents revealed that, between 1995 and 1997, he spent $230,000 on cellphones and pagers, threw a birthday party costing $410,000 and bought cars for sixteen friends and acquaintances (although it didn't specify, one can safely assume the cars weren't Neons). His company Mike Tyson Enterprises Inc. owed $8,100 for the care of his pet tigers and $65,000 for limousine services. Turner said she watched helplessly as Tyson squandered over $140 million of his boxing earnings. The court documents showed that, in January, 2003, he was $18 million in debt.

None of this implies that Tyson kept Turner tethered to the sink and made her save coupons for grocery shopping. She had quietly "amassed a fortune", according to Tyson's attorneys, who calculated that he had given her more than $17 million in cash and personal property. The catastrophic tax situation he was in was, in part, attributable to her neglecting to mail a $5 million check to the IRS, they claimed. Easily done, as we all know. Far from being on the breadline, Turner was raising the children with "considerable domestic help" at the Bethesda estate and driving "any number of fancy cars," including a Rolls-Royce and a Mercedes 600.

———

The world heavyweight title fight between Tyson and Lewis was held on June 8 at the Pyramid Arena in Memphis, Tennessee. It nearly didn't come off when a bank refused to issue a letter of credit to local promoters, citing "moral issues." The group of promoters were allowed more time to come up with the $12.5 million site fee (what the venue charges for using its facility). Finkel was probably on target when he argued that the postponement from the original April 6 date and the vast publicity generated by, at first, the press conference, then Nevada's refusal to let Tyson fight, had stimulated even greater interest in the fight.

It was, as expected, a sell-out, the 19,185 tickets generating more than $23 million in revenue, a record gross, the previous highest being $16.86 million set in 1999, when 17,078 fans saw Lewis-Holyfield II in Las Vegas. Ringside tickets were $2,400. The state and local sales tax produced about $1.9 million, more than any single event's total gross revenue in the Pyramid's history.

The television revenues were divided between AOL Time Warner's subscription channel HBO and Viacom's Showtime, which co-operated in a unique joint-venture. Lewis was contractually obligated to HBO and Tyson had a similar arrangement with Showtime. Neither side was willing to allow its fighter to appear on the other network. Such was Tyson's appeal that Showtime could have continued profitably to feature him against the likes of Andrew Golota and Brian Nielsen in nontitle fights. But, with the kind of revenues expected from a title fight of such magnitude, the networks agreed to a co-production. As Rich Thomaselli of *Advertising Age* put it, "half the pie is better than no pie at all" (June 3, 2002). The networks priced the ppv at an all-time high of $54.95 and split the revenue 50/50, except that the losing fighter's network received $3 million extra to compensate for the fact that the winner's network could replay the fight at a later date. Overall, the fight grossed $103 million.

The front-end money was $17.5 million each, this being the amount guaranteed to both Tyson and Lewis. In addition, each would take a percentage of gate receipts, foreign television rights, sponsorship and merchandise (which in this case ran as high as $7.5 million). Tyson's take-home pay was slashed by having to repay an existing $12 million debt to Showtime, though he would probably have ended up at least $8 million better off after being pummelled for eight rounds. Lewis couldn't have hoped to make close to his end with any other opponent. Yet, three years before, the possibility of his ever fighting Tyson was remote; not because he seemed incapable of giving Tyson a competitive fight, but because Tyson was approaching another of his many crises, this time one that appeared to be terminal.

―――― four ――――

LIKE WATCHING A SERENGETI
LION RIP INTO A WARTHOG

He must have felt like he was emerging from a sensory depri-
vation tank. Tyson roused himself for action after a long period
of quietude. It had been over a year since the second Holyfield
fight. Tyson had been on Zoloft, an antidepressant medication,
for much of it. He'd also been attending weekly psychotherapy
sessions, sessions in which, as his lawyers put it, he'd made
"immense progress." Toward what, they didn't specify, but sufficient, it seems, for him to be able to stop taking the medication
periodically. "I'm taking Zoloft . . . and it probably is making me
feel a little better," said Tyson. "But it makes me feel bad because
I like to, you know . . . I'm penis-centered."
 Whether he was on or off his medication on March 1, 1998,
is not known. Tyson was dining at Au Pied de Cochon, a
restaurant in Greenbelt, Maryland. Among the other diners were
Sherry Cole and Chevelle Butts, who were with a local comic
named Michael Colyear. They ran into Tyson's party and
decided to sit together at four two-top tables pulled together. The
waiters brought their food, Tyson signed a few autographs and
happily allowed a woman at a nearby table to take a photograph
of him. When a man at another table took a photograph without
his permission, Tyson became irritated, though calmed down
when the photo-taker was asked to leave.
 Butts and Tyson started arguing. Butts alleged that Tyson
grabbed Cole and requested sex. On learning that Butts was
a correctional officer, Tyson, they claim, swore at her. On the
women's account, the terms "bitches," "sluts," and "ghetto
whores" were used. The women filed suit in the US District

Court, seeking $7.5 million in damages. They reckoned Tyson moved toward Butts in a threatening manner and, to defend herself, she threw a cup of coffee at him. Tyson's bodyguards stepped in after he turned over a table.

For most men, the shame and ignominy attending such accusations would be reason enough to occasion anxiety. For celebrity athletes and entertainers, the infamy that often follows these kind of slurs can cause colossal embarrassment. But for Tyson it was just one of a catalog of allegations he had been fielding pretty much since he first rose to public prominence. It was almost two years before he reached an undisclosed settlement with the women. In papers filed by Tyson's lawyers, six witnesses confirmed that Tyson was verbally harassed by his accusers, but was not abusive in return.

Later in 1998, on August 31, Tyson was traveling by car in Gathersburg, Maryland, a suburb of Washington, DC. He was sitting in the passenger seat of his wife's Mercedes convertible when the car behind rammed into it. It was a chain-reaction: the car behind was itself rearended, shoving it into the Tyson vehicle. Tyson himself seemed to respond as if in a chain-reaction: he leaped from the car in a fury and lashed out, striking Abimelec Saucedo, a 62-year-old man, in the face and kicking Richard Hardick, 50, in his groin. Returning to the car, Tyson raced away with Turner at the wheel. Police stopped the car soon afterward, not far from the Montgomery County Airpark. According to the officers who stopped him, Tyson complained of chest pains then made allusions about racial profiling. They described Tyson as "combative."

Tyson was on probation for rape at the time of the incident, so, even for a headstrong guy like Tyson, this was irrational in the extreme. Even though he was unarmed, his fists might well have been construed as dangerous weapons by the courts. Boxers' sometimes are.

The hearing was scheduled for February, 1999. The month before, Tyson was in the ring against Francois Botha, who was known as the "White Rhino." Despite coming off two defeats and looking forward to his 33rd birthday, Tyson was able to command $10 million. It was Tyson's first fight in nineteen months (only his seventh in as many years) and the ringrust had shown. He labored terribly against the willing, if limited, South African. At 32, Tyson seemed sluggish as he pursued Botha, eventually catching him in the fifth round with a short right that traveled about six inches and connected conclusively with Botha's head.

It may not have been vintage Tyson, but it offered a reminder of at least one reason why he was so mesmerizing: "The wonder of so much force materializing out of thin air and the delicious destruction of another human being," as *Sports Illustrated*'s Richard Hoffer put it (January 25, 1999). "Botha's collapse incorporated all the important themes of the Tyson Mystique, the ability to generate so much danger on demand being the principal one." Another, we might add, was unpredictability: a Vesuvian eruption of terrifying power at a moment when it was least expected surprised and perhaps dumbfounded those who had or were beginning to write off the aging Tyson. And an even greater surprise followed: as Botha disintegrated under the weight of his own body, Tyson, having separated him momentarily from his senses, stooped to support him in an effort to cushion his fall. As Hoffer observes, he revealed himself as "monstrous, but human too."

The fight, which took place in front of a disappointing crowd at the MGM Grand, Las Vegas, went some way to restoring Tyson in the public's imagination. But this was not a fully restored Tyson. Not technically, anyway. Prior to the pulverizing end, Tyson had not won a round. There again, the Tyson of the imagination does not have to win rounds and, at one point during the fight, there was a tiny glimpse of what some might think of as the essential Tyson. Toward the end of the first round, the two boxers went into a clinch and Botha grimaced – an unusual reaction when boxers are holding each other and catching their breath. Botha later claimed: "He was trying to break my arm." Later confronted with this accusation, Tyson merely confirmed it with a perfunctory "Correct." Although he didn't say it, he might just as well have added: "Next question?"

Tyson seemed in defiant mood after the fight, reminding the media "I'm a man," and that "when I die I'm going to paradise and I'm not worried."

With the money he earned from the fight, Tyson was able to pay the US government a chunk of the $14.3 million he owed in back taxes, though he still had assorted creditors – including his former trainer, Kevin Rooney, whom he owed $5.1 million – and would need, according to his manager of the time, Shelly Finkel, "three to four fights for him to become solvent again."

Solvency is not the kind of problem typically associated with someone whose gross earnings over the previous two-and-a-half years were about $140 million.

Three weeks after the fight, he was in court, listening to his lawyer trying to put the assaults on the motorists in context. Tyson himself pleaded *nolo contendre* to two misdemeanor charges of second-degree assault, meaning he did not contest the charges; but nor did he admit or deny guilt. He settled out of court with the two recipients of his blows. Both Saucedo and Hardick were ready to say that Tyson should not go to prison. The expectation was that he would receive a lenient sentence. Plea agreements often mean that there is not a prison sentence in Maryland, and Tyson's lawyers negotiated such an agreement with State Attorney Robert Dean.

A memo from Tyson's lawyers to the Montgomery County Court sent prior to the hearing suggested that Tyson was on his way to becoming a "useful and contributing member of the community" as long as he continued to receive psychiatric treatment and performed more volunteer work. The lawyers, Paul Kemp and Robert Greenberg, focused on their client's mental health, noting that, at the time of the violent incident, Tyson was not in training for a fight: he was under suspension. "It was unclear whether Mr. Tyson would ever fight again," wrote Kemp and Greenberg. As boxing was Tyson's means of support, he had grown anxious about his ability to take care of his family financially. "Everything in his life and career were in chaos," Kemp and Greenberg concluded, offering this as context rather than excuse.

The memo to District Judge Stephen P. Johnson came in response to the State Attorney sentencing memo, in which Tyson was described as a "bully" and a "timebomb" with a "propensity for violence" (not an uncommon trait for a boxer, of course). Tyson had "continually bizarre and frightening outbursts", the prosecutors claimed, backing up their argument with magazine and newspaper stories of his previous indiscretions. As further evidence, the prosecutors, Douglas Gansler, who succeeded Dean as Montgomery State Attorney, and Assistant State Attorney Carol Crawford, invoked Tyson's past criminal record from his youth and references in the media. They recommended "incarceration" for Tyson. "He's paid off the complaining witnesses," said Gansler. "You don't get attacked and beaten to the ground by a random person and them come in and testify on their behalf without a large incentive to do so, such as a large sum of money."

His lawyers argued that incarceration could be interpreted to mean home detention, a community facility or even community service. They were presumably mindful that second-degree assault is punishable by up to ten years in prison.

Gansler resisted attempts by Tyson's lawyers to use the mental state of their client as part of an argument for clemency: "Whether mental issues mitigate [a person's behavior] or make someone more dangerous is a philosophical issue."

Tyson's attorneys countered that "rampant inaccuracies" about Tyson's background, social and psychological, marred the District Attorney's case and referred to the Nevada Athletic Commission's finding that Tyson suffers from low self-esteem and has "significant problems with trust, as he fears being betrayed." Leaving aside the self-esteem, Tyson's insecurity about being betrayed was based less on a pathological condition, more on an accurate appraisal of his experiences over the previous decade.

Saucedo, the 62-year-old whom Tyson had struck, bore a cut on his lip. Comparing the fate of Botha a few weeks before to that of Saucedo, Tyson's lawyers concluded that their client had made no "significant" contact. "If Mr Tyson had intentionally struck Mr Saucedo, one need only look at the crumpling of Francois Botha as a result of the single punch from Mr Tyson to envision the result."

Despite their differences, both sets of lawyers seemed agreed on a number of points. In their own ways, they both conjured up an image of Tyson as a lethal, unstable intimidator. Their differences lay in how the legal system should handle him. Their image was shared by Judge Johnson, who characterized Tyson as someone who "acts compulsively and violently, especially when not under supervision."

Johnson continued: "Unfortunately, this court cannot look into Mike Tyson's soul and so we have two conflicting views of this defendant . . . but, reviewing his prior conviction of a crime of violence – rape – and a juvenile record of theft and violence and the fact he lashed out at two people unknown to him in ways that were assaultive . . . the court sees this as a tragic example of potentially lethal road rage."

There was an audible gasp from nearly all of the 190 spectators who packed Courtroom 1 of the Montgomery County Courthouse as Johnson sentenced him to two years in jail on each count of assault (the punch and the kick), with one year suspended, running concurrently. He was also fined $5,000, ordered to serve two years' probation and perform 2,000 hours of community service on release. The court granted the prosecution's request for no bail.

Plans to appear in an April 24 fight to be shown by the cable television network Showtime were ruined, though his boxing license remained valid for the rest of the year. After that, said Keith Kizer, Deputy Attorney General in Nevada, which restored his license after it had been earlier revoked, Tyson would have to reapply in 2000. If he was out by then.

Complicating Tyson's plight was his parole violation, which could have landed him with another four years inside. An appeal would have meant giving up his no-contest pleas and facing trial on more severe charges that carried up to twenty years. Judge Patricia Gifford, who presided over Tyson's rape trial in Indiana, granted an appeal by Tyson to modify his probation so that he could serve the rest of it in the Montgomery County jail. Gifford added a 60-day sentence to Tyson's time, which amounted to 30 days with good behavior. Tyson was led from the court in handcuffs destined for the Montgomery County jail.

He had remained silent throughout the hearing, though he had written a letter that Judge Johnson read out aloud. Tyson maintained: "Jail would mean I lose everything."

He was wrong: he did not lose his potency to fascinate. If anything, his power to enthrall was enhanced. On May 21, less than four months after the sentence had been handed down, the Maryland Parole Commission voted 5–1 in favor of granting Tyson's release. Four days later, Tyson left the jail in Rockville, Maryland, sporting a tee-shirt, gray sweatpants, and prison-issue sandals.

Twenty-one-year-old Amadou Diallo was from Guinea, West Africa, and worked in New York as a street vendor, selling hats and clothing. In the early morning of February 4, 1999, he returned from work to his apartment in the Bronx. Four white police officers investigating a cab shooting approached him. They later said that they believed Diallo motioned his hand toward his pocket, reaching for a gun. He was subsequently found to be unarmed. The officers, who were members of the NYPD's Street Crime Unit and carried nine-millimeter semi-automatic weapons, opened fire, discharging forty-one shots and killing Diallo instantly.

"Even an execution squad would not have fired so many shots," said the Reverend Al Sharpton, who had staunchly supported Tyson throughout his travails. Sharpton asked: "Are we talking about policing or are we talking about a firing squad?"

The sheer quantity of gunfire turned what would have been a controversial case into a *cause célèbre*, with inchoate protests escalating to a fully fledged campaign after the acquittal of the officers. Over a thousand arrests were made in the aftermath of the killing.

The trial of the officers was moved from the Bronx to Albany, where the jury was mainly white. The prosecution didn't raise the possibility of racism during the trial. Unlike the initial absolution of the four Los Angeles police officers who were acquitted after the Rodney King trial, this did not touch off riots (the King riots left fifty people dead). There were street marches involving thousands, mostly in New York. Banners bearing "Jim Crow Justice" and "KKK Cops" were carried.

49

But perhaps the most significant event in helping raise awareness of the killing was the performance of a song by Bruce Springsteen, who wrote "American Skin (41 Shots)" specifically about the Diallo case and sang it at a number of concerts. Although the song wasn't recorded, it was downloadable from the internet. It included the line: "You can get killed just for living in your American skin." By the time of Springsteen's appearance in a concert in New York in June, 2000, the police officers had been acquitted. Diallo's parents praised Springsteen for keeping the memory of their son alive, but the police and the mayor condemned him.

The Diallo killing came within two years of another globally publicized case involving a black suspect and the police. In 1997, Haitian migrant Abner Louima was arrested, taken into custody and sexually assaulted by police officers in Brooklyn.

Tyson may not have had the Diallo incident specifically in mind when he counseled his children, "you're a nigga and the society will treat you like a second-class citizen." But, his words would have gained force as a result. Tyson himself may have borne many of the costs of an image of black people that's indexed to what Jan Nederveen Pieterse, in his 1992 book *White on Black: Images of Africa and blacks in Western popular culture* calls the Brute Nigger, a "black male stereotyped as beast, who is 'tamed' by means of lynching (emasculation)." There were countless others who bore a much greater cost. Nederveen Pieterse writes: "The American complex about race is geared chiefly to suppressing black males" (p. 178).

The suppression takes different forms. Whether you're an iconic athlete who charges millions to exhibit your talent or a street vendor who ekes out a living selling cutprice trinkets, the fact remains: you will be contained, restrained, or else crushed. The links between Diallo and Tyson are not as tenuous as it might appear. Savagery, bestiality, promiscuity, cannibalism: attributes such as these sustain an unbridgeable difference between blacks and white America. Forget how bogus and antiquated the attributes may seem. They live and draw subsistence every time a black person does or is just thought to have done something that might be seen as vaguely negative. In Tyson's case, he rarely stopped.

———

No sooner had Tyson surfaced than Finkel was inundated with offers, and the speculation about his next opponent started. The announcement of the Felix Trinidad vs. Oscar de la Hoya megafight was eclipsed by news of Tyson's liberation. Dates that were booked for other fights suddenly became unbooked, pending information on Tyson's intentions. No promoter or television channel wanted to risk clashing with a Tyson fight, especially a Tyson comeback fight – and there had been two others, both of which excited global interest. Up to 1999, Tyson had appeared in six of the eight most-viewed ppv fights ever. His fights accounted for one-third of all ppv boxing revenues and 17 percent of all monies from non-movie events (including rock concerts and wrestling shows): $461 million of a total of $2.7 billion.

Finkel told the media that Tyson had made no decision about whether he would even fight again, though, given the scale of his debt, only boxing would provide him with enough money even to approach clearing it. The only one thing for certain was that a Tyson comeback fight would not clash with another premier sports event. As Ron Borges of the *Boston Globe* explained: "October is generally avoided by the pay-per-view industry for big fights because of the competition with the baseball playoffs and it does not generally put competing pay-per-view boxing events in the same month because subscribers tend to buy only one major event in a billing cycle" (May 22, 1999). Tyson's comeback fight was on October 21, 1999.

It was billed as a fight, but, in truth, the encounter with Orlin Norris was a débâcle. Norris, a decent cruiserweight but with neither the power nor the resilience of a full-blown heavyweight, disintegrated almost immediately, hurting his knee as he fell so badly that he was unable to continue. The fall happened after the bell to end the first round. The anticlimactic affair was declared no-contest. Somehow, it seemed to chime. A straightforward knockout, a points decision, or an injury stoppage just wouldn't work; there almost had to be something bizarre about a Tyson fight, even if it meant an absence of conflict.

While ostensibly a free man, Tyson was subject to urine testing at least twice a week and unannounced home visits by state authorities. He also needed permission before leaving Maryland. He underwent an anger management program and completed a psychiatric evaluation. The conditions of his parole also stipulated that he perform 200 hours of community service over two years following his release. He remained on parole until February, 2000.

One of the effects of infamy is that your world becomes a Panopticon – an ideal prison where cells are arranged around a central watchtower in which a concealed authority figure or several of them can inspect without being inspected. Everybody could see Tyson, but he couldn't see all those who were watching him. His behavior was observed, monitored, and chronicled. Virtually every movement, every twitch, was broken down into minute fragments, each analyzed and subject to media surveillance. Another effect is that the media become a kind of seismograph, recording the direction, force and degree of severity of each action. A push in a crowded bar might register more of a reading than an accidental brush in a shopping mall or an angry glare. But less than a fullscale Tyson transgression.

Long before June, 2000, the sheer presence of Tyson seemed enough to provoke some sort of incident. So there was a predictability about the commotion before Tyson's intended match against Lou Savarese in Glasgow, Scotland. Tyson had been in Britain six months before to dispatch the appallingly overmatched Londoner Julius Francis. His reception had been so encouraging for promoter Frank Warren that a swift return was arranged.

Tyson's earlier visit was portentous: protesting groups complained that a convicted rapist shouldn't be granted a work permit. The British Home Secretary of the day, Jack Straw, was lobbied before he eventually approved Tyson's visit. And, when Tyson did arrive, the crowds greeting him were hysterically reverent, especially in the predominantly black district of Brixton in south London. Here, the crowd could not have been more enthusiastic if Nelson Mandela had arrived. It made nonsense of the speculations of some civic leaders who warned that his presence could provoke unrest.

The return was less controversial to begin with, though the actual fight against Savarese was thrown into doubt when promoter Warren threatened to file assault charges against Tyson. Prior to the fight, Tyson had spent $630,000 on jewelry and charged it to Warren. A row over who was liable for the jewelry broke out; according to newspapers, including the British tabloid the *Sun*, Tyson attacked Warren. What actually happened may never surface, but Tyson agreed to pay Warren $3 million, effectively reducing his purse for the fight to $5 million. It still worked out at over $131,600 per second: Savarese lasted only 38 seconds before he crumbled under a fusillade of Tyson's shots, an errant one of which hit the referee.

It was after this fight that Tyson uttered the words that were to hunt and haunt him forever: "I want Lennox Lewis. *I am going to eat his children*. I will rip out his heart and feed it to him," then added curiously: "Praise be to Allah."

This wasn't the first time he'd used the "eating children" phrase (in fact, his former trainer Teddy Atlas reckons he got it from a movie). Tyson had made frequent use of vile and repellent invectives that seemed to go way beyond the more traditional bad-mouthing of boxers. But, the suspicion grew that Tyson was not so much spontaneously combusting as responding in a calculated and judicious manner. Judicious because it was both sensible and prudent in the particular context it was used.

Think of the reaction: outrage, offense, abhorrence. Another Tyson transgression. More infamy for Tyson. By this stage, Tyson had grown weary of trying to live down his reputation, or even avoiding embellishing it. He seemed to be embracing the image, what *New Republic*'s Robert Wright once called "middle America's nightmare, a crude, violent, sexually aggressive black male – threat to home, wife, daughter" (in his 1995 article, "Tyson vs. Simpson," April 17).

Far from fleeing his nightmarish rep, Tyson wanted to act it out. Further proof of this came in September, 2000, when he exploded at a Los Angeles press conference to announce his fight against Andrew Golota, a fight billed as "the matchup of the heavyweight world's two dirtiest practitioners" (Golota was a serial grantee of disqualifications). In a passage of either piercing self-reflection or freakish self-parody, Tyson yelled: "I'm a convicted rapist! I'm an animal! I'm the stupidest person in boxing! I gotta get outta here or I'm gonna kill somebody." Maybe it was neither self-reflection nor self-parody; maybe it was an artifice, contrived and built by the corporeal Tyson for the delectation of others.

This was surely Tyson serving up *Tyson*, the latter a hideous monster of the imagination made flesh by the former. In other words, the 33-year-old former champion, denuded of his dignity and denied anything resembling respect, decided to cash in whatever saleable items he had left. Looking back on his career, he realized that the one thing that endured, regardless of his successes or failures in the ring, was how others thought of him – as a beast. "My doctors are concerned about the fact that I'm a violent person, almost an animal," he told the gathered media at the press conference, adding that the Zoloft he was taking was the only thing that prevented him from killing all of them.

Some measure of Tyson's complicity in a stratagem – and it was surely that: a device for deceiving an enemy – can be divined from his consenting to an interview with *Maxim*, a glossy magazine specializing in features on the likes of Christina Aguilera and Carmen Electra and with regular columns such as "World O' Sex" and "Girls of *Maxim*." Around the end of 1998, when in the midst of a nineteen-month period of inactivity and presumably weary of weathering media assailment, Tyson decided not to grant interviews. After two-and-a-half years, he invited a reporter, Albert Baime, and a photographer to spend 36 hours with him, following his daily routine as he prepared for a fight scheduled for June 2001 (which didn't materialize).

The ensuing article appeared in the July edition of *Maxim* under the title "Mr. Nice Guy" and was later described by Huel Washington, of *The Sun Reporter*, as "one of the most disgusting, degrading, despicable, unflattering, racist articles . . . for years" (July 26, 2001).

"Raised in a Brooklyn ghetto, he was arrested 38 times by age 13," Baime restates what surely everyone already knew, before moving on to describing trainer and surrogate father Cus D'Amato's providential interception, removing Tyson from the streets and installing him in a mountain retreat in the Catskills.

"Secluded there in the mountains like a Frankenstein project, D'Amato molded a monster," writes Baime, invoking a clichéd analogy, though one that might be a little too revealing to be lightly dismissed. He also alluded to Tyson's animalism when he described his dining habits: "Watching Tyson eat is like watching a Serengeti lion rip into a warthog."

"Dark, unhinged, uncontrollable," is how Baime sees the "old Tyson," who occasionally surfaces to remind the writer of "the gruesome incidents in this man's past life."

It was, as Washington suggests, "degrading"; but "racist"? Washington argued that "members of the media who have a darker pigment would not have crucified Tyson because they have traveled the same route and know how he feels being ostracized." Baime points out: "I'm a Jew."

According to Washington, Tyson was "devastated at being a victim of such deceit," though there are enough direct quotes in the story to conjecture at least that Tyson was an active participant in the trickery, if indeed that's what it was. "Listen. I'm crazy. Whoa! *I'm fucking crazy!*" replies Tyson after the interviewer asks for an elaboration of his statement "I'm on the verge."

Tyson also reflects on his past mistakes. "There was so *much damage*," Tyson recalls on the effects of his actions, adding: "But my only regret is infidelity. When I was younger it was all about pussy." In his maturity, he was able to cite Alexander the Great as one of his heroes, the reason being: "Alexander got all the bitches and they weren't all whores!"

At one level, this was the unspeakable degenerate revealing his primal self. Yet Tyson was probably fully aware of the effect such apparent depravity created. Self-parody it may have been. Tyson's problem was that there was never enough distance between the image he wanted to create and what others saw as the true Tyson. He was no Ali: he had neither the aplomb nor the history to get away with mockery of this kind. Whereas Ali always managed his image in a way that allowed his audience to glimpse a space between the theatrical performance and the man, Tyson hamfistedly confused the two. Or, more accurately, gave others only source material and no way to separate the role from the role player.

If Tyson was devastated by the *Maxim* rendition, he must either have learned very little from his fifteen years' experience with the media or have become thin-skinned in his late thirties. After all, he'd been annihilated in one way or another by the media since losing his title in 1990 and maybe even before. His entry into the public consciousness was not via his eloquence, intellect, or wit: it was through his uncommonly destructive capabilities. In 1986, when Tyson pronounced that, with every punch, he had "murderous intentions," he was presenting the world's media with enough raw material to start building a new icon.

Baime's stated intention was to discover whether the older "volcano of a man" had reformed into a "new gentler Millennium Mike." On this account, the answer would be emphatically "No." Though the suspicion persists that Tyson was acting reflexively: he was looking back on his own career, in particular the image that had brought him infamy, and was living it. This was Tyson addressing himself as an object. Far from being devastated, Tyson was more likely beaming and self-satisfied with the results.

———

There are also costs in perpetuating an image that has been bounteous in many respects and they are the litany of accusations that are leveled at the image rather than the human being. In the same month as the *Maxim* article was published, the Sheriff's Department of San Bernadino County, California, opened an investigation into a woman's allegation that she was sexually assaulted by Tyson. The allegation was described as "without merit" by one of Tyson's representatives. Tyson was in training in Big Bear Lake, to where he had fled "devastated" after reading the magazine.

By August, San Bernadino County prosecutors had decided that they did not have enough evidence to pursue rape charges.

Speaking to the *Los Angeles Times*, Deputy District Attorney David Whitney, perhaps ingenuously, announced: "Because of his past, we looked extremely carefully at the case, because of his reputation for violence and his prior rape conviction" (August 18, 2001).

Tyson's attorney, Darrow Soll, argued that: "Initially, there were reports that he [Tyson] is a convicted rapist, so he must be guilty of this." Later, he announced that he was satisfied that the investigation was "based on facts, not on public sentiment." Tyson refused to be interviewed by law enforcement officers.

Allegations of sexual assault against Tyson were, by this time, legion; and they would continue. In 2000, a Vegas topless-bar manager fired a dancer who accused Tyson of hitting her during a scuffle at the club's bar. "Mike never struck her or pushed her in any way," the club owner confirmed. "She's in it for the money." Acting for Tyson, one of his associates, Peter Seligman, concluded that it was "another case of a celebrity being hunted down for money. There's no bigger target than Mike Tyson" (quoted in the *Chicago Defender*, May 11, 2000).

By the end of 2002, two separate allegations were issued by women in Las Vegas. Both cases were dropped, prosecutors concluding that there was not enough evidence to warrant charges.

The spiral of allegations against Tyson continued, raising the suspicion that they were leveled at the image as much as, if not more than, the man. In case this appears too lenient a suggestion, we should stay mindful of the point made by Jeff Benedict in his 1997 book *Public Heroes, Private Felons: Athletes and crimes against women*: "In an attempt to counter the growing public perception that athletes receive preferential treatment, law enforcement officials often overcompensate in their efforts to maintain impartiality" (p. 79).

Allegations against athletes, especially high-profile, not to say notorious, athletes like Tyson, are investigated seriously and, where appropriate, prosecuted aggressively in the effort to nullify popular ideas about the reluctance to disgrace popular celebrities. Tyson would never have been the beneficiary of the doubt. So it was no surprise to discover more accusations of wrongdoing in the first two months of 2002. Again there was more than a hint of a man acting out his public persona, perhaps confused as to whether he should play to the gallery or resist the ceaseless intrusions of the media into his life. There seemed no middle way.

The retreat to the mountains was, it seems, no solution. Even in the solace of his Big Bear camp, the attentions of others proved an irresistible attraction and Tyson was never able to recover the self-discipline he had in his late teens. Self-discipline is perhaps the wrong choice of term, as we will see in later chapters: externally imposed discipline spiced with occasional indulgences serves better.

The fight against Andrew Golota, in Detroit in October, 2000, had been another disappointment on a par with the Norris non-event. Golota quit on his stool at the end of the third round and the result was later changed to no-contest. The Michigan Athletic Commission also fined Tyson for failing to take a drug test. The one-round blow-outs against Francis and Savarese in London and Glasgow respectively were hardly competitive. Effectively, his only genuine outing since November 1996 had been the win over Botha in January 1999. So the sixth-round stoppage win over Brian Nielsen in October, 2001 worked like a tonic.

Relieved of rape allegations, Tyson, then 35, turned his attentions to the Danish boxer, who enjoyed homefield advantage in the packed 21,000-seater Parken football stadium in Copenhagen. Admittedly, Nielsen was limited and a year older than Tyson, but he had previously been beaten only once in 63 pro fights. Tyson seemed better focused than he had been for years – which was not the case for Nielsen, who explained: "From the start of the fifth round, every time Mike hit me in the head, I couldn't see for about ten seconds." Tyson immediately began planning a January date with Ray Mercer.

The Mercer fight was intended to be Tyson's last fight before a matchup with the then heavyweight champion, Lennox Lewis. While challengers are traditionally meant to pursue champions, the process was reversed in this case. Sensing that Tyson was a far greater boxoffice draw than himself, Lewis insisted that Tyson, as a mandatory challenger, avoid Mercer and proceed straight to the ring with him. Lewis had temporarily lost, then regained, his title after a contretemps with Hasim Rahman (and, before him, Oliver McCall). The Mercer fight was canceled after Lewis went to court to file an injunction on the grounds that, as champion, he had the right to make a mandatory defense against the number one contender. It was an extraordinary, if logical, move.

Win, lose or draw, Tyson virtually guaranteed a career-high payday for whoever stood in the opposite corner. A fighter of the caliber of Evander Holyfield or Lennox Lewis, or way before them (in 1988) Michael Spinks adds value to a Tyson fight, of course. But, essentially, the opponent is exactly that: an opponent. In his mid-thirties, with his peak years perhaps over a decade before, Tyson remained the world's foremost sports attraction. Lewis was aware of this and, having been twice deposed by modest boxers, searched for a career-defining, credibility-building, hugely enriching fight with Tyson.

Tyson, for his part, could have lived without Lewis, or without a world title. "The planet's most violent celebrity," as Baime had described him, drew attention like a magnet draws iron filings. $5 million fights against modest fighters like Nielsen and Golota would have helped chip away at the tax debt and contribute to the impossibly lavish lifestyle Tyson had created for himself. But a single fight against Lewis offered the riches of Croesus: before a contract was signed, television networks were rubbing their hands at the prospect of pay-per-view revenue in the order of $150 million.

five

HIS VITAL ORGANS IN EXCHANGE FOR FORGIVENESS

Evander Holyfield had once been told he had a heart condition that would threaten his future as a professional boxer. Stubborn to a fault, Holyfield continued to fight. He'd also been told that little men can't become heavyweight champions. So he set out with a rigorously demanding conditioning program designed to transform him from a cruiserweight into a fully fledged heavyweight without a corresponding loss of speed or endurance. When he was told that, at 34, he was too old, too small, too slow and too weak to withstand the onslaught of the resurgent Tyson, he knew he had a challenge. There was, it was thought, no stopping Tyson: apparently getting stronger with every fight as his comeback progressed, he would easily overwhelm a fighter four years his senior whom he'd been favored to beat five years earlier when their matchup was originally scheduled. It had been postponed, after Tyson suffered an injury in training, then canceled completely after Tyson was convicted of rape.

Ordered by a federal jury to pay his former trainer, Kevin Rooney, $4.4 million for breaking a "lifetime contract" in 1988, Tyson showed no signs of resentment and revealed that he would have written Rooney a check for the same amount if he had asked him. Instead, Rooney sued him for $49 million, this being the rough equivalent of 10 percent of his earnings. While the amount may not have been significant in terms of Tyson's overall earnings, it raised the hackles of Jesse Jackson, who said it "should have been dismissed as a nuisance suit;" Al Sharpton, who complained that the all-white jury's verdict was racially charged; and *Hyde Park Citizen* writer Sylvester Leaks, who likened it to the Dred Scott decision of 1857 (which involved a fugitive slave who lived in a free state but was told that the Constitution did not protect blacks, either free or enslaved, as they belonged to "a subordinate and inferior class of beings"). The lifetime contract was a verbal one made in 1982 when Tyson was 16. There were no witnesses to the agreement, apart from Rooney and the late Cus D'Amato, who guided Tyson's early career. In October 1996, at the time of the ruling, Tyson was too focused on other matters to be distracted.

Tyson had fought four times since his release from prison in March 1995. It was his most active period since 1990/91. Still beaten only once in his life – and that defeat retrospectively rationalized by reference to a disordered domestic life that upset his training – Tyson was looking more dangerous than ever. So much so that the Nevada State Athletic Commission insisted that Holyfield should undergo a series of medical examinations to determine his fitness to face Tyson. The Commission took the unusual step of arranging medical visits to his training camp to monitor his performance. Presumably fearful that there could be a tragedy, the Commission wanted to cover itself. While Holyfield came through all the tests with flying colors, the fact that he was under such close scrutiny by the organization charged with responsibility for the sport's and its athletes' well-being was ominous.

Some pay-per-view retailers in Cleveland and on Long Island offered customers a special deal of $9.95 per round, so that they would not feel short-changed if Tyson finished the fight early. If, as many suspected, Tyson finished off Holyfield within a round, the viewer got change from ten dollars.

Compounding the feeling that Holyfield would be eaten whole by the reawoken monster was his indifferent form of late. Of his previous seven fights, Holyfield had won only three. He'd looked unconvincing in his fight immediately before meeting Tyson. A fifth-round win over Bobby Czyz in May 1996 did little to help his credibility.

The most-asked question about Holyfield was "why does he carry on?" He was, by 1996, one of the richest athletes of all time, accumulating $120 million in ring earnings. So the extra $11 million he stood to earn from facing Tyson was neither here nor there. His ability was beyond question. A bronze medalist at the 1984 Olympics, he had won a world cruiserweight title before making what many thought was an impossibly hard transition to the heavyweight division. But he proved his doubters wrong by beating Tyson's conqueror Buster Douglas for the world title in 1990 and, after losing it in 1992, regained it, then lost it again in 1994. In the process, he helped set a pay-per-view record, attracting 1.36 million viewers at an average cost of $36 to produce a gross take of $48.9 million for his 1991 fight with George Foreman.

Compared to Tyson, Holyfield may have been dull out of the ring. But inside, he gave full value and featured in some of the most rousing fights in heavyweight history. In particular, his three fights with Riddick Bowe and his dramatic win over Michael Dokes in 1989 were among the best heavyweight fights of the late twentieth century. His ne'er-say-die attitude drove him to the most improbable comebacks. Time and again, critics had pronounced his career effectively over, only to be proved embarrassed by Holyfield's indestructible resolution.

He could have retired, his credibility intact, in the safe knowledge that he would be remembered as one of the best heavyweights of the modern era. Yet here he was, at an age when many men are barely energized enough to make the trip to the gym, confronting Tyson. "Mismatch" did not quite capture how one-sided this contest appeared. And for this Tyson was to receive $30 million.

The bookmakers' odds were 25–1, though a shrewd punter could have got even longer odds if he or she shopped around Vegas a few weeks before the fight. As the fight approached, the odds shortened, as they always do, though a Tyson win inside the first three rounds was favored.

Yet, in previous fights, Holyfield had shown estimable resolve and staggering powers of recuperation in the most unpromising circumstances. He also seemed to relish the kind of trench warfare in which technical skills were subordinate to determination. There was also a historical reason to believe Holyfield might have a chance. In *A Savage Business*, Richard Hoffer tells an instructive tale from Holyfield's youth when both he and Tyson were at an amateur training camp at Colorado Springs. "In a rec room one afternoon Tyson was taking his turn on the pool table," Hoffer relates. "He scratched and, refusing to sit down and wait another turn, started to rack them up" (p. 209). Holyfield reminded Tyson that it was his turn at the table. The two squared off for a few seconds before Tyson fled to his room, leaving Holyfield to set up the table and play his game. Holyfield, by all accounts, was always motivated by the prospect of belittling a bully. He may well have been on the night of November 9, 1996.

It was instantly clear from the opening bell that Holyfield was no more intimidated by a seasoned 30-year-old Tyson than he was by the untutored rascal who shot his mouth off around the pool table. Tyson stomped out as usual, all swagger and minatory stare, only to be met halfway across the ring by a rival who was so pumped he was willing to risk getting knocked out in order to unload his own shots. If he was surprised by Holyfield's sheer appetite for a fight in the first, Tyson was stunned into disbelief in the second when Holyfield – not known for his punching power – made him lurch with a left hook to the head.

The unlikely pattern was set: Holyfield stamping his authority by dominating every facet of the fight. Far from waiting for Tyson to initiate attacks, Holyfield marched forward, pushing back Tyson so that he could rarely establish leverage enough to make his own punches effective. Holyfield's pressure was hardly interrupted: the occasional Tyson shot would bring back memories of the power he still possessed. But, for the most part, it was Holyfield who summoned more force. Continually, he pressed Tyson against the ropes and punished the peculiarly ineffective Tyson, whose facial expression turned from menace to bewilderment. How could Holyfield boss him around like this?

Tyson's torture was ended in the eleventh after Holyfield sent him reeling to the ropes, prompting the referee to call a halt and register one of boxing's biggest upsets in years. Later, Tyson claimed he couldn't recall any part of the fight after the third round. He would have forgotten the blow that sent him to the canvas in the sixth, the twenty-three unanswered punches he took toward the end of the tenth and the constant appeals he made to the referee about Holyfield's illegal use of the head. It was puzzling to see Tyson turn to the ref for help; it was like an anarchist calling 911.

Even after all the post-fight dissections, the fight remained mysterious. Holyfield had been unpredictable in recent years, but no one could have expected such a ferociously effective performance, better than anything he had produced in at least five years. Conversely, why had Tyson submitted so – dare it be said – tamely? After a frenetic start, Tyson seemed subdued and unwilling. Nobody really dominated Tyson, surely: he allowed himself to be dominated.

In the absence of rational explanation, Holyfield's seemed as reasonable as any other. "This fight is blessed," he said before the fight. "I will beat Mike Tyson. There is no way I cannot, if I trust in God. God is that good." And after it: "I came up to the fight and I was led by the spirit."

The belief that God is in your corner can function as a motivating instrument, of course. Many athletes over the years have competed as if divinely inspired. Faith works. Of course, it may not make up for a shortfall in ability, but, when combined with the kind of technical proficiency that Holyfield possessed, it occasioned a competitive performance of the highest rank. Tyson, despite being an avowed Muslim, had no belief powerful enough to resist Holyfield, who became only the second man in history to win the world heavyweight title three times. The other was Muhammad Ali. Holyfield won Tyson's World Boxing Association (WBA) title; there were other claimants due to the proliferation of boxing titles in the 1990s.

Holyfield's win was a popular one, though it would be misleading to assume Tyson, in 1996, was detested; far from it. As Robert Lipsyte wrote in the *New York Times*: "For those who love Mike Tyson – and there are more than you might think – his abandonments, humiliations, betrayals, persecutions and prosecutions are theirs writ larger, their rap opera, too. He gives them heart because he has not quit, he has not stopped boxing, and he has remained true to his posture: he has not begged forgiveness, turned to crack, committed suicide, or dumped his old friends" (November 17, 1996).

Holyfield was, indeed is, a decent man, a pious Christian with family values. Every victory was credited to God rather than the three or four months of unflinching preparation that he put into every fight, the courageous manner in which he fought and the masterly craft he acquired over a career spanning more than two decades. Even a suspected heart condition couldn't deter a boxer whose nickname, for once, did actually reflect his character: the "Real Deal." Holyfield was a genuine, honest-to-God, fearless combatant who fought long, long after he'd earned enough for a comfortable retirement.

Yet Holyfield was no hoarder. He was an original board member of the Major Broadcasting Cable Network (MBC), the USA's only African-American-owned and operated 24-hour cable network, an organization with a brief "to broadcast the positive aspects of African-American culture, which are too often ignored by other networks," according to fellow board member Willie E. Gary. Among MBC's other founders were Marlon Jackson, formerly of the Jackson Five, and ex-baseball player Cecil G. Fielder. It started operating in 2003. Never one to attract publicity, certainly not in the way Tyson did without trying, Holyfield quietly involved himself in worthy projects. For instance, he addressed the Congressional Task Force on Fatherhood and advocated Christianity in a number of public forums. True to his commitment to parenthood, marriage, and what became known in the 1990s as family values, he decried Tyson's behavior and, in 1992, told *Flash*, a US mail-order boxing magazine, that: "It would be wrong for me to be fighting somebody convicted of such a crime as rape" (February 29).

When reminded of his apparent change of heart, Holyfield could not remember his statement. Nor were there any signs of outrage from the church about a man of God doing business with the somewhat ungodly Tyson. For all his beatific posturing, Holyfield never tried to project himself as a standard bearer of Christianity. A deferential supporter of black enterprise, he would have been a model civil rights champion if he had been around in the 1960s. Christian decency and integrationist resolve would have equipped him well. It's easy to imagine how well he would have personified Martin Luther King's Southern Christian Leadership Conference. Hailing from Georgia, Holyfield strove for exactly the kind of integration King sought. Never a radical, Holyfield sunk his energies into his progress as an individual who wanted to be judged only on the "content of his character." Maybe racism still hindered the progress of African Americans, but Holyfield was not one to complain about it: his alternative was to work around it or through it, or perhaps, more accurately, just make so much money that it didn't matter.

Tyson could never relate to Holyfield. They were similar in two respects: they were both African American and they were both boxers. Beyond that, there were few points of contact that would have made meaningful communication possible. Holyfield claimed that, when they were amateurs, he had looked after Tyson, who was four years his junior, though Tyson said he couldn't remember this happening. Tyson was as prodigal as Holyfield was provident. Holyfield's piety jarred with Tyson. But even more jarring was the dignity that Holyfield maintained through all his exertion. Most boxers who insist on prolonging their active careers long after their peak years become parodies of themselves, pathetic beings vainly seeking former glories and trying to recapture something that time has taken away. They're almost invariably chasing a lost cause. Not only are their efforts to no avail, but they become recipients of a sentiment that's anathema to any athlete: pity.

Think of 38-year-old Muhammad Ali being battered by Larry Holmes, who took breaks from the execution to ask the referee to stop a grotesquely unbalanced contest. Think of Mark Spitz, winner of seven gold medals at the 1972 Olympics, trying to revive his efforts two decades later, his gray hair colored to conceal his age, but his physical decline painfully in evidence. Think of Ben Johnson, disgraced by his disqualification from the 1988 Olympics, yet still refusing to give up the ghost ten years on. Pitiful.

Holyfield was 34 when he beat Tyson. He'd been written off several times before, like when he'd lost to Riddick Bowe and when he'd lost to Michael Moorer. He could have withdrawn from boxing a rich man and people would have respected him. But, he couldn't countenance retirement. He shared this inability with a great many other athletes. With Holyfield there was no public disapproval, less still condemnation and never the slightest hint of the dreaded sentiment. What must have stuck in Tyson's craw was the quality that Holyfield always seemed to have and yet which had never been even remotely within his own reach, dignity. Survivor that he was, Holyfield hadn't survived the kind of adversity Tyson had. True, much of Tyson's adversity was the product of his own enterprise, but there was an object lesson somewhere in him. Redemption surely awaited him. There's nothing like a crushing defeat for instilling humility and, at the post-fight press conference, Tyson asked for Holyfield's hand, but not in friendship: "I have the greatest respect for you."

Tyson seemed less involved than usual. Not exactly fatalistic, but free of the rancor that might be expected of a boxer who had just lost both his title and his claim to be the best heavyweight on earth – a claim that had been largely accepted by everyone. "I'm just here to render my services," he suggested and he alluded to the inevitable rematch that would follow. The numbers made it inevitable.

When the counting was over, it was announced that the fight had grossed over $100 million. A return contest practically guaranteed a similar figure. Both fighters were, on paper, wealthy: Tyson's total ring earnings had passed the $300 million mark, and Holyfield had earned over $130 million.

Tyson, perhaps with one eye on his rival, introduced a more instrumental mentality to his approach, reminding everyone that, in defeat, he had earned $30 million: "Monday, I'll sign up for another $30 million."

And so he did. Seven months later, the two would meet again in a fight that would effectively affix to Tyson a mask behind which he would both perform and recoil, crumble and rebuild.

———

1962. A segregated United States moved agonizingly towards civil rights, but remained ripped by racial divisions. Malcolm X warned of "social dynamite" in the ghettos waiting to be detonated, while JFK struggled to defuse it. James Brown's soul classic "Night Train" evoked the unstoppable motion of black protest. White America watched fearfully, as the inevitability of desegregation became manifest. There was another fear, this one shared with black America.

Boxing's heavyweight championship of the world has always held an expressive value that goes beyond sport. A largely American possession, the title's holders have for long been typically vested with moral leadership, an authority informally conferred on them by blacks and whites alike. The prospect of Charles Sonny Liston becoming champion terrified almost everyone.

Far from welcoming the formidable black fighter, who had emerged from the ghetto via the penitentiary, "Black leaders and their followers feared the prospect of Sonny Liston as champion," according to Nick Tosches, author of *Night Train*. "It was believed [Liston] would bring disgrace and trouble; would impugn and abrogate black respectability; and would be like gasoline to bring white hatred flaring forth anew" (p. 159).

Liston was, as Nick Tosches describes him, "the big bad nigger who looked at you like he didn't know whether to drink your blood or spit on you . . . something that was inhuman, but also something in which humanity was not even vestigial" (p. 46). Today, such a person might be highly marketable; intimidating African Americans from sport and show business are regularly turned into commercial products that exploit racist fantasies about black bestiality. But, as Tosches points out, "In those days, bad niggers were not the darling middle-class iconic commodities and consumers of a white-ruled conglomerate culture" (p. 159).

The towering, illiterate Liston came from Arkansas, though he spent most of his life in St Louis, where he became a habitual larcenist. Imprisoned in 1950 after a violent robbery, Liston – then aged 20 (though there are doubts about his birthdate) – was taught how to box by the prison's chaplain and began fighting professionally in 1953, shortly after his release.

At the time, boxing was largely under the control of organized crime, Frankie Carbo, aka "The Gray," being the supreme overlord. All manner of recondite deals were made to ensure that Liston became the property of the Mob, though Liston himself was probably unaware of his virtual serfdom. By 1960, when he surfaced as a contender, Liston had probably only a dim awareness of who owned what pieces of him. Nor, it seems, did Liston himself much care. "As long as I'm fighting and making money and driving a good car and eating regular, nothing much is bothering me," he declared.

Floyd Patterson, from whom Liston took the world title, was, like the earlier black champion Joe Louis, often lauded as "a credit to his race." With civil rights so near, white leaders as well as black organizations, including the National Association for the Advancement of Colored People, supported Patterson. They were crushed as helplessly as Patterson himself was once the indomitable Liston had finished his business: he blasted Patterson within a round and repeated the feat in a rematch.

In 1964, the year of the Civil Rights Act, Liston defended his title in a spectacle that seemed like a foregone conclusion. The challenger was voluble, perhaps too voluble for his own good. Most suspected whistling in the dark. Whistling bravely, or perhaps tremulously, was Cassius Clay, hopelessly overmatched and destined to go the same way as other Liston opponents – so it was popularly thought. Unbelievably, Liston surrendered his title; then, in a second fight, meekly lay down for the count after what seemed an innocuous blow ("the phantom punch," as it became known).

Few were convinced that the fight had been honestly fought: why would the hitherto ferocious and apparently invincible "King of the Beasts," as *Look* magazine called him, succumb so tamely? Tosches has no definite answer, though he reasons that the substantial amount of money gambled on the rank underdog Clay shortly before the fight supplies a clue. Even at the zenith of his career, it seems, Liston was under the domination of others and his destiny linked to their material interests.

The Mob's involvement in his life ended only with his death in 1971. His body was found in his Las Vegas home, and, though traces of heroin were found in his corpse, a verdict of "natural causes" was ruled.

"As soon as a black person starts looking for acceptance from white America he will never be at peace with himself – because they will never give that acceptance to him." John Horne, a member of Tyson's management team, was dogmatizing to Donald McRae, author of *Dark Trade: Lost in boxing*. Bilious prejudice unsupported by evidence, or piercing insight?

Liston had never looked for acceptance, nor had Tyson. If either of them had, it wouldn't have done them much good, though, in Tyson's case, he gained an acceptance of sorts. Not the kind he would have sought, perhaps. He was accepted as evidence of the animal that lies dormant inside all African Americans. Liston's experience must have touched Tyson. Comparisons between the two were not new, though Tyson himself had limited his comments to Liston's fighting prowess. He discussed him in much the same way as he did other fighters: in terms of his athletic abilities.

Then, during the build-up for the Holyfield rematch, Tyson became quite explicit, acknowledging a felt affinity with Liston. Most athletes align themselves or identify with great champions of the past who have covered themselves in glory or have led an exemplary life, the kind of life that qualifies them as role models. Liston didn't fit the bill at all. He was perhaps the least-liked champion of all time. Even Jack Johnson, at the depths of his popularity, enjoyed the support of African Americans during the first two decades of the twentieth century. Liston was liked by practically no one. Apart from Tyson, it seems.

"This may sound morbid and grim," announced Tyson, "but I pretty much identify with [Liston's] life. He just wanted people to love and respect him and it never happened" (quoted in Hoffer's *A Savage Business*, p. 242).

Holyfield had never outwardly solicited acceptance either. In a way, it just descended on him. His faith, his values, his prudence and his enterprise was admirable. His doggedness in returning to the ring to fight what appeared to be lost causes and winning them earned him esteem. And yet, he was never, as Horne put it, at peace with himself. Other fighters in their mid-thirties with several million in the bank, directorships, and a portfolio of investments might regard a win over Tyson and a third world title as the consummation of a glittering sports career. Not Holyfield.

Tyson's options were more clear-cut. He'd carry on boxing. He'd earned plenty of money, but he'd also blown most of it, and the IRS was on his back. Besides, he was Mike Tyson, the most marketable athlete in the world. Who could turn their nose up at $30 million? The aura of invincibility had now been smashed into a thousand pieces, but people would still cough up big money for the rematch. It was as if the Holyfield fight was one of those freakish events, like Bob Beamon's 29 feet 2.5 inch long jump at the Mexico Olympics of 1968. Tyson must have drastically underestimated his opponent, or maybe slackened off his training after the easy wins over Bruno, Seldon, and the others. These possibilities added to the curiosity. And the curiosity was so great that a rematch offered even greater riches for the contestants.

Tyson's marketability was still strong enough to justify another $30 million, but, this time, Holyfield wanted and got parity. The deal done, the two fighters went in separate directions. Tyson replaced his trainer with Richie Giachetti, a former debt-collector and associate of Don King, and retreated as far as possible from public view, while Holyfield became more accessible than ever, launching a line of sports apparel, granting interviews at every request and, generally, making the most of his new-found recognition: he had finally won over his doubters by providing indubitable, irrefutable, and conclusive proof that he was the top heavyweight in the world.

"Tyson has dug himself deeper into his personal world, surrounding himself with a Tonton-Macoute-style crew," wrote John Lombardi of *New York* magazine (June 23–30, 1997). He prepared secretively, his managers John Horne and Rory Holloway becoming his conduits to the outside world. He even got married in the most un-celebrity-like circumstances: privately. It was a Muslim ceremony and the media were not invited.

Tyson's seclusion didn't hurt the fight. His name alone ensured that the rematch would be a commercial success, though Tyson seemed intent on not doing the promoters any favors. In one memorable statement, he told reporters that, as a Muslim, he didn't drink alcohol. St Ides malt liquor was one of the sponsors of the fight. "I'm not sponsoring St Ides," Tyson stressed. "I don't believe in it." The promoters had to grin and bear it. Tyson appeared to have no interest in aiding the fight. What interviews he gave were laced with bile: he complained that he'd been "dehumanized" and "betrayed," especially by the media. He described himself as "bitter and angry," though at no specific individual and about nothing in particular; just his life.

It was during this interlude that Tyson acknowledged that he felt a strong affinity with Sonny Liston. It wasn't the first time people had compared Tyson with Liston. But to hear Tyson himself make the connection was not exactly startling, but, well, unexpected. Liston was demonized during his rise to power and scandalized during his fall. The manner in which he retired sitting on his stool at the start of the seventh round of his first fight against Clay elicited an odor that hung in the air for many months and actually needed a Senate Antitrust and Monopoly subcommittee investigation to remove it. After all, the fearsome Liston had not been knocked down, nor had he appeared in any serious trouble in previous rounds. Surrendering the heavy-weight championship of the world in such circumstances was inexplicable.

Unloved before the fight, Liston was damned after it. Presumably, Tyson felt the same kind of processes at work on him. In his book *King of the World: Muhammad Ali and the rise of an American hero*, David Remnick quotes *Sports Illustrated*'s description of Liston as he prepared for a second fight with Clay, now Muhammad Ali: "Socially primitive and sadly suspicious and forever the man-child" (p. 250).

The similarities can be exaggerated. Liston, for all his menace, was never subject to the same kind of vilification as Tyson. True, Liston was disliked, though largely because of his connections with organized crime and his sullen, brooding manner, not on account of his deeds. He didn't actually do much apart from fight. It's also misleading to believe that Liston suffered by comparison with his conqueror. Ali, while venerated today, was in the early 1960s hated much more than Liston ever was. He converted to Islam and began to use his position as heavyweight champion to advance his views on civil rights issues. Going against the grain of Martin Luther King and the integrationist movement, Ali aligned himself with his friend Malcolm X, preaching separation and the subjugation of women. He talked of white devils. "Ali is a vicious propagandist for a spiteful mob that works the religious underground," wrote Jimmy Cannon, a sports writer of the day.

Those that had found Liston an unattractive champion might well have wished for him back after Ali began his reign. Liston, at least, filled the obligatory stereotype role: dumb, inassimilable, but entirely controllable.

There is, however, a compelling symmetry about the rematches, Holyfield vs. Tyson and Ali vs. Liston. Not only were the conditions under which they were staged similar, but their outcomes both incited disbelieving reactions.

In 1965, there was still a feeling that lightning wouldn't strike twice. Liston's astonishing withdrawal from combat in the first fight was one of those anomalies that sports throw up every so often. Liston would almost surely set the record straight and assert his authority over the upstart. Ali had enjoyed his moment in the sun to the full, but it was soon to end. Holyfield too had been the beneficiary of an athletic oddity. The reasons for Tyson's lackluster effort had never been disclosed. But there were reasons – surely. And they would not remain for the rematch. Both Liston and Tyson started favorites, reflecting the view that the results of the first matchups were not accurate indicators of genuine ability. Liston was 9–5, Tyson 5–2, according to Vegas bookies.

Ali–Liston II took place in the incongruous setting of an ice hockey arena in a small textile town called Lewiston, 35 miles from Portland, Maine. It had a capacity of 5,000, making it one of the smallest venues for a world heavyweight title fight. The money wouldn't be made on the gate: it would come through television, radio, and closed circuit. On the night of May 25, the arena was not even full. The 4,280 fans who attended didn't see much of a fight; they certainly didn't see the punch that ended it. That was visible only with the benefit of slow-motion replay. Liston barely landed a punch before disintegrating. Ali had circled him for a minute or so before firing over an almost inoffensive right hand that seemed only to graze Liston. But that was all there was. Liston remained motionless and the fight was over.

It was perhaps the most pathetic challenge for a heavyweight title in history.

The cries of "Fix!" rang out when the crowd realized that Liston, for all his horrifying reputation, had folded, apparently without taking a solid shot. Footage of the fight would be replayed over and over again in an effort to discern if and how the punch connected. Remnick reckons that the film of the fight has been studied with the same fanatical attention Kennedy assassination scholars have given the famous Zapruder film. "But, unlike the Zapruder film, with its bleeding colors and blood clouds, the films of the Ali–Liston fight actually erase some of the mystery that supposedly enveloped the event as it happened" (p. 256).

It probably looked to ringside spectators as if Liston had been shot by some sniper in the rafters, so suddenly did he drop to the canvas. But slo-mo reveals Ali throwing a short, whipping punch that "profoundly affects" Liston. Ali was still champion, though even he could hardly believe the manner of his victory. One of the abiding sporting images of the twentieth century is the one of Ali standing over the prostrate Liston, urging, no, beckoning, no, commanding him to get up and fight. He seemed as incredulous as the viewers.

Doomsayers always argue that boxing will either take a long time to recover or will never recover from a fight such as this. What they fail to recognize is that boxing actually thrives off controversy. The enduring appeal of Tyson himself is testimony to that. Boxing's popularity depends less on the technical ability of boxers, more on their ability to enrage, incense, provoke, or in some other way grab the attention of the public. A fight that ends unsatisfactorily stimulates endless argument long after the fight itself, sometimes after the boxers themselves have disappeared. People still talk about Ali vs. Liston II, as they do about Holyfield vs. Tyson II.

Everyone knows what happened on the night of June 28, 1997. No one actually knows why. Not even Tyson himself, it seems. At the press conference after the fight, he looked at Holyfield and said: "When you butted me in that first round, accidentally or not, I snapped in reaction. And the rest is history."

It was actually the second round when Tyson first appealed to the referee Mills Lane. (Tyson's team had initially objected to Mitch Halpern as referee as they believed he had been lax in allowing Holyfield's headbutting to go unpenalized previously; Halpern stood down.) Blood spilling from above his right eye, Tyson fought heedlessly and ineffectively as Holyfield nullified his power, much as he had done in their first fight. Those who believe Tyson was temporarily out of control in the third neglected that, at the very start of the round, he left his corner without his mouthpiece. It was Holyfield who pointed this out to the referee, who then motioned Tyson back to retrieve it. This might have been an oversight on Tyson's behalf. Or it might have been deliberate.

With less than a minute left in the third round, Tyson spat out his mouthpiece while in a clinch. Viewers then witnessed the extraordinary sight of Holyfield jumping in the air clasping his glove to his right ear. Amid the confusion, few noticed Tyson releasing a piece of flesh about the size of a razor blade cartridge from his clenched teeth. As in the Ali–Liston confusion, few people knew precisely what was going on: Tyson pushed Holyfield in the back, Lane struggled to restore order by separating the fighters. Once the realization had dawned, Lane deducted two points from Tyson, cautioned him and gestured the fighters to resume action.

Within seconds, the two fighters became intertwined again and Tyson, with no apparent attempt at concealment, repeated his anthropophagous maneuver, this time on Holyfield's left ear. Lane dived between the boxers and disqualified Tyson, though it was several minutes before the ensuing pandemonium subsided and an official verdict was announced. And what a verdict it was: "Referee Mills Lane has disqualified Mike Tyson for biting Evander Holyfield on both his ears."

Despite what people think, sports rarely provide a level playing field. Holyfield in victory was a footnote, while the defeated Tyson made the headlines. He wasted no time in publicly apologizing to Holyfield, and his family, and Showtime, and anyone else associated with the promotion, which had been seen by 16,331 at the MGM Grand Garden Arena and 1.95 million

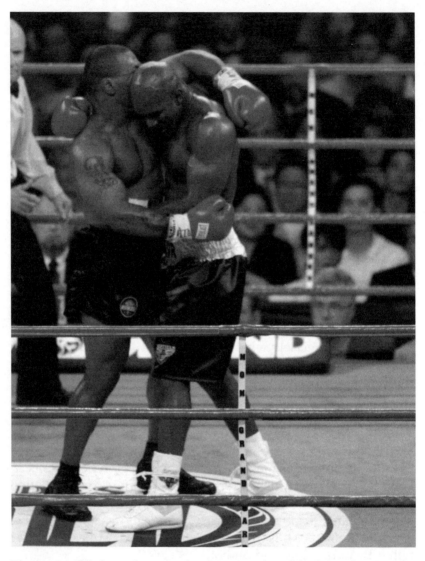

Figure 3 "He butted me in the first round and he butted me in the second," Tyson said of Evander Holyfield after their infamous fight in 1997. "What am I supposed to do? I've got children to raise. I have to retaliate." Tyson did so, but in a manner that earned him disqualification.

pay-per-view viewers plus whoever watched it with them. It was screened in 100 countries, generating almost $95 million.

The missing portion of Holyfield's mutilated ear was recovered and, later, surgically reattached. Tyson was immediately suspended by the Nevada State Athletic Commission and, as is usual following disqualifications, his purse was withheld pending an investigation.

Every so often in history, an athlete undergoes a process in which he is represented or portrayed as a malevolent, noxious fiend, whose very presence offends, contaminates, and debases. Ben Johnson was demonized in the late 1980s after becoming the first globally high-profile athlete to test positive for dope. His athletic career was effectively extinguished and, though he made several attempts to rehabilitate himself on the track, he never succeeded. In the eyes of the world, he was "the world's greatest cheat." He might just as well have checked in his Diadora spikes for a pair of cloven hooves. Until Tyson, no other athlete had approached Johnson.

Other athletes have transgressed, of course; some quite seriously. Tyson himself alluded to this when he said: "I reacted and did what many athletes have done and have paid the price for." Roberto Alomar, when a second baseman for Baltimore Orioles, spat in an umpire's face. Latrell Sprewell attacked his coach when he was with Golden State Warriors. When playing for Manchester United, Eric Cantona leaped into the crowd and assaulted a heckling spectator. Unauthorized violence is not an unusual occurrence in sports, though it typically draws a lot of publicity to the sport and a lot of notoriety to the perpetrator. Condemnation of Tyson was leavened by the jokes. Jonathan Demme's 1990 movie *The Silence of the Lambs* was still reasonably fresh in people's minds, so Hannibal Lecter gags did the rounds. But, the possible repercussions were no laughing matter for Tyson. His license would surely be revoked: for how long? There would be a sizeable fine: how much? Civil action was a possibility: would Holyfield sue? Tyson was still on probation at the time of the incident: had he violated it?

The ghost of Liston would have provided little succor: Liston himself had little interest in continuing his boxing career and slid toward oblivion, his death only six years away. In any case, Ali, in the late 1960s, attracted controversy so effortlessly that there was no inclination to dwell on a discredited has-been. With Tyson, it was different. The best-known sportsman in the world, he was at the stage in his life when, as one commentator put it, he couldn't go out to buy a carton of milk without prompting a media frenzy. He was unlikely to gain a sympathetic hearing from any quarter.

Unlikely, perhaps, but, in the narrow cracks between the slabs of denunciation there were attempts to balance an episode that had become as one-sided as a bear-baiting. Even *Sports Illustrated*'s Richard Hoffer, whose writing on the later Tyson was unswervingly critical, in reporting the fight, concluded that: "It was easy to lament his [Tyson's] miserable exploitation" (July 7, 1997).

More sympathetic was George Wilson of *The Washington Informer*, who wrote of what he called in the title of his story "Selective Outrage" (July 9, 1997). "What has been particularly dismaying is the reaction as chronicled in various media outlets," wrote Wilson, surmising that: "Tyson is expected to give his vital organs in exchange for the possibility of forgiveness" (p. 11).

Wilson compared the furious reaction to Tyson's infraction to those that greeted others outside the world of sports. "NBC sportscaster Marv Albert will soon face trial for allegedly biting a woman on her back and forcing her to engage in a certain kind of sexual activity. From the time charges were filed, Albert has been able to keep his job and be treated with respect from the media and public," Wilson observed. "On the other side of the coin, Tyson seems to be more vilified than Timothy McVeigh."

Tyson's behavior was the "bitter fruit of a mentality that urges athletes to give it all for their respective sport." In an age when athletes do not simply give of their best and shake hands after a good clean contest, Tyson was, in a way, exemplifying the win-at-all-costs approach that pervades all professional sports. So was Ben Johnson. "You can't pay two men huge sums of money to engage in 'legalized assault' and then become offended when one of the combatants goes over the line," Wilson argued.

In much the same way, Jane O'Hara, of *Maclean's*, reflected that: "In the world of boxing, where jaws are broken, skulls fractured and brains emulsified, where fans pay good money to see blood flow like the Ganges, biting an ear or two seems a minor infraction" (July 21, 1997). She may well have added that in boxing, a sport in which competitors try to inflict as much physical damage as possible, deaths often occur and boxers who kill are never culpable.

Writing for the British publication *The Voice*, Tony Sewell offered a comparable argument in his approvingly entitled "Live and kicking: Why Iron Mike was right to take an earful." The outrage that followed Tyson's actions was due to the fantasy of boxing becoming its reality. In Sewell's eyes, the appeal of boxing is essentially the same as that of the gladiatorial contests of ancient Rome, though, instead of slaves and trained gladiators, "we get two big Black guys to act out the nation's inner desire for violence" (July 7, 1997).

"As the world rises in moral indignation and demands that Tyson be banned for going berserk, I smell a distinct waft of hypocrisy," detects Sewell. "Tyson was a gladiator who broke the rules. The real savages are the audience which now wants to feed him to the lions."

After the fight, Tyson had claimed: "He [Holyfield] butted me in the first round and he butted me in the second round. What am I supposed to do? I've got children to raise. I have to retaliate" (quoted in the *Los Angeles Sentinel*, July 9, 1997). It seemed a lame excuse, but it speaks to Sewell's point about the blood lust that maintains interest in boxing. While he doesn't actually spell this out, Sewell's argument could be construed to mean that transgression in any field of competitive endeavor is actually an extension – perhaps an illogical one, but an extension all the same – of the basic impulse to win. Tennis fans don't shield their eyes when one player throws a tantrum; soccer fans don't turn away when fighting starts; NFL watchers delight in those highlight tapes that show the illegal hits as well as the legal ones. Maybe there is something basic and gladiatorial about our interest in sports. Maybe the games that capture our imagination today are not as distant from the ones that drew the crowds to the Coliseum 2,000 years ago as we like to think.

Sewell's argument has a racial component, of course. "Boxing sets up Black men as modern-day gladiators who will eventually be shelved – minus their brain cells – once they've lost their ability to thrill." African Americans are expendable. This includes Tyson, though his capacity to excite emotions was enhanced by the second Holyfield fight. A dangerous black male barely able to control his rage may not be a welcome presence in most contexts. But, in the security of an organized competitive environment, it is richly agreeable.

"For me, whether intentional or not, this was the most radical political action of Tyson's career," Sewell contends. "It sends out a clear message, particularly to a White world that ultimately sees all Black men as savages." The message was that the "sanitized version" of violence, as he calls it, is a lot less feral than the real thing "as it is played out in the brutal ghetto."

If this was indeed the import of Tyson's message, however unwittingly it was sent, it surprised a few people. The lasting appeal of Tyson lay in his ability to expose his audiences to a different world, one in which violence was endemic and the "have-nots" habitually used it in their efforts to become the "haves." Tyson personified this. And still he kept adding to it. He may have sounded like whites' worst nightmare: a violent, misogynistic black multi-millionaire willing to resist the forces of law and order even if it meant his own physical annihilation. But, he was also a dream. Living proof that African Americans were genuinely dangerous, even under the most controlled conditions.

Middle America consumed Tyson with the kind of voyeuristic pleasure patrons of the minstrel shows of the late nineteenth century took from their entertainment. Watching white and sometimes black artists clowning as they portrayed ridiculous caricatures, audiences were satisfied that they were witnessing aspects of African-American life. Absurdly and grotesquely distorted as the minstrels' performances were, they provided what audiences took to be amusing insights into the happy-go-lucky, pumpkin-eating world of black people, where the misery of slavery was conquered by an all-purpose insouciance.

Biting an opponent's ear in mid-fight was unusual and even bizarre, but perfectly consistent with the behavior patterns of a man who was never fully in control of himself. This is what made Tyson *Tyson*. Control him and he was no longer a source of such curiosity. Render him predictable and there was an automatic reduction in his allure. Take away his ability to provoke denunciation, disapproval, and damnation and what was left?

———

Barnett Wright, a writer for the *Philadelphia Tribune*, reported that in an internet poll conducted after the fight, 70 percent of respondents believed Tyson should be banned from boxing for life (July 4, 1997). Wright didn't specify what percentage thought he should receive a shorter ban, but it seems a fair assumption that the majority of them would have favored some sort of suspension. Tyson himself expected this and in the post-fight press conference attempted a pre-emptive response: "To those of you who say that I should never fight again, I can only say that I am just 31 years old, in the prime of my career and I have made it this far because I had no other way."

Trying to set his seemingly irrational action in context, he explained: "I grew up in the streets. I fought my way out and I will not go back again" (quote in the *Hyde Park Citizen*, July 3, 1997).

Yet the reaction was uproarious. "Horrified ... horrified!" President Bill Clinton may have been describing his emotional response to the atrocities in Rwanda or ethnic cleansing in the former Yugoslavia; but he wasn't. Nevada state legislators, within 48 hours of the fight, began framing a new law that would allow for the withholding of all of a boxer's purse if he committed an act "detrimental to the interests of boxing."

The Nevada State Athletic Commission called Tyson a "discredit to boxing" when it revoked his license to box for at least one year and fined him $3 million. While this was 10 percent of his gross earnings for the Holyfield fight, it left Tyson with about $2.3 million clear: $9 million of his gross purse went to Don King and $6 million to Tyson's two co-managers, leaving $15 million, of which the IRS demanded $6.3 million. The fine was deducted from the remaining $8.7 million, reduced by tax to about $5.3 million.

Had a suspension for a fixed period of time (five years was the maximum) been issued, Tyson would be reinstated after serving it. A revocation was harsher. It prevented him from fighting and so earning his living for at least a year, after which Tyson could apply for reinstatement, but without any guarantee that he would be successful. In effect, this was indefinite. Technically, he could have fought in another state, though other regulatory federations tended to honor Nevada's decisions. He may also have sought to fight outside the USA, though it was unclear whether Tyson would be allowed to leave the country on account of his parole conditions. On the whole, this was a punitive package. Tyson accepted it with some resignation. There were no protests, appeals, or even muttered doubts over the fairness of the penalty.

At least one critic believed the penalty was "racially inspired." Larry Reeves compared Tyson's punishment to those handed down to other rule-violating athletes, such as Dale Hunter of the Washington Capitals National Hockey League team. In 1993, Hunter struck New York Islanders' Pierre Turgeon from behind, sending him sprawling into the boards and leaving him with separated shoulders. Hunter was suspended for twenty-one games and lost salary valued at $150,000. Back in 1977, Kermit Washington became involved in a fight during a Los Angeles Lakers–Houston Rockets game. Rockets coach Tom Tomjanovich ran on the court to break up the fight and was hit in the head by Washington. He suffered a fractured skull, fractured jaw, broken nose, facial lacerations, concussion, and a leakage of spinal fluid. The National Basketball Association fined Washington $10,000 and suspended him for sixty days.

While Reeves doesn't mention it, the 1972 incident involving Bobby Clarke provides further perspective. Playing for Team Canada against Russia, Clarke broke Valery Kharlamov's ankle with a violent sweep of his hockey stick. Clarke received no punishment and, in fact, was the hero of the hour. Every season in every sport, there is at least one violent incident that prompts earnest soul-searching and an exemplary punishment. Increasingly, violators are dealt with by the law as well as sports federations. Several have ended up behind bars, but typically for offenses of much greater severity than Tyson's.

Reeves cited a survey conducted by his publication, the *Tri-State Defender*, in which 200 African American adults were asked for their reactions to the verdict. In all, 47 percent felt Tyson's actions did not justify the penalty; 43 percent believed the fine was justified but not the license revocation; 37 percent thought the Nevada Commission's response to Tyson was "racially motivated" (July 23, 1997).

Whatever others thought, Tyson accepted his fate. But he refused to take back his accusation about Holyfield's deliberate illegal use of his head and, later, broadened his complaint to include the referee, who, he claimed, simply disregarded Holyfield's fouling.

In March, 1998, in the midst of his enforced inactivity, Tyson became estranged from Don King, who he thought had exploited him more ruthlessly than anyone. "Don King isn't the worst person who's fucked me," said Tyson. "He probably fucked me more royally." He filed a $100 million lawsuit against King alleging fraud, and further lawsuits against Rory Holloway and John Horne, his $7,000-per-week aides. The changes in personnel were probably related to Tyson's discovery that he owed the IRS $13 million in back taxes. The enmity appeared at the same time as the *Wrestlemania* show in Boston. Tyson was to be a "special enforcer," as referees are known in these circles. His fee: $3.5 million. Tyson, already dissatisfied by the tax debt, found that King had collected $300,000 for the rights to Tyson's likeness produced in a line of action man-style dolls. As Jim Brady put it in his 2002 book *Boxing Confidential*: "Tyson had been sweating and bleeding as a pro since 1985, but under King, he didn't even own the rights to his own face" (p. 350).

Tyson confronted King physically, at one point kicking him as he demanded to know what was happening to money he thought rightfully his. The more he probed, the more he suspected that Holloway and Horne were in cahoots with King. Of a total of $168 million Tyson earned while working under King's guidance in the previous two years, King himself had kept $91 million, over 40 percent of his ring purses plus a cut of millions more from foreign broadcast rights and expenses charged to Tyson. The maximum managers ordinarily take is 33 percent. It took Tyson only six fights to make this kind of money and King may be credited with negotiating an excellent deal. But Tyson seemed to end up furthest from the money. Interestingly, African American leaders, such as Jesse Jackson and Al Sharpton, continued to support King despite what seemed well-founded allegations of exploitation and fraud.

Tales of Tyson's heroic extravagance had circulated for years. His stable of cars included top-of-the-line Rolls-Royces, Lamborghinis, and practically every other prestige marque. One call at an LA dealership cost him $2.2 million in new cars: he liked the look of a Bentley Azure, the most expensive production car in the world at the time, so he ordered four. A visit to a clothes store usually left him a couple of hundred thousand lighter – more if he took friends along (he was prone to ask Rodeo Drive stores to lock the doors so that he and his entourage could shop peacefully; everything went on his credit card). Then he had several homes to run in Connecticut, Maryland, Nevada, Ohio, and elsewhere. His penchant for keeping Bengal tigers and African lions was costly, as was his appetite for exorbitant jewelry. Tyson's was serious profligacy. Even so, his earnings suggested that he could support this kind of wasteful lifestyle. So it must have surprised even Tyson himself when he discovered that his fortune had shrunk while under the control of his management team.

Tyson had been with King for ten years, having left his previous management team amid a legal conflagration. The switch coincided with his short and tempestuous marriage to Robin Givens. After splitting from his wife, Tyson committed himself to King, at times appearing to surrender his free will in order to satisfy King's ambitions to remain the world's premier promoter. His worldview colored by King's conjectures on how America clamps down on any successful black person, Tyson hitched his wagon to King's star. Trusting King implicitly and, it seems, naïvely, Tyson thought only to examine what King had earned out of him when the relatively minor matter of the dolls came to light.

"Eaten up by rage . . . hostile, despondent and absolutely convinced of his irredeemability." That was how the writer Mark Kram described the state of 32-year-old Tyson at this stage. Still without a license, bereft of his usual management team and vilified like no other athlete in history, he was at what Kram called the "crossroads in his life and career." The writer's interview with Tyson took place days before his bid to regain his license and appeared in *Playboy* (November, 2000).

What surfaced from the interview was a character who thrived on the very thing that was denied him: activity. "What produces the self-doubt is boredom and idleness, when you're alone, when you're with your thoughts. In the midst of the action, I never have self-doubt."

Nor, according to Tyson, was he "manic-depressive," as many amateur and, indeed, professional psychiatrists had suggested. Like anyone else, he conceded, he became depressed every so often. Tyson said he was not on medication, though later reports indicated that he had been taking Zoloft. He had also been in therapy for over three years, though he remained unsure of whether he actually needed or wanted to. "When people think of Mike Tyson in therapy, they think of extreme psycho, the walking timebomb. I say to those people, 'You don't know me. Fuck you! You can't define me' . . . They just go by what they see in the paper, what people say."

Impetuous, fiery, agitated, certainly. But, perceptive enough to see how popular conceptions of him had taken on a life of their own. He felt powerless to do anything about them. Hence Kram's remark about "irredeemability": Tyson had arrived at the point where he felt that anything he did or said was liable to be interpreted as evidence of his psychopathic condition. He could do nothing to redeem himself. It's easy to imagine how, having reached this conclusion, Tyson gave up on trying to reclaim a sense of approval, admiration, respect, less still affection or dignity in the eyes of the public. His alternative was to play up to the image that had been made for him.

———

Tyson decided to apply to the New Jersey Athletic Commission for a boxing license. This was not a straightforward application form-filling exercise. Tyson was summoned to appear and answer questions for thirty-five minutes. There was a moment during the interview when the fighter, till then contrite to the point of being submissive, clasped the palms of his hands to his temples and turned to his attorney. Forgetting that his microphone was still switched on, Tyson clenched one of his fists and brought it thundering down on his desk, asking angrily: "Why do I have to go through this fucking all the time?"

It was essential Tyson: penitent one second, ferocious the next. Tyson reminded the world that he was still uncontrollable. No amount of regulation could subdue him; his nature, red in tooth and claw, could always overpower his cultured being. Tyson's minor outburst of frustrated aggression disclosed a feature of a very singular individual and perhaps something about the condition of African Americans.

Shortly after, Tyson's legal team, realizing the damage done by his incautious moment, withdrew his application for reinstatement. Later, Tyson applied to the Nevada Athletic Commission, which insisted on psychiatric evaluations before reaching its decision to allow him to box. Six clinicians administered a series of tests that included brain scans and drugs screenings. It was then that Tyson made his famous observation: "I feel like Norman Bates surrounded by all these doctors." The clinching testimony was apparently that of Dr David Medoff, who concluded that he could not discover "the presence of any major mental illness or personal disorder." His license was restored in October 1998. Tyson's restless career resumed.

six

GOD'S PLANNING TO SCREW HIM

To spare him the indignity of having his hands bound by LAPD-issue handcuffs in front of the world's media and the West Los Angeles paparazzi, the accused was fitted with a concealed electronic belt. In the event that he tried to flee, a remote control could be activated and an electric shock would stun him motionless. He arrived in a motorcade of presidential proportions, jurors arriving in a sheriff's department bus used for carrying prisoners, shielded from the media by heavily tinted glass and a mobile cordon of 240 police officers. It was February 1995: they were on a field trip, a maneuver common to California murder trials. The scene in this case was the Brentwood home where Nicole Simpson and her friend Ronald Goodman were found dead.

Johnnie Cochran Jr objected when jurors were denied access to a trophy room. He objected that it was unfair to exclude areas that reflected well on his client. The trial judge agreed, but insisted that a life-sized statue of the accused in football uniform be covered. It was a sheet, though it might just as well have been a sacramental pall that was draped over the icon.

Cochran, LA's, probably the world's, leading African American lawyer, led the defense of O. J. Simpson, the ex-football star, sports journalist, and movie actor, who was accused of the murder of his former wife and her friend. At times during the trial, Cochran's rhetoric was that of a nonconformist preacher. Robert Shapiro, a white attorney, was Cochran's righthand man. Both attorneys became internationally known figures in a matter of weeks. Yet they were bit-part players in one of the greatest real-life dramas.

It's been argued that the O. J. Simpson case was America's defining cultural experience of the decade. It claimed the front page of every newspaper in the USA, Britain, and many other countries round the world. The television companies gave it gavel-to-gavel coverage and were rewarded with record-breaking viewer ratings. Even the soaps were eased aside to make room for a story that was every bit as involving as *Days of Our Lives* and had an extra dimension – that of race.

While both sets of attorneys publicly announced their intention not to exploit the race issues, one of the defense's strategies was to shake the credibility of Detective Mark Fuhrman, one of the first police officers to arrive at the scene, at first by hinting at his racism. Soon, the entire focus of the case shifted to the detective's racial slurs, and it was he rather than the defendant who began to dominate the front pages and lead stories. No matter how they may have tried – and that was not very hard at all – they couldn't help playing the race card.

If everyone in the courtroom had been instructed not to think, less still utter, the word "race," the trial would have been a masked ball, the players presenting themselves behind false faces. The world knew this was about race. As the trial started to dictate every day's news agenda through 1994 and 1995, research indicated a curious difference in the interpretations of evidence and testimony presented. A majority of African Americans believed Simpson to be innocent of the fatal stabbings that took place on the night of June 12, 1994, while a majority of whites thought he was guilty. It was as if whites and blacks were looking at the same thing, except through different lenses.

Near the end of the trial, a perverse symmetry reared itself. Sixty-four percent of whites interviewed for a study found the evidence against Simpson convincing and would have returned a guilty verdict had they served on the jury; 59 percent of African Americans, when presented with exactly the same evidence, opted for an acquittal.

Four years before, in 1991, a *Wall Street Journal*/NBC News poll revealed a "chasm in attitudes" between whites and African Americans. Whites saw a country where relations between blacks and themselves had improved over the previous decade;

blacks saw the opposite. One of the most contentious issues dividing the two groups was federal government assistance. Many blacks welcomed the government's efforts, especially affirmative action, but whites were skeptical of such efforts and thought it time for blacks to be allowed to fend for themselves.

The acquittal was widely seen as an expression of outrage at the racism in the Los Angeles Police Department, racism that had been brutally exposed in the amateur videotapes that recorded the beating of Rodney King three years before. The Simpson case unearthed the possibility – however unlikely – that a racist plan had been hatched by the LAPD to frame Simpson, a conspicuously successful millionaire African American who could lay legitimate claim to being one of the USA's most decorated and celebrated sports stars ever. Without his kind of fame and money, Simpson might have become just another inmate in a prison system already scandalously overpopulated by black males: about one in three young black Americans are in prison, on parole or on probation at any one time. In many states, five to ten times as many black men under the age of 30 are in prison as whites. Not Simpson, of course: he had sufficient funds to hire a top defense team. His legal fees are thought to have been in the region of $10 million.

Time magazine, in its first issue following Simpson's arrest, featured his police mugshot on the front cover. This was hardly surprising: the same shot was ubiquitous, adorning virtually every news publication. It was a powerful image: Simpson staring out through hooded eyes, his arrest sheet number BK401397006179 strapped across his chest and "Los Angeles Police: Jail Division" framing the shot. But *Time* added its own Stygian touches. Apart from its headline AN AMERICAN TRAGEDY, it artificially darkened Simpson's face and surrounded it in murky shadow to produce a representation that resonated with menace.

"No racial implication was intended," the magazine's editor assured 800,000 computer bulletin board readers. The doctored photo was just "a work of art." Not so, answered an assembly of black interest groups led by the National Association for the

Advancement of Colored People (NAACP). The cover presented a stereotype that pandered to white racism. Here was the surly black brute, dark, sinister and dangerous, a throwback to days when lynching or emasculation were the prescribed methods of taming bestial black males, especially those who messed with white ladies. Even a naïve reader would have got the sense: O. J. used to thrill whites with his athleticism, then make them laugh in his movies, but now he goes after white women. He's as black as sin itself.

Some accused the magazine of a scabrous attempt to crank up circulation figures by appealing to the latent racism of white America. This was the line taken by a rival magazine, *Newsweek*, which published the same picture, but without the brushwork. *Time*'s editor, James Gaines, would not apologize for the tampering and actually tried to reverse the tide by prompting the query: is it not racist to say that being blacker equates to being more sinister?

Around the same time as the Simpson hearings, another image of a black male filtered through the night air of Indiana and into the world's media. As he left the medium-security prison where he'd been for the past three years, Tyson was enveloped by a swarm of bodyguards and swiftly ushered to a waiting car. His first public appearance for years was brief. It had been anticipated with a mixture of celebration and dread. Those who celebrated knew that Tyson was a victim: wrongfully imprisoned, not for rape, but for being a black male. Those who dreaded his re-emergence into civilized society knew he was no such thing: he was a rapist who got less than he deserved.

Now 29, Tyson had lost three years of his athletic career. Three years when he should have ruled the roost, almost certainly would have ruled the roost. Plenty of athletes have done time. None of them at a time when they dominated their sport. Even if O. J. had been found guilty, he would have been imprisoned long after his sports career was over. If anything, by this time he was known more for his exploits in the *Naked Gun* movies than on the football field. Black America had either forgiven Simpson or suspected he was framed by a racist police force. He was accused of killing a white woman and her white friend. Tyson was convicted of raping a black woman.

———

There were no speeches and no interviews when Tyson was released from the medium-security prison in Indiana. He shot straight toward Don King's stretch limo, which carried him to a nearby mosque. Tyson praised his new god, Allah, before boarding a plane for his 90-acre estate deep in Amish territory in Southington, Ohio. Liberation must have been sweet, though, according to *Newsweek* writers John Sedgwick and Alison Samuels, Tyson had merely "substituted a whole new prison for the old one" (in their article "He's back," August 21, 1995). While Sedgwick and Samuels don't expand, we can assume they meant that his freedom would be a limited one. Life, for Tyson, would remain a Panopticon.

Three years out of the loop. No media cameras, no prying eyes, no stories. Well, just one story, really: it related to a conversion to Islam and a newfound appetite for reading literature. Diverse literature too: from the works of Tolstoy to that of Mao Zedong, the latter the inspiration for a new tattoo. Celebrities live on publicity. Few can survive being out of focus for long. Greta Garbo did, of course: sequestering herself away helped build a mystique so that the myths about her eventually became more important than Garbo herself. Howard Hughes, too, vanished, leaving his public to make up its own stories about his eccentricities. The public did the same with Michael Jackson, who spent much of life corralled in his heavily guarded Neverland estate saying nothing, while the rest of the world speculated about his bizarre dispositions. Invisibility and silence can work like a charm for some. For most, it can mean just plain obscurity.

In his absence, Tyson had drifted way past his athletic prime. Some might argue that he reached that in his early twenties and was on a downslide from 1989. Now approaching 30, inactive and with his previous fight an uninteresting ten-round decision three years before, he might have returned from exile an inconspicuous figure, remembered for his disgrace more than his achievements. He might then have slid unnoticed toward oblivion.

"Listen, I understand these people. They want to crush me, they want me to cry, to beg on my knees," said Tyson shortly after his release from prison. He seemed to have a new perspective. He may have been right. But, if "they" – by which he meant not just the media, but the public they served – wanted to destroy him in the way he imagined, why were they prepared to pay so dearly to watch him do it to himself? Within weeks of his release, he had signed a deal with Showtime that was worth, on his own account, $600 million over six fights.

Some of this might have been explained by the virtual torpor that had afflicted heavyweight boxing during Tyson's absence. Riddick Bowe, whom most believed the division's premier fighter, lost to Evander Holyfield, who himself lost to Michael Moorer, who found himself unconscious after taking a right hand from the aged George Foreman. No one had emerged from the three years with much credibility. In boxing terms, even an over-the-hill Tyson appeared like a redeemer of old values. Any other athlete would have been written off after three years of enforced inertia.

Tyson's constituency went far beyond boxing, though. Even in his absence, he could lay claim to being one of the most famous people in the world. So his re-emergence was a hugely anticipated event, something like Richard Nixon's resignation speech or the funeral of Princess Diana. The void of inactivity that might have finished off other celebrity athletes, or celebrity anythings, actually worked to pump up interest in Tyson. Why? Because, in the absence of information, people just joined up the dots themselves. In his book *A Savage Business*, Richard Hoffer puts it this way: "The public was forced to fill this empty vessel with meaning, to take his violent history, his horrifying successes and equally terrifying failures, and the perverse glamour of his prison term, and construct its own terrible attraction" (p. 35).

Nothing was on offer, save fragments of information about his conversion to Islam, a few new tattoos and, of course, the new-found literary bent. But there was just about enough memory to prompt dark, delicious thoughts of Tyson ripping disabling shots into the body of Michael Spinks, of his sitting humbled on a couch while his then wife Robin Givens described her living hell with him to a nation of tv viewers, of his traipsing to prison, hands cuffed, head bowed, but still claiming a miscarriage of justice. The "terrible attraction" superseded all other forms. After all, curiosity, even morbid curiosity, in athletes usually tapers off as they advance in years and regress in skills. Michael Jordan, on the face of it, appears an exception, generating colossal interest when he made his second comeback with the Washington Wizards. But this was still never as great as the interest that surrounded him during the 1990s.

Even then, the public was pretty certain that Jordan's lifestyle would equip him handily for a return. Not one prone to drinking or other sorts of revelry, Jordan, even at 75 percent of his peak, was still a formidable athlete. Tyson did just about everything an athlete can to dissipate himself – apart from succumbing to drugs, of course. Already showing signs of decay before his incarceration, he hadn't sparred for three years and had, after all, spent that time in a cell, not a health farm. The "terrible attraction" was nothing to do with sports. America welcomed back a figure who reminded it of the reason why civil rights had not brought racial equality. Liberalism and inequality were consistent. Tyson was proof. He imbued whites with spiritual contentment: "We've done all we can. We've bent over backwards to help. You can give them money, status, even power and what do they do with them?"

Tyson supplied an answer of sorts. Rescued from the ghetto, a millionaire before he was old enough to drink, he earned himself every privilege going. He met corporate leaders, politicians, and civil rights leaders. He was fêted everywhere. But the beast within was never completely under control; and every so often it reasserted itself with a preternatural fury. Once again, he was out of his cage and, once again, middle America could savor his rage.

At first it looked unpromising. In an interview for *Ebony* shortly after his release, Tyson reckoned he had changed. "I don't get arrogant about nobody," he told Robert E. Johnson. "I won't say anything a dignified man won't say . . . I just want to be humble at all times." He listed his priorities as: to be a good Brother and to be a good father. Monica, not yet his wife, was going to be a powerful positive influence. "I just look round and say 'I'm a mess, baby. I don't know why I do things.'"

The last thing America, perhaps the world, wanted was a dignified Tyson, who was both humble and intent on straightening himself out. And the prospect of Tyson without that streak of defiance, insolence, and rudeness that he called arrogance was unthinkable.

African-American responses to Tyson's return were ambivalent. A press conference in Harlem resembled an evangelical meeting, with thirty-odd religious ministers from a diverse range of churches, Christian and Muslim, assembling to hail Tyson's return. Dr Benjamin Hooks, the former executive director of the NAACP, addressed the crowd. The banners conveyed the message: "Welcome home."

The celebrations were condemned by various organizations, which sensed that making Tyson a martyr would effectively condone rape. "As black men, we are victims," observed Donald Suggs of the organization African Americans Against Violence. "But we are also victimizers."

———

Odds of 22–1 against Peter McNeeley beating Tyson seemed a fair reflection of his chances. The intangibles that make gambling so fascinating were, in this case, age, inactivity and motivation. Not only was McNeeley younger (26), he was fresh from a one-round win over Frankie Hines and could look forward to very big paydays if he could upset Tyson. His end of the purse was a career-high of $540,000 and he added $150,000 from some advertising spots. Even after deductions, it was big money for the Massachusetts boxer with no hope of ever becoming a contender.

The fight on August 19, 1995, at the MGM Grand Hotel, Las Vegas, lasted eighty-nine seconds. If there had been erosion of Tyson's skills, it was not visible; a later count revealed that he had actually thrown only ten punches. Ringside tickets for the fight were $1,500 and pay-per-view was $39.95. The Grand was sold out and ppv sales were $1.4 million. Gross revenue: $63 million. McNeeley's quick demise might have disappointed boxing fans, but this was never intended to be a boxing match: it was entertainment and, as such, it served notice – Tyson was going to be as functional as ever. He'd never left the popular consciousness, but, in captivity, he was less engaging than he was unchained.

Against McNeeley, Tyson was in no more trouble than he would have been in a pillow fight with his children. Even so, there wasn't a genuine credibility problem: Tyson was the attraction; Tyson in an actual competitive fight was of supplemental importance only. Still, his next opponent needed to represent some sort of progress toward a full restoration. Buster Mathis Jr had a marquee name, principally because his namesake father was a top-class heavyweight of the 1960s who had fought and lost creditably to Ali and Joe Frazier. Mathis Jr wasn't as good a boxer as his dad. But he did have a *name*, and, as such, it made good marketing sense to match him with Tyson. Good boxing sense too: Mathis was a step up from McNeeley and boasted a better record of twenty straight wins. Yet Tyson was still an overwhelming favorite to win their fight.

Tyson was then 29, an age when many heavyweight fighters have reached their peak. Some, like Lennox Lewis, peak even later, in their thirties. With typical extravagance, Tyson had bought two $3 million homes and was planning to marry Turner, at that time pregnant with his child. The plan was to ease Tyson back into the groove with a couple of undemanding fights, then recapture the world heavyweight title, which had by then fractured into several versions, one being held by Britain's Frank Bruno, another being disputed by Evander Holyfield and Riddick Bowe, who were to meet on the same night as Tyson's mooted fight with Mathis.

The plan to clash with Holyfield–Bowe was hatched by Don King in concert with Rupert Murdoch. Unexpectedly deviating from the pay-per-view route to the title, King took the Tyson fight to Fox, by 1991, a proper rival to the established television networks of ABC, CBS, and NBC. A free-to-air Tyson fight added value to Fox and guaranteed it enormous viewing ratings. It also helped position it as a major sports network.

Tyson earned $10 million for the Mathis fight, which was a reduction from the $25 million he had taken from his previous encounter. Mathis was due to earn $700,000. Without ppv revenue, an important income stream was dry. This was one of the costs of transmitting the fight on Fox. The benefit was the exposure to a wide viewing audience. Seeing Tyson for free was an enticement few would resist. Also it gave King a chance to stymie the Holyfield–Bowe fight, which was broadcast by HBO's ppv arm, TVKO. King and Tyson were contracted to HBO's deadly rival Showtime.

Ticket sales for Holyfield vs. Bowe held up surprisingly well. It was the third time the two heavyweights had met, each holding a decision over the other. Both previous fights had been compelling and there was every reason to think the rubber would be just as entertaining. One thing was for sure: it would be competitive. Tyson's fight, by contrast, wouldn't be. There was also something disarmingly rational about Tyson when he talked about himself. "I'm still pretty much confused over what I want to do in boxing in general. I'm back in civilized life and it's difficult," he confessed quite reasonably. Coupled with the fact that he was about to marry and, again, become a father, this almost reflective Tyson contrasted with the animal that had been incarcerated three years before. And the public was not responding to him, at least not in the kind of unchallenging matchups arranged by King for Fox viewers.

The venue for Tyson vs. Mathis, the MGM Grand, reported disappointing ticket sales, while over at the Caesars Palace, where the Holyfield fight was to take place, a sell-out looked likely. TVKO confidently projected in excess of 750,000 ppv buys (the record then stood at 1.4 million for Holyfield's fight against George Foreman). Fox was initially anticipating a viewing audience in the order of 17 million, but was perhaps scaling that down as interest in the Holyfield fight built.

When Tyson pulled out of his fight with a hand injury, it relieved King, the MGM Grand and Fox of a possible embarrassment. There was understandable skepticism: the injury seemed a little too fortuitous, though X-rays later confirmed the damage. Injuries had forced Tyson to postpone four previous fights, so it was not atypical. Still, rumors circulated and the convenience was undeniable. The Holyfield fight lived up to expectations, with Bowe prevailing amid the drama of changing fortunes, each fighter staggering the other repeatedly. Tyson's fight was rescheduled for December 16. It was also relocated from Vegas to Philadelphia, where the CoreStates Spectrum could house 18,000 people.

Las Vegas is an almost natural home of boxing. Quite apart from the congruent qualities of corruption, vice, and sundry iniquities, Vegas casino owners can furnish promoters with site fees of $20 million or more just to stage a big show on their premises. A fight lures the high rollers to the city and their losses are the casino owners' gains. The change of date meant that Vegas could not offer an appropriate venue at such late notice. Atlantic City in New Jersey would have been a possibility: gambling is legal and big fights have much the same effect on business as they do in Nevada. The trouble was that the New Jersey Casino Control Commission had banned King from promoting in 1994.

The original date was in a sweeps week, when television ratings are monitored and the results used as a basis for negotiating advertising rates. The new date wasn't in a sweeps week, but Fox still bought the fight, though at a reduced undisclosed price, thought to be around $4 million. Mathis took $100,000 less, though $600,000 was still his career-best purse. He lasted three rounds against a ragged-looking, but too powerful Tyson, who later maintained his wild punches and carelessness in the first two rounds were tactical ploys: he was, as he put it, "lullabying" Mathis before he put him to sleep. "It was a plot, a setup," claimed Tyson, adding somewhat cryptically: "Just like society."

The Philadelphia arena had 10,000 empty seats, suggesting either that Tyson's pulling power was in decline or, more likely, that the prospect of watching for free on tv was a more appealing prospect than paying up to $500 for a seat. Fox garnered a record high 29 share of the viewing audience during the broadcast, the actual Tyson fight itself attracting a 34 share.

While the heavyweight title had split three ways, none of the champions generated anything like the interest that appeared to be developing about Tyson. In fact, few people outside the fight trade could name all three champions. They were: Frank Bruno, of England, who held the World Boxing Council (WBC) version of the title; Francois Botha, of South Africa, the International Boxing Federation (IBF) champion; and Bruce Seldon, of the USA, the World Boxing Association (WBA) title-holder. On the evidence of his first two comeback fights, Tyson had slid back some way. Yet he was still popularly acknowledged as a superior to any of the three champions and he would start a firm bookies' favorite no matter which of them he fought. In the event, it was Bruno.

This was a fight that Bruno, in common with all other heavyweight boxers, dreamed of: anybody stood to earn his highest-ever purse against Tyson. After all, they were strictly there to support the main attraction. Chances were that they'd be soundly beaten and possibly hurt. But, they'd be an awful lot richer. Bruno would be $6 million richer. For this he took a merciless hammering until his resistance, such as it was, subsided in the third round of a pitifully one-sided transfer of title.

Some indication of Tyson's mounting value was his purse – $30 million. A champion can typically expect to receive 60 percent of a total purse for a fight, in this case $36 million. If this convention had been observed, Bruno would have got $21.6 million and Tyson $14.4 million. Hoffer also makes the revealing comparison between Tyson's earnings when he met Bruno in a fight in 1989: he earned $3 million. Tyson was then unbeaten and, at 22, at the height of his fighting powers. Against Bruno the second time, he was seven years older, showing palpable signs of decline and was challenging for rather than defending a title. Something had happened in the intervening period that served to justify an appreciable gain in market value.

In 1995, Tyson was the top-earning athlete with $35 million. This was at a time when Michael Jordan was in his prime in both playing and earnings mode, bringing in an annual bundle of $30 million, Deion Sanders was hot enough to command $5 million a year and Arnold Schwarzenegger was picking up $12 million a throw for movies such as *Eraser* and *Junior* (the one where he gets pregnant).

"What O. J.'s doing is sickening. The man has no dignity." Tyson was talking to *Esquire*'s Mark Kram. "The way he's trying to win public opinion. That's making him look very unstable," argued Tyson, who, for all his sins, had never tried to "win" public favor. He seemed hellbent on losing it most of the time.

"People like a vicious fighter in life," Tyson told Kram. Looking at a tv screen showing Simpson during his trial, Tyson said: "I'm not saying O. J.'s a bad guy. Look at this, he's laughing. He's not dealing with a situation that calls for that. I believe the more he keeps his mouth shut, the more it'll go away . . . God's planning to screw him" ("The tiger king," *Esquire*, April, 1996).

If God wasn't planning on screwing Tyson, several others were. "Mike Tyson continues to be a target of media, legal and female harassment," wrote Howie Evans in the *New York Amsterdam News*. It was an unusually considerate evaluation. Most other media were all-too-ready to chart his catalog of dishonor with almost prurient glee. Bad Tyson news was news indeed. For example, in April, 1996, LaDonna August, a 25-year-old hairdresser/beautician, was in a Chicago nightclub called Le Clique. So was Tyson. August claimed that Tyson sexually assaulted her and he was charged. This quickly became the stuff of headlines. Tyson was still serving four years of probation and, if convicted, could have returned to prison.

According to August, the club's owner, Calvin Hollins – an old friend of Tyson – sent a security guard to her under the pretense of wishing to introduce her to Tyson. She claimed to have been unaware of the fact that Hollins was "offering" her. Through her lawyer, she claimed that Hollins extended to Tyson the use of a private VIP facility in the club, where he could have sex with a woman of his choice. He chose August. She voluntarily followed Tyson to the VIP room on the third floor, but, as her lawyers stated: "She didn't know the circumstances of why she was going up there and wasn't aware that she would be expected to perform sexual favors."

Two friends of August claimed that she came running downstairs, her face flushed and eyes watery, alleging Tyson had grabbed her and forced her to touch him. A third friend, however, reported that August was lying and said she would testify to that in court if necessary.

The next month, the case was dropped: the Chicago Police Department found no grounds or witnesses who would corroborate August's story. State attorney Jack O'Malley announced that the police "did a thorough investigation," which included interviewing witnesses and had decided not to prosecute. It was not big news. As Evans wrote: "When Tyson was charged with sexual harassment it became front page news around the world. It was the lead story on tv newscasts. And now, the fact that Tyson has been cleared is just another small hidden news item" (May 4, 1996).

Public interest in Tyson was greater than it had ever been. Kram, in his *Esquire* interview in 1996, reminded Tyson that he was bigger and had "more power" than at any stage in his life, to which Tyson snapped back: "Power corrupts the soul." "A soul?" asked Kram sarcastically. "That's going to surprise so many who think you don't have one."

Contemplating the implications of the remark, Tyson agreed: "Yeah. All those who expect me to be what they want – The Beast" (April, 1996). He might have discerned how others visualized him and what they expected of him, but he couldn't have known to what extent he would eventually be prepared to meet their expectations.

Tyson's next fight was for another version of the world heavyweight title, the World Boxing Association championship held by Bruce Seldon. Seldon had won his belt after the WBA had stripped George Foreman of the title after he had defied the organization, arranging to defend the title against German Axel Schultz instead of either Tony Tucker or Seldon. In November, 1994, Foreman, at 41, had become the oldest heavyweight champion when he knocked out Michael Moorer, who had beaten Evander Holyfield earlier in the year.

Seldon couldn't have been described as a good, or even decent champion: mediocre would be more appropriate. Tyson gave him short shrift, dismantling any pretensions Seldon may have had in just 109 seconds on September 7, 1996. It was barely a fight: as Ron Dungee of the *Los Angeles Sentinel* put it, despite holding two versions of the world title, Tyson was "still untested."

The 17,000 crowd at the MGM Grand roared "Fix!" though, in truth, Tyson was just so rampant that he swept away his opponent with his avalanche of punches. In common with all of Tyson's opponents, Seldon had his highest payday: $5 million. "I didn't train for twelve weeks to take a dive," claimed Seldon after the fight. "I didn't realize how hard the guy hit and how fast he was." Many wondered why not. Everyone else had realized exactly that. What's more, there was a feeling that, even at 30, Tyson was returning to his vintage form.

The MGM Grand's sports arena emptied quickly after the disappointing decomposition of Seldon. The crowd, like that of any big fight night in Vegas, was jammed with high rollers, Wall Street tycoons, showbiz celebrities, and entertainment moguls. The fight also attracted an assortment of underworld figures, including mobsters from Chicago, drug dealers from New York and gangstas from Los Angeles. Among the fans leaving the Grand was a crew of gangsta types, all elaborately adorned in chunky jewelry, some dressed in expensive-looking suits, others in the more colorful attire favored by rap artists. As they crossed the lobby, they became involved in an exchange of words so loud that they could be heard above the ringing cacophony of thousands of slots. A scuffle broke out near a bank of escalators. This was quickly broken up and the adversarial groups went their separate ways.

Among those involved in the altercation was Tupac Amaru Shakur. He'd just left Tyson, having congratulated him on his succinct demonstration of absolute superiority. A rap artist of some renown, Tupac Shakur had dedicated one of his numbers, "Knock You Out," to Tyson. "Did you see that?" he asked, looking into a ringside camera: "Fifty punches I counted. I knew he was gonna take him out. We bad like that – come of prison and now we running shit."

When things had subsided, he accompanied rap mogul Marion "Suge" Knight to a BMW 750 that Knight drove along the Vegas strip away from the hotel. Other members of the crew drove nearby in their own luxury sedans, all black. It was just after 11 p.m. The convoy of cars headed north on Flamingo Drive on the way to Club 662, owned by Knight's company Death Row Records.

Tupac Shakur, then 25, stood up through the open sunroof. It was not a wise move, considering the man who was driving was known to have had three contracts out on him. Shakur himself was mindful that he was also a target and often wore a bullet-proof vest. But not on this night. Suddenly, a white Cadillac carrying four black males raced up alongside Knight's car. A gun appeared from a rear-seat window and gunfire shattered the windows of the Beamer. It was all over in about three or four seconds of continuous gunshots. The Cadillac screeched away, leaving the bullet-riddled BMW and its occupants. Knight, bleeding from the head but conscious, turned his car around and drove back to Strip where he rammed his car onto the kerb.

Shakur was taken to the University Medical Center, where surgeons removed his right lung in an attempt to stop internal bleeding. When his condition deteriorated, they put him on a ventilator. He died six days after the shooting, his mother at his side. Six years later, the killing of the world's most famous rap star remained officially unsolved. Las Vegas police never made an arrest and conspiracy theories continued to circulate in the music media and beyond. Like: Knight arranged the murder so that he could exploit his rapper's martyrdom. And: Shakur faked his own demise and secretly escaped to an obscure island, where he lives well on the posthumous royalties, which actually outweighed royalties earned during his life. The *Los Angeles Times*, in a detailed two-part investigative report, "Who killed Tupac Shakur," advanced the plausible account that the shooting was carried out by a gang from the Compton area of LA to avenge the beating of Orlando Anderson, who had been kicked by Shakur in the conflict earlier in the evening and who was later killed in an unrelated incident (September 6 and 7, 2002).

There was a weird parallelism between Shakur and Tyson. Both were brought up in the tough Brooklyn ghetto, mainly in the absence of their natural fathers. Shakur's stepfather was a member of the radical Black Panther Party and was on the FBI's Ten Most Wanted register until the early 1980s, when he was imprisoned for robbery and murder. His mother, also a Panther, was charged with conspiring to blow up a block of New York department stores and acquitted a month before Tupac was born in 1971.

Like Tyson, he showed a raw talent, in his case for drama, and, for a while, studied at the Baltimore School for the Arts. In 1988, his mother sent him to live with a family friend near Oakland, California (where the Black Panthers started), and, as Tyson had discovered his potential in the relative seclusion of Catskill, Shakur revealed his talent as a rapper in a band called Digital Underground. By 1991, he was finding his feet as a solo artist and signed a record deal, the first fruits of which were the album *2Pacalypse Now*.

In common with much of the rap output of the time, the lyrics were effectively invectives against the police: they explored such subjects as gang violence, teenage pregnancy, single mother-hood, and racism. His reputation grew with an appearance in Ernest Dickerson's 1992 movie *Juice*, which was about the implosive relationship between four black youths, who botch an attempted hold-up. It was one of several films of the time that tried to disclose the aspects of the African-American experience in a way that avoided both condemnation and sentimentality. John Singleton's 1991 *Boyz N the Hood* was perhaps the most successful, though the Hughes Brothers' 1993 *Menace II Society* also drew acclaim. There was symmetry between these movies and rap in that they introduced the viewer to concealed areas of ghetto life, though without exposing the same viewer to the attendant dangers of actually visiting places like Brownsville or Compton.

Rap related stories against a background of poverty, rancor, and the internecine killing associated with drug dealing. One of the enduring sources of conflict was the feud between the Crips and the Bloods, two gangs, or, more precisely, gang networks that connected multiple gangs, such as the Mob Piru Bloods, of Compton, whose members worked for Knight's Death Row operation. The Crips and the Bloods have a rivalry spread over at least three decades. Based mainly on turf, or territory, their hostility is merciless, involving beating and drive-by shootings. Shakur was aligned with the Bloods, whose color is red, while

Crips favor blue. His affiliation to the Bloods seems to have strengthened during his youth, when he was sentenced to ten days in jail after attacking a rapper with a baseball bat at a Michigan concert in 1993. In LA, he was convicted of assaulting a music video producer. A 19-year-old fan also accused him of sexual assault. During the trial of this case, Shakur was shot five times and robbed of his jewelry. He insisted that another rap artist, Notorious BIG, was behind the attack.

Notorious BIG, a.k.a. Biggie Smalls, aka Christopher Wallace, was himself a victim of a gangland shooting which resulted in his death outside an LA nightclub in 1997. Unlike Shakur, Smalls came from a middle-class New York neighborhood; his street persona BIG was an affectation. He became a successful rapper with Bad Boy Entertainment, the label owned by Sean "Puffy" Combs, also a man of many aliases, like Puff Daddy and P. Diddy. His death was often linked to that of Shakur, Chuck Philips, of the *Los Angeles Times*, suggesting that: "The murder weapon was supplied by New York rapper Notorious BIG, who agreed to pay the Crips $1 million for killing Shakur" (September 6).

Convicted of sexual abuse, Shakur began a four-and-a-half-year prison sentence, and it was during this time that he struck a deal with Knight, who financed the appeal for his conviction in return for his signature on a Death Row Records contract. Knight posted a $1.4 million appellate bond and Shakur was released in 1995. Within hours, he was in Knight's studio working on a double album, *All Eyez on Me*, which was to sell five million cds and establish Shakur as the leading rapper. This was the meaning of his allusion to the camera after Tyson's win: "We bad like that – come of prison and now we running shit."

The friction with Wallace began as two rap artists from either side of the US and belonging to rival gangs and, eventually, rival labels, ridiculing each other. Even though there was no official proof that Wallace was behind the attack on Shakur, he seemed to claim responsibility eight months later, when he released a track called "Who Shot Ya?" Shakur retaliated through another track, "Hit 'em up," in which he bragged about having sex with

Wallace's wife and warned, "you're about to feel the wrath of a menace."

Wallace wasn't at Tyson vs. Seldon. His family maintained that he was at his Teaneck, New Jersey, home. Philips holds that he soon learned that one of his Crip comrades, Anderson, had been abused in the MGM lobby and initiated a swift and fatal revenge. As often happens with gangland slayings, official investigations faltered, possibly because of the silence that impedes inquiries or maybe because Crips and Bloods are not priority when they kill each other. Whatever the reasons, they stayed in place: Wallace was gunned down in March, 1997, and that case also remains unsolved.

The violence that repeatedly struck at rap stars returned in November, 2002, when Jason Mizell, better known as DJ Jam Master Jay, a member of Run DMC, was killed by an intruder in his New York recording studio.

Shakur and Tyson were products of a common culture, one that applauds black men who pander to the imagination. Shakur was no prizefighter, but he was a fighter nevertheless: most of his fights were conducted with weapons on the streets of LA. He wasn't an athlete, but he was an entertainer and, like Tyson, the delectation that he served up was consumed overwhelmingly by whites. Rap is not a genre for minorities: its global success is based on its appeal to whites. *Yo! MTV Raps*, which started in 1989 and built a demographic profile out of white, suburban youths aged 16–24, was the cable tv station's top-rated program. Eminem – a white rapper, of course – became the most popular recording artist in the world in the early twenty-first century, helping push the genre into the musical mainstream. Its appeal recognized no barriers of class, gender, or ethnicity.

Why? Because rap was supposed to be authentic. It was meant to express the way underprivileged blacks look at the world, portraying an accurate reflection of black underclass life and its values. Walter Farrell and James Johnson of *The Michigan Citizen* go so far as to single out Shakur as "The Paul Revere of the inner city, chronicling the most socially and economically distressed aspects of life" (in their article "Who will heed the alarm?", October 26, 1996).

Most purveyors of rap had long since left the ghettos of the inner city and bought homes in the altogether more salubrious environs of the LA hills, but this didn't stop them claiming their music was "real." Writing in a 1994 article, "Jazz, rock'n'roll, rap and politics," M. Bernard-Donals argued that rap exposed to white consumers what we might call a subaltern consciousness: an expression of the way poor African Americans look at the world. The vision was intended to unsettle and, in this, it achieved its aim.

David Samuels complemented Bernard-Donals' interpretation in 1991 when he wrote in *The New Republic* of "a highly charged theater of race in which white listeners became guilty eaves-droppers on the putative private conversation of the inner city" (p. 26). It was as if, by buying a cd, you were given an invitation to inspect life in the ghetto complete with all its gangbanging, crack slinging and bitch slapping. All this without leaving the comfort of your home.

But whose blood curdled? If these were true characterizations of black life, they suited whites' images almost perfectly, confirming the quality of Otherness. They stabilized the feeling that, on one side of the divide, there were whites – civilized, urbane and respectful – and on the other were violent, misogynist black men, willing to resist the forces of law and order even if it meant their own physical annihilation, full of prejudices, phobias, and seemingly unaware of a common humanity. Alongside them were their women, erotic, licentious, good primarily for sexual gratification and procreation, and prepared to put up with the insults and disdain of their men.

Think about the representations of black males in rap: aggressive and threatening. Exactly the kind of qualities imputed to brute niggers in colonial days. Whites consumed rap with a voyeuristic pleasure, devouring images that corresponded with those once conveyed by colonial observers of non-Western people. The cutouts that had once been functional in justifying oppression and captivity were dusted off and brought back into service, this time by blacks themselves.

And Tyson was right there with them. A black male slipping in and out of control, barely restrained by civilizing forces and always liable to self-destruct or, perhaps, submit to the kind of fate that met Tupac Shakur. Tyson's similarity with rappers went beyond social backgrounds, entertainment values, and violence: he mined the same vein of historical types. Brutish, vicious, primitive, and uncontrolled, these were types that endured for centuries and had been all but discarded in the aftermath of civil rights. But, not quite. While there were still black men prepared – or perhaps unable to resist the appeal – to conform to images of brutality and danger, there was a market ready to exploit the demand for them.

seven

TO RAPE THE VIRGINAL
BLACK PRINCESS

In 1991, Tyson was probably the most famous man in the world. Even the recently liberated Nelson Mandela, who was then preparing to become the first leader of post-apartheid South Africa, might have had to settle for a close second place. Tyson was pre-eminent. He helped usher in and provide a focus for a new era, the era of celebrity in which a different type of being was introduced to popular culture.

Celebrities were not just famous people who had distinguished themselves by great deeds, like rock stars, movie actors, military heroes, political figures, inventors, heads of businesses, or even sports stars known for their accomplishments, though, of course, they included all of these. They were figures who were just *there* on our screens, in our magazines, in our papers. Whether anchoring tv shows, hosting quizzes, forecasting the weather, fighting court cases, celebrities became part of our lives. Images of them circulated in the electronic and print media, so that following the lives of celebs became a collective preoccupation.

Unlike earlier objects of our attention, celebs relied less on doing, more on being noticed. It wasn't simply a case of accomplishing something great: to be a celeb, you had to be seen, read about and, importantly, talked about. Joe Louis was a great heavyweight champion in the 1930s and was universally respected as such. But, no one was really interested in him as anything other than a boxer. Even in his most symbolic fights, such as against Max Schmeling – who was portrayed, perhaps unfairly, as the embodiment of Nazi Aryanism – Louis was still an athlete, albeit one freighted with additional significance for the duration of his big fights.

By complete contrast, there was insatiability about the way we craved information about Tyson. Like Louis, he came to prominence as an athlete. But interest in Tyson went far, far beyond his fighting abilities. There is probably no individual in history who has commanded more curiosity than Tyson. Just watching him fight didn't come near satisfying the interest. We wanted to know everything about him, everything. Would it be possible for someone with Tyson's profile to have a dependency on heroin, as Louis did, without the world knowing it?

The start of the 1990s was a watershed, when celebrity culture began to take shape. The proliferation of global media created new requirements, the main one of which was to create content for the zillions of channels, websites, and stations that seemed to multiply as prodigiously as those furry creatures, "tribbles," in the classic *Star Trek* episode. The dizzying number of people who were thrust into our lives via media reflected a new hierarchy, ordered alphabetically. A-list members were the elite celebs, of course.

Numero uno of the A-list, to mix the classification schemes, was Madonna, a celeb of such sublime chameleon qualities that the media were forever trying to invent new frames of reference. She not only personified the new age, more than anyone else, she initiated it, negotiating a Faustian pact with media that allowed them to pry, probe, investigate, and inquire, salaciously if need be, into the innermost parts of her life. The quid pro quo was: she wanted media coverage the likes of which had never been seen. Both parties lived up to their side of the bargain and Madonna reigned.

Like a Prayer, the album cover of which featured La Ciccone wearing rosary beads around her waist, was released in 1989, and heralded the start of a long and productive relationship between the archetype celeb and the media that both lapped her up and lifted her to the cultural stratosphere. She'd been making records since the mid-1980s, but as the 1990s approached, interest in her in particular veered toward the prurient. Far from shielding herself from the intrusions, she laid herself bare.

Literally so: her book *Sex* revealed her shamelessly but astutely, beguiling her global following.

Describing Madonna as a singer, or, for that matter, Tyson as a boxer, is like describing Tony Soprano as a waste disposal operative: technically accurate, but nowhere near adequate for understanding why we are so enthralled by them. By 1991, Tyson was established as a full-blown, all-round celebrity. His fights were moments of high drama. But, not necessarily the moments of highest drama. Incidents involving Tyson typically provided the raw material of scandal, gossip, and outrage so beloved of journalists in the era of celebrity.

Tyson didn't seek to ingratiate himself with the media, or even coax them in the way that Madonna had essayed so ingeniously. He just had to exist. The stories seem to arrive ready-headlined: TYSON FOUND GUILTY OF BREAST-FONDLING or TOPLESS DANCER SAYS, "TYSON IS FATHER OF MY CHILD." These were actual stories. There was no need to dig for dirt on Tyson: he seemed to serve it up.

There were other men who commanded the media, of course. Still, it's difficult to imagine anyone who provided so much scandalous copy as Tyson. Michael Jackson maybe: as reclusive as Garbo, Jackson contrived to become enthroned as the King of Pop and vilified as a freak at the same time – and without actually doing or saying much at all. His absence allowed the media license to concoct all manner of extravagant narratives about his apparently bizarre lifestyle. And while he remained hidden from view, the stories grew ever more fabulous (and I use the word in its original sense: celebrated in fable).

Tyson was much more accessible. When he wasn't on public display fighting, he was in public training sessions, or giving interviews. These were all good for news copy, especially when Tyson blew up spontaneously, as he did after one training session in 1991. Another great headline: TYSON PUNCHES OUT $20,000 TV CAMERA AFTER SPARRING.

The Western world was changing as the 1980s turned into the 1990s. As faith in traditional leaders slid, people began to look to alternative sources, not of inspiration but of fascination. In his 1998 book on the Arizona Diamondbacks baseball club, *Big*

League, Big Time, Len Sherman maintains that in the past our heroes came from the ranks of great political leaders, explorers, scientists, even philosophers. Now they have been replaced by pure celebrities, which Sherman describes as "the most watched, admired, privileged, and imitated people" (p. 189).

Celebrities, especially sports celebrities, have a kind of exemplary authority that they don't usually use to promote change or good causes, as some heroic figures of sports have done in the past. Instead, they promote commodities. They do this directly through endorsements – Tyson had deals with, among others, Kodak, Nintendo, and Pepsi (which also had Jackson under contract) – and indirectly through creating stuff on which media thrive. Sherman's view is that, at some point during the 1980s, the public turned cynical and gave up on its traditional leaders, either because they suspected they were lying or had just grown out of touch. So they looked elsewhere and found a substitute in celebrities who supplied endless gratification and demanded little in return.

As our confidence in government, state, and church receded, so "the two modern industries of communication and entertainment (whose corporations and personnel are frequently one and the same) have increased in autonomy and power," argues Sherman (p. 188).

Celebrities emerging from the early 1990s were, at once, anonymous and intimate. People didn't actually know them on a personal basis, but they were made to feel as if they did. This, remember, was a culture that threw up the *Jerry Springer* Show, in which people were prepared to disclose deep and usually excruciatingly embarrassing details of their private lives in front of millions of strangers whose prurient interests were equally unconcealed. Of course, the assumption was that, if the roles were reversed and members of the audience were invited onto the stage, they would be equally candid and unreserved about their innermost secrets.

This is why Tyson, though once honored as an athlete, was by 1991 regarded differently – as someone the public wanted to know better, demanded to know better, insisted on knowing almost as an intimate. They didn't necessarily want to like him.

They may even have taken pleasure from the many other emotions associated with him: fear and loathing being two of the more obvious ones. But few people remained unmoved by Tyson. He had the knack of stirring people one way or another. One thing you couldn't do was remain indifferent. Springer's show started airing in 1991.

In Michael Jordan, the other celebrity athlete who had emerged in 1991, but not yet ascended to the vertiginous peaks he would reach later in the decade, people saw a more uniform character. Jordan was perhaps the most controlled athlete in history. The impression he gave was of an overstuffed suitcase, nearly bursting apart, but with several straps fastened around it to prevent its opening fully. Nike had the sturdiest of all straps around Jordan. The clean, wholesome, and genial image was vital to the success both of the man and the brand with which he lived symbiotically. Tyson had no such ties. If the suitcase wasn't open, it was crowbarred open by meddlesome media. And when it was open, all the contents on view were unpleasant.

Reputations are essential to celebrities. They don't refer to what a person does, or thinks about doing, or even thinks about thinking about doing. What counts is what others say or believe they are doing or thinking. Tyson's reputation was based on three widespread beliefs, according to Randy Roberts and J. Gregory Garrison, authors of *Heavy Justice: The trial of Mike Tyson*: "First, he was the meanest, toughest man on the block. Second, he had money to burn, which was perhaps the only way he hadn't tried to rid himself of it. Third, he was attracted to women who believed that their reason for being was to dispose of his fortune" (p. 82).

Like air travel, reputations help get you from A to B much more quickly than other means; but they carry similar residual dangers. The third of the three beliefs about Tyson was always going to be the most dangerous of all. Molestation allegations were commonplace. Most of them were bogus. Some of the several paternity suits filed at intervals over the years were bogus too. Tyson didn't always insist on paternity tests and was found to be paying child support for other men's children.

Money tended to make most of the accusations disappear. One, in particular, didn't.

———

Four impressive wins in 12 months had cleared the way for a spectacular matchup against the current world champion, Evander Holyfield. The date was set: November 8, 1991. The venue was to be Caesars Palace, Las Vegas. When the live gate receipts, foreign rights, pay-per-view revenues, merchandising and delayed broadcast fees were added up, the fight would be the first $100 million attraction in boxing history. Tyson was guaranteed $15 million, while Holyfield would earn the then unbelievable purse of $30 million. Few doubted that Tyson was the real drawcard.

On Friday, October 11, the fight was postponed. Tyson had suffered a rib injury two weeks before, and though he continued to train in the expectation that the injury would heal, it didn't. Holyfield accepted Francesco Damiani as a substitute opponent, but his purse shrank to $8 million (Damiani later pulled out, leaving Bert Cooper as the opponent). The Tyson fight would have to wait. But no one could have predicted for how long. It was five years before Tyson and Holyfield climbed into the same ring.

"Stardom, by nature, dulls adherence to social norms, luring athletes to overindulge in illicit temptations," writes Jeff Benedict in his *Public Heroes, Private Felons: Athletes and crimes against women* (p. 215). Tyson was invited to appear at the Indiana Black Expo in Indianapolis. The exhibition featured a beauty pageant as well as a speech from Jesse Jackson and a concert by singer Johnny Gill. There are competing accounts of the events that followed; though everyone agreed on some points.

Facts. Tyson flew in on July 17 to be greeted by a throng of fans. With his bodyguard, Dennis Hayes, Tyson traveled by limo to a hotel, where he met with Angela Boyd, a rap artist, who worked under the name B Angie B. She would later say that they had sex. After stopping by a nightclub for drinks, Tyson headed for another club, where he signed autographs before checking in at the Canterbury Hotel. The following day, Tyson met the Reverend Charles Williams, one of the event's organizers, and

Gill. All three of them went to the Omni Severin Hotel, where a rehearsal for the pageant was in progress. It was here that Tyson first met Desiree Washington, an 18-year-old contestant from Rhode Island. He asked for and received her phone number.

After meeting and talking to several other contestants, Tyson had dinner, went back to his hotel to change, then went to the Gill concert at the Hoosier Dome. He watched the show from the wings. After the show, Tyson rode the limo toward the Canterbury. En route, he called Washington, asking if she would meet him. "Can you come out?" he asked. "Please, please, I just want to talk to you." He suggested that they could see some of the sights. When she raised the possibility of doing it tomorrow, he told her that he would be gone by then: "It will be too late."

Washington left her own hotel, the Omni Severin, to meet his limo outside. The limo then went to Tyson's hotel. Washington followed Tyson to his suite, number 606. Tyson invited her to his room and she went without duress. She sat next to him on the bed. Tyson told her: "You're turning me on." Accounts as to what happened next differ.

Washington's version. "I just got really nervous and started babbling," Washington is quoted in Roberts and Garrison's book (p. 223). "I said, 'I need to go to the bathroom. When I come out, I want to see Indianapolis, like you said.'" But, when she returned, Tyson was sitting on the bed wearing only his undershorts. "I was terrified. I said, 'It's time for me to leave.' He said, 'Come here,' and he grabbed my arm. And he was like, 'Don't fight me. Come here.' And then he stuck his tongue in my mouth. He was disgusting . . . He put his hand into me, his fingers into my vagina . . . He grabbed my legs and he lifted me up . . . and he licked me from my rectum to my vagina . . . He pulled his penis, exposed his penis . . . jammed it into my vagina." Later, she said on television: "I begged. I cried. I said, 'Please, I want to go to school. I don't want a baby.'" Rape.

Tyson's version. "She [Washington] comes to my room and takes off her panty shield ready to fuck. I fuck her, suck her on her ass, suck all over here. I perform fellatio [sic]." This is how he described it to *Playboy* (November 1998), adding "she planned it from the beginning." Consensual sex.

Figure 4 Desiree Washington met Tyson when she was an 18-year-old contestant at a beauty pageant in 1991. She accepted an invitation to his hotel room, but became "terrified" by his behavior. He was later convicted of rape.

On leaving, Washington appeared, to the limousine driver who drove her, upset, asking indignantly: "Who does he think he is?" She was occupied all the following day with duties relating to the pageant. On July 20, shortly before 3 a.m., Washington reported to the Indianapolis police department that, in the early hours of July 19, Tyson had raped her. She then went to the Methodist Hospital emergency room, where a doctor found two small abrasions on her vagina. By this time, Tyson had left the state: in fact, he checked out of his hotel at 4.45 a.m., barely two hours after Washington had left. Because the "do not disturb" sign was still hanging outside, the housekeeper didn't clean the room, enabling the unlaundered bed linen to be used later as forensic. The formalities of the rape charges were processed by July 22 and Tyson was subpoenaed to appear before a six-member grand jury that had been empanelled to investigate the allegation.

It was not the only allegation to arise from the Black Expo: three weeks after the pageant, Rosie Jones filed a $100 million lawsuit against Tyson, maintaining that he touched her buttocks and made sexually explicit suggestions to her. Another contestant, Artavia Edwards, claimed that Tyson had grabbed her backside. And yet another, Pasha Olivier, who, at one stage during the grand jury testimony, described Tyson as a polite gentleman, later filed a civil suit against him, accusing him of making advances toward her. But, everyone was accustomed to these slurs. When, on July 27, the Indianapolis police announced that it was investigating a rape accusation against Tyson, it was unexpected.

On September 9, Tyson was charged with four felony counts: rape, confinement and two counts of deviate sexual conduct. Collectively, they carried a maximum penalty of sixty-three years in prison. Tyson gave himself up and was released on $30,000 bound. The trial date was set for January 27, 1992. While many argued that the planned fight with Evander Holyfield should have been called off immediately, interested parties, including HBO's ppv division TVKO and Anheuser-Busch, one of the corporate sponsors, insisted that it proceed. When the fight was eventually called off, it was for pragmatic rather than moral reasons: Tyson's injured rib. Even then, Tyson, presumably anticipating a collapse of the prosecution's case against him or an acquittal, agreed to reschedule the fight in late January. His lawyers filed motions to delay the start of the trial, which was due to begin on January 27. When that motion failed, there seemed no alternative but to postpone the fight indefinitely.

Tyson protested his innocence. "I didn't hurt anyone," he maintained, adding that he respected women. "Unfortunately, every time I get involved with one something happens."

He hired Vincent J. Fuller to represent him. Fee: $5,000 per day. A prominent lawyer from Williams & Connolly, of Washington, DC, who registered in the public consciousness as the man who had defended John Hinckley, who got off on an insanity plea after he'd attempted to assassinate President Ronald Reagan. Fuller had also successfully represented Don King in a tax evasion case.

In Indiana, juries are drawn from voter rolls. Three African Americans were selected (one female) so that the composition of the jury reflected the demography of the surrounding population, of which 22 percent was African American. One of the black males was later excused and replaced by a white male.

Fuller's defense was organized around the not-so-innocent-as-she-looks motif. Washington was a 5 foot 4 inch, 108-pound teenager from a religious family who, when she turned up at the trial, radiated wholesomeness. But, asked Fuller, what was she doing, going to the hotel room of one of the world's most notorious womanizers? "Consent can be expressed," Fuller reminded the jurors. "It can also be implied."

He embellished a popular emerging image of Tyson as big, brutal, priapic, prone to fits of spontaneous violence and motivated only by the satisfaction of his own desires. Other pageant contestants were brought forward to testify that Tyson had been vulgar and suggestive with them. When questioned, Tyson declared that he had been similarly coarse with Washington. "I explained to her that I wanted to fuck her," Tyson told the jury. "She said, 'Sure, give me a call.'"

The basis of Fuller's defense was that, if he knew about Tyson and the jury knew about Tyson and the other contestants knew about Tyson, surely Washington knew about him too. She'd even seen him in action earlier in the day, when he was groping and messing with other contestants at the pageant. Washington would have gone to his hotel suite voluntarily – there was no question of force – in the full knowledge that she was not going to admire the view of the city, certainly not to "talk and watch television," as she indicated.

There were also the questions of why she removed her panty liner and why she went to the bathroom at all, even after Tyson had signaled his intentions. Her answer was that she intended to change her sanitary pad rather than just remove it, but had left a replacement in her purse, which was in the bedroom. Washington acknowledged her naïveté in the episode as a way of rebutting the suggestion that she'd schemed the whole evening.

Fuller's effective dehumanization of his client may have complemented the media representation of Tyson as a great athlete gone wrong, but it may also have alienated the jury. "Tyson's defense trafficked in racial stereotypes; it drew on images and notions that many Americans, black and white, had been struggling against for more than three hundred years," wrote Roberts and Garrison, the defense attorney. "The defense robbed Tyson of his individuality and turned him into a cardboard figure from a racist X-rated cartoon" (p. 245).

Appealing to racist images by dramatizing a black male as at the mercy of his genetic stock has proved reliable in the past. But, in this case, the theorem may have been a little too sophisticated for its own good: paint the most abominable, most depraved, most evil picture of Tyson imaginable, then instill a doubt – would she really have gone this far with a creature such as this if she wasn't up for it?

"In other words, both principals were animals – the black man for the crudity of his sexual demands, the black woman for eagerly acceding to them," wrote Sonja Steptoe, in her article "A damnable defense" in *Sports Illustrated* (February 24, 1992). Fuller "was pandering to bigoted perceptions about blacks, apparently hoping that the jurors would buy into those perceptions and vote to acquit Tyson." (Fuller had unsuccessfully tried to introduce expert testimony about the size of Tyson's penis as an explanation of Washington's vaginal abrasions, though, in this instance, it seems his intention was to undermine the popular archetype about size.)

Washington was described by Roberts and Garrison as "bright, outgoing, attractive, athletic, gentle-mannered, considerate"; she was a freshman class president, National Honors Society member, varsity cheerleader, member of her highschool softball team; she'd represented the US on a summer tour of the USSR, met Soviet diplomats, Vice-President Dan Quayle and several business and church leaders; her plan was to attend Providence College on a Martin Luther King scholarship. The jury couldn't believe that this same girl would brazenly answer, "Sure, give me a call," when faced with Tyson's not-so-subtle approach. In fact, the exact wording of Tyson's initial approach was contentious: only later did Tyson say that he explicitly used the word "fuck" to Washington.

"I didn't violate her in any way," said Tyson on the stand. "She never told me to stop and she never said I was hurting her. She never said 'no'." Basically, it all came down to this. In the event, the jury believed Gregory Garrison, who argued that it was inconceivable that the sweet, slight, girlish, well-educated, church-going teenager who was actively involved in charity work would entertain willingly having sex with Tyson, whether for pleasure, bragging rights, money, or any other kind of motive. Inconceivable.

As the jury deliberated for ten hours, thoughts must have turned to an earlier case involving a celebrity and a little-known accuser. In December, 1991, William Kennedy Smith, the nephew of Senator Edward Kennedy and a member of the illustrious extended family, was acquitted of rape in Palm Beach, Florida. The thrust of his defense was that the accuser wasn't credible, having had abortions and been abused as a child. There was also the matter of the skimpy black underwear she favored: this was used by the defense to signify intention. While some felt that the ruling in favor of the accused boded well for Tyson, there were several significant differences, the obvious one being that Kennedy Smith was white.

The judge, Patricia Gifford, sentenced Tyson to ten years for each of the felony convictions and fined him $30,000. The sentences would run concurrently and four years ,was to be suspended. Six years, three with good behavior. Fuller had, inadvertently perhaps, provided not so much new evidence as confirmation of existing evidence about Tyson, "that he was always something less than human," as Montieth Illingworth puts it in *Mike Tyson: Money, myth and betrayal*. Returning to Steptoe's critique of Fuller's racially riven defense, which she calls a "travesty": "He [Tyson] was the stereotypical savage black man run amok, this by the characterization of his own lawyer . . . The defendant was affixed with a label: BEWARE – DANGEROUS SEXUAL ANIMAL" (p. 91).

Steptoe's commentary on Fuller concludes that his "misguided and contemptible defense fanned the fires of racism by perpetuating the worst kind of racial stereotypes." Later, in 1995, Robert Wright, of *The New Republic*, complemented this view in his article "Tyson vs. Simpson" in which he described the impression of Tyson left by the trial: "Middle America's nightmare: a crude, violent, sexually aggressive black male – threat to home, wife, daughter" (p. 4).

In 1994, Abraham Abramovsky, a law professor at the Fordham University Criminal Law Center, added further criticism in an article published in the journal *Crisis*, entitled "Tyson was denied a level playing field in Indiana" (vol. 101, no. 1). Abramovsky lists a catalog of legal irregularities, the most serious of which was Judge Gifford's failure to use permissible discretion when the defense asked to introduce witnesses who would have testified that they saw Tyson and Washington embracing in the limousine as they arrived at the Canterbury Hotel. One witness would have stated that she saw Washington enter the hotel holding Tyson's hand. Abramovsky also believes the arrangement that Washington had with attorney Edward Gerstein, if known at the time of the trial, would have led the jury to question her motives and credibility. Gerstein was hired on a contingency basis, assisting in handling the rights to Washington's story as well as handling the civil case that was to follow. Cumulatively, these points added up to an unevenness that should have provided grounds for appeal. Yet Tyson was denied this two to one.

Tyson's later appeals to both the Indiana Court of Appeal and the US Supreme Court were based essentially on the exclusion of the three witnesses and the selection of the trial judge. Both appeals were turned back.

These points open up the possibility that Tyson was standing trial for the others' infractions. Kennedy Smith was fresh in people's minds, but so too was Clarence Thomas, who was accused of sexual harassment by Anita Hill in what he famously called a "high-tech lynching." Even as jurors deliberated, there were suspicions that these two had tested the elasticity of reasonable doubt. Did Tyson serve as some sort of atonement? During his trial, he, abetted by his lawyer, may have morphed into every man who has ever molested a woman and got away with it. He was made for the part. "It is difficult to think of a celebrity defendant who had more to lose," wrote Tom Callahan, of *US News & World Report* (February 2, 1992).

He meant that transgressors are seldom so young, so close to their peak and so well placed to make a bundle (from the proposed Holyfield fight). A long prison sentence would mean freedom only at an age when his physical prowess was in decline and his earnings capacity was diminished if not finished. The guilty verdict may well have had symbolic meaning far beyond the case itself.

———

Washington agreed to have her name and photograph appear on the cover of *People* magazine; she also went on the tv show *20/20*. Neither assignment carried any fee. Earlier, in fact, before the trial started, "Washington was offered $1 million to drop the charges and settle the case privately," according to Jeff Benedict. She turned down the offer, though in June, 1992, with Tyson serving his prison sentence in Indiana, Washington filed a civil lawsuit against him, seeking damages for several offences, including the infliction of emotional distress. No monetary amount was specified for the punitive and compensatory damages, but the suit included a request for a jury trial to consider the new case. This wasn't settled until July, 1995, by which time Tyson had been released, still insisting he was innocent. The deal to pay an undisclosed sum averted a trial that was set for Indianapolis.

One of the most interesting facets of the aftermath was the rapidity with which the jurors changed their minds. All twelve were contacted with a view to assessing their thoughts on the trial and six of them expressed concerns over whether Tyson had received a fair trial. There were probably two reasons for this. Some had, after all, received uneasy receptions when they returned to their homes and places of work. They were also presented with the claim that Washington had falsely accused someone of rape years before the Tyson case. Although this was never substantiated, it introduced doubts about the accuser's trustworthiness. While Washington hadn't had her credibility undermined during the trial, every effort was made to do so after it.

A year after the sentence had been handed down, Alan Dershowitz had an appeal turned down by Indiana's Supreme Court. Dershowitz had been retained earlier and had filed a twelve-point appeal at the Indiana Court of Appeals the day before Judge Gifford passed sentence.

Dershowitz believed Fuller's approach had been flawed: instead, he opted for trying to discredit Washington as a groupie who had failed to communicate her true intentions to a man who was habitually entertaining admirers in his hotel rooms. "She *appeared* to be consenting," Dershowitz told Benedict (p. 160). Washington may have changed her mind, of course, but Tyson may genuinely have not understood this.

Dershowitz may have been right, but his appeal foundered because the testing question was not "What would Mike Tyson do in that position?" but "What would a reasonable person do in that position?" Tyson's specific background and experience did not serve as divining rods. Just because he was a celeb and found most women amenable didn't mean Tyson could determine whether or not consent was implied.

In August, 1994, the appellate lawyer's son, Nathan Dershowitz, who was also representing Tyson, announced that one of Washington's lawyers, Michael Weisman, had suggested terms for a settlement of the civil lawsuit against Tyson. If Tyson accepted them, Weisman indicated that he would encourage an early release from prison for Tyson. Dershowitz conveyed his client's response to the *Los Angeles Sentinel*: "Mr. Tyson has uniformly directed us not to 'buy' Ms Washington's cooperation" (August 4, 1994). It was eventually settled a year later, as suggested above.

Only two months before, Tyson had been denied an early release date by Judge Gifford for failing to meet minimum educational requirements for rehabilitation. During his appearance, Tyson steadfastly refused to admit guilt or apologize for a crime he insisted he did not commit: "I'm innocent of the charge. I don't take responsibility for raping anyone." He had served 26 months of his sentence.

There is no way of knowing what this statement cost him, but the chances are that he would have hastened his release had he been repentant. Throughout the term of his imprisonment and beyond, Tyson continued to deny that he had raped Washington or, indeed, done anything wrong at all. He remained convinced that he had been set up. In an interview five years on, Tyson was to muse: "It's easy to hate Mike Tyson, to do something to Mike Tyson and get away with it" (in *Playboy*, November, 1998).

In January, 1996, the US Supreme Court refused to review the rape conviction. The court turned away arguments that Tyson was denied a fair trial, finding no constitutional violations in Tyson's trial. The appeal raised essentially the same points as did an appeal the high court rejected in 1993: it allowed the prosecutors to select the judge who presided over the trial; it barred three crucial witnesses because they came forward too late.

Despite a series of appellate court rulings turning down Dershowitz's various petitions and confirming the veracity of the original verdict, research suggested that there were divisions among the population over Tyson's guilt. Many of the surveys were of uncertain validity. Like the Cleveland radio station 93-fm WZAK's call-in poll in 1992, in which 80 percent of listeners felt that Tyson didn't get a fair trial. More valid was the National Prisoners' Rights Union and National Prison Lawyers' Guild survey that revealed 78 percent (mostly women) questioned the verdict. Perhaps the most valid was the research conducted by Indiana University Public Opinion Laboratory for the *Indianapolis Star*/WRTV, which highlighted a division: while only 28 percent of white respondents believed that Tyson hadn't received a fair trial, 67 percent of African Americans thought that he had been wronged. The racial asymmetry reflected that laid bare at the time of the O. J. Simpson trial.

Two theories were developed in the aftermath of the trial. One involved a conspiracy designed to disable black men who had been conspicuously successful. The other was the "set-up" hypothesis favored by Tyson himself ("she planned it from the beginning"). Evidence, while not tangible, could be inferred from recent history. Clarence Thomas and Marion Barry, two prominent African Americans, had both been pulled through the wringer. Tyson himself was like a magnet for gyp merchants trying to squeeze money out of him (many of them successfully).

Neither theory reflected well on Washington. In fact, the conspiracy version had wider ramifications: "The allegation that Black men are being targeted for special oppression carries with it the implicit notion that African American women are exempt from special abuses and inadvertently renders the suffering of Black women invisible," wrote Aaronette M. White in her 1999 article "Talking feminist, talking Black" in *Gender and Society*.

White describes how a coalition of women's groups grew concerned over the endorsements of Tyson, many of which came from unlikely sources. For example, nearly a year to the day since he had first appeared at the Black Expo, supporters gathered at the steps outside Marion County Courthouse where Tyson had stood trial. Among the thousand protestors carrying FREE MIKE TYSON banners were Louis Farrakhan, Councilwoman Patricia Moore, and Don King. Moore's presence was especially interesting: a prominent African American woman defending a man convicted of raping a black woman was a provocative statement.

Tyson had never been short of supporters. Spike Lee had been outspoken in his defense, and T. J. Jimerson, the former president of the National Baptist Convention, supported the campaign to release him.

White's article tracks the evolution of a protest movement, at first to counter the mounting support for Tyson and, later, to raise awareness of the "myths about rape." When a black man rapes a white woman, it reiterates a centuries-old fear about the propensities of black men and the vulnerability of white women. When a black man rapes a black woman, again it summons up a history, this time about the propensities of black women. The coalition sought to challenge what White calls "the privileging of Black men's suffering." As support for Tyson grew, it was he rather than Washington who was seen as the victim. "Washington and [Anita] Hill [who claimed Clarence Thomas had harassed her] were trapped by the slave mythology that Black women are sexually loose and promiscuous," Earl Ofari concluded in his *Pittsburgh Courier* column, "Assassination of the black female image" (December 18, 1996).

But was Washington formulated in this way? Was she seen as "black" at all? Although he relegates what seems a crucial assertion to a footnote of his 1997 essay "Mike Tyson and the perils of discursive constraints," John M. Sloop maintains that: "Washington was repositioned 'away from' the ordinary discourses that surround African American women (i.e. promiscuity, primitivism) and positioned instead as, arguably, 'white'" (p. 121).

Sloop points out that the media constantly played up the fact that she was a Sunday school teacher, upper middle class, a college student, naïve, and "easily taken advantage of by the more knowledgeable and hostile Tyson." These worked like "links to Caucasians," according to Sloop. Perhaps this had a bearing on the ambivalent reaction to Washington from African American women.

Reading between the lines of White's article, it's possible to peek at a reality that was typically obscured by the mainstream media. Remember that the popular image of Tyson had mutated during his trial. Influenced by his own defense's powerful caricature of him as an instinct-driven primate, the media had moved away from the indestructible "Iron Mike" who was liable to lash out at the slightest provocation and toward a dangerously unstable creature, prone to use violence indiscriminately to satisfy base urges. Yet, in chronicling the obstacles the women's coalition faced, White reveals a support for Tyson from many sections of the African-American population, male and female, young and old, of all classes. "I agree with everything you said. I think I may even be a feminist, but there are too many men in my household who think Mike Tyson is a hero and if I signed that ad and they saw it, I would never hear the end of it," explained one woman who refused to sign a petition to run in a newspaper (p. 87).

The two most common reasons for women not signing up with the coalition were fear of reprisals from men and "not wanting people to think that they weren't loyal to the [race] Black community." Siding with Washington or even with black women was tantamount to disloyalty.

Some of the jurors who had found Tyson guilty were given uncomfortable rides by neighbors and colleagues after the trial. A UPS worker complained that he was ostracized when he returned to work. In other words, while Tyson was being variously cast as the villain by the mainstream media, he was anything but that in the eyes of many people, black and white.

If one woman's stance dramatized this, it was that of Khaliah Ali, daughter of Muhammad Ali, who complained of the "misrepresentation" of Tyson as a "heartless, animal-like womanizer" during and after the trial and of the "indefensible" behavior of Judge Gifford.

———

"The photos of Tyson in handcuffs appeared more prominently than the ones when he became the youngest man in history to become heavyweight titleholder," wrote Barnett Wright in his *Philadelphia Tribune* story, "Media assassins open fire" (June 24, 1994).

If there were any doubts that the image of Tyson created in the trial had no lasting effect beyond the courtroom, they were dismissed by two reports, one from a *Business Wire* scan of media coverage and the other the result of scholarly research that appeared in an academic journal.

At the height of interest in the Simpson trial, Lexis/Nexis, the online news service, asked the question: "Which sports figure is the undisputed champ in generating the most negative media coverage for off-the-field incidents?" After surveying print and broadcast media, the research showed that, up to August, 1994, the media had reported 9,906 stories about Tyson, comfortably more than the widely disparaged Simpson (6,754) and Ben Johnson (6,688), whose use of steroids earned him universal opprobrium. While the search was confined to non-sports stories concerning athletes, it's doubtful whether even killers like Timothy McVeigh and Jeffrey Dahmer would have challenged Tyson (*Business Wire*, August 29, 1994).

Throughout and after the trial, Jack Lule had been conducting research into how the media had reported the case, in particular, how they had depicted Tyson. The results of the research were published as "The rape of Mike Tyson: Race, the press and symbolic types" in the June, 1995 issue of *Critical Studies in Mass Communication*. The title of Lule's research alerts the reader to the nature of the treatment dealt Tyson by the media: he was, according to Lule, "violated and debased."

Deriving his arguments from a systematic review of the media's coverage of the trial, Lule suggested that: "The large drama of his [Tyson's] degradation shaped and was shaped by American press mythologies about African Americans."

More specifically, Lule concluded that "prefigured patterns that influence and shape understandings of the present" have been passed down the generations virtually unchanged and, as such, carry symbolic importance. Media portrayals of Tyson drew on "just two, crude, dehumanizing and – paradoxically – opposing archetypes for African Americans: the animal savage and helpless, hapless victim" (p. 177).

Lule describes the former as "A crude, sex-obsessed, violent savage who could barely control his animal instincts." The animal trope is a popular one. A sample of headlines and comments includes: THE "ANIMAL" IN MIKE TYSON; "the animal within"; "changed completely from a sweet, nice person into an animal"; "Mike Tyson is an animal."

As such, Tyson was reported as being a "danger to society" and "filled with anger toward all women," an "attack dog, trained to be vicious and rewarded for it, but unfit to be around innocent people." Lule notes, as others have, that the portrayal was "aided and shaped" by Fuller: "Press reports simply extended Tyson's defense" (p. 181).

There was a mix of sadism and smugness in the way the media greeted his imprisonment. The humiliation of confinement among other offenders was no more than Tyson deserved, if not for this crime, for the countless others he had got away with over the years. Front page pictures of Tyson in handcuffs, being led away by law enforcement officers, enhanced this image. "Life for Mike Tyson as a jailhouse celebrity will be hard and humiliating," wrote the *New York Times*'s Dave Anderson, anticipating a terrifying obstacle course, with prison guards and inmates lining up to get a piece of him.

Lule presents evidence of a consensus: media applauding the sentence, at the same time deploring a man they had praised only a few years before. Yet there was a different, more sympathetic portrait that emerged during the trial, one that emphasized the parts played by Tyson's background in determining his fate. In this characterization, Tyson became a victim, struggling through an orphaned childhood on the streets of Brooklyn, punished by an unforgiving penal system, cruelly deprived of the stabilizing effect of a father. The Tyson trial had not one but two victims. The abundant money Tyson had earned couldn't help him escape his past: it haunted him to the point where he was a "victim, not a victimizer," as *Washington Post* columnist Tom Boswell wrote.

Yet, there is more than sympathy on offer in this account: there is a conception of someone stripped of any meaningful power to guide his own destiny, someone just swept along by at first adverse, then favorable circumstances without being able to exercise any control over himself. Just like all the other feckless African Americans brought up in the ghettos, their lives wasted on drugs and crime, Tyson found himself ultimately unable to steer his life in the direction he wanted. No amount of money could help him abscond from his circumstances. It was a description that symbolically disempowered Tyson, argued Lule, and, in this sense, was yet another "racially charged" type.

Either way, Tyson was guilty of something. The question was: did the "black, savage, sex-driven former heavyweight champion use his animal strength to rape the virginal black princess?" Or: did the "dumb, innocent but well-hung black boxer get manipulated again, this time by a promiscuous black gold-digger who had knowingly thrown herself at him only to be hurt by the size of his organ?"

It would be tempting to conclude from Lule's study that the reporters and commentators who collectively presented Tyson in these terms were a bunch of racists. It would also be wrong. Lule isn't suggesting the representations were the result of journalistic bias, prejudice, or bigotry. Narratives about Tyson were conducted according to unquestioned and unnoticed conventions that may have had racist outcomes, but were not necessarily racist in production. The reason the portrayals rang so true is that they appealed to common sense. How else could you understand a guy like Tyson?

Alternatives were just illogical, according to Sloop, whose previously quoted essay supports Lule's findings: "Playing into the myths of the black male and the black athlete, it becomes only logical that Tyson is guilty . . . Tyson is faced with . . . the charges brought on by a miasma of cultural stereotypes" (p. 112 and p. 114).

Miasma is an interesting choice of metaphor. It refers to an infectious or noxious outflow, a pollution. Tyson was infected by an entire cultural tradition. Sloop avoids commenting on "the absolute guilt or innocence of Mike Tyson" and concentrates only on how the boxer was contaminated by ideas, images, and statuses about blacks that have been transmitted by history, but spread by media representations that were as diffuse as common cold germs before and during the trial. For a long time after, too.

The particular combination of being a black man, a heavyweight boxer and a fighter whose style was based – at least, according to many in the media – on "ferocious aggression" was such a powerful one that Tyson, on Sloop's account, collapsed "under the weight of past discourses." The discourses in question consist of prejudices, images, and symbols that have been recycled through the decades and centuries, always being modified, yet always remaining essentially the same.

The 1962 John Ford movie *The Man Who Shot Liberty Valance* has a conceit: the character of the title is not actually the man who did the deed. Although the peaceable attorney, played by James Stewart, gets credit for killing Valance, a murderous scoundrel who had terrorized locals, the crucial bullet is fired by John Wayne's less cerebral character, who prefers to leave this fact obscured. If the accounts presented by the likes of Lule, Sloop and others are to be accepted, Washington may have drawn the applause and brickbats for a deed she didn't actually commit. Of course, she made the initial allegation and will be remembered as the woman who, as one headline writer put it, KO'd Tyson. But his own reputation defeated Tyson. It was a reputation forged in the heat of celebrity culture, hammered, beaten and stamped out by his own defense counsel, the media, and a global audience willing to believe just about anything of the "walking keg of testosterone," as *Time* magazine described him in August, 1991.

A *Los Angeles Times* story headlined "Boxing, the public are not blameless" by M. Penner captured the ambiguous and paradoxical responses to Tyson's conviction: "A sports champion is charged with rape, and then convicted, and we are simultaneously disgusted and intrigued, appalled and enthralled" (February 12, 1992). There are events that both horrify and bewitch us, drawing us to them as a car wreck entices gaping bystanders filled with feelings of attraction and repulsion, but unable to determine which one, if any, takes precedence. The Tyson rape case was one of them.

—— eight ——

IN HANDCUFFS IN THE BACK OF A POLICE CRUISER

It took centuries to perfect the vision of American righteousness. But it was worth it. After all, God blessed America, bestowed on the young nation divine approval. This wasn't just a land of opportunity: it was *the* land of opportunity. Americans believe in their constitution. They believe in the freedom to vote and the freedom to worship according to one's own beliefs. They believe in a free marketplace. Freedom forms a big part of the American ideal. There is a visionary greatness about the nation. Yet, every so often, an alternative vision appears and forces earnest reflection. The sources of the alternative vision are usually improbable. Take the case of George Holliday.

Holliday was the manager of a plumbing company in Los Angeles. On March 3, 1991, he was experimenting with a new toy, a camcorder that he'd recently bought in order to make home videos. Twisting knobs, rotating lenses, pushing buttons, he hadn't completely mastered how to use the technology, but he was getting to grips with it; enough to make a recording, anyway. Little did he know that he was about to record a piece of footage that would become as famous, as iconic and as historically significant as the film of the Kennedy assassination.

Still trying to fathom out exactly how the camcorder worked, Holliday was distracted by the sound of screeching car wheels. He looked up to see a scene of total confusion, police cars, sirens, shouting and, in the midst of this, an African American man who was, Holliday presumed, being pulled over for something or other. Worth recording, maybe.

For 81 seconds, he left the camcorder in "record" mode and pointed it at the bewildering frenzy. In that time, the black male was beaten to the floor and dealt 56 baton blows, punches and kicks by police officers. He was, of course, Rodney King, and he ended up with a broken leg, shattered eye socket, broken cheekbone, split lip, multiple skull fractures, and partial paralysis of the face.

The following April, four white LAPD officers were brought to trial at Simi Valley, California, a predominantly white area where African Americans make up only 2 percent of the population. It was an area in which, in the judge's estimation, the police officers could expect fair treatment. The jury, comprising six males and six females, one of whom was Hispanic, another Filipino, the rest white, watched the tape of the beating, listened to testimonies and brought back a verdict that resonated all over the US and beyond. The officers were acquitted. There was protest outside LAPD headquarters.

The protest was a prelude to three days of violent unrest in LA and elsewhere in the United States, resulting in 50 deaths, with 4,000 more injured, 1,100 arrested and $1 billion in property damage. King eventually received compensation of $3 million. The LAPD deployed only two officers per 1,000 residents, the lowest ratio in the United States (New York City deploys 3.7) and 15 per square mile (compared with 89 for New York). Neighborhood involvement was sought through community policing, but, with so few officers, the approach was largely ineffectual. When the LAPD failed to quell the initial violence, 1,000 federal law enforcement officers and 4,000 Army and Marine troops were sent to Los Angeles, ready to move in at the express command of the President. One thousand four hundred Californian National Guard members were placed on stand-by. California Governor Pete Wilson declared a state of emergency. Even when President George Bush arrived in LA on May 8, 1992, the seared buildings were still smoking.

Racial schisms in America had not been in full view since the 1960s, when a violent incident in the Watts district of South-Central LA ignited riots across the nation. Then, the cycle of expectation and disappointment that accompanied the civil rights movement was the underlying source of the upheavals. Again, it was an episode involving African Americans and police officers that precipitated the disturbances. The aftermath of the King case suggested that racial tensions had abated rather than disappeared.

After the riots of 1965/67, race became a "wedge issue" in the USA: something that forces sections of the population apart. Many whites may have felt encumbered with guilt during the 1950s and 1960s, when the new deal of the postwar period was anything but that for most blacks. Segregation remained virtually unchanged and racism was still a potent force. But, the pangs of guilt became less tormenting: the grievances aired dramatically in the mid-1960s were being dealt with through school integration, preferential hiring and higher taxes to fund ethnic group-specific programs. In other words, the idea that *something* was being done diffused so quickly and effectively that whites believed they were bending over backward to help African Americans. Civil rights laws smoothed off the rough edges of racist discrimination, and though no one deluded themselves that racism would retreat overnight, there was a sense in which the issue was being managed.

Beatings, like the one administered by the police to Rodney King, were probably commonplace. The difference was that this one was videotaped. It was shown time and again around the world. Hearing and reading about the treatment blacks alleged they received from white police officers made people aware. Seeing it actually happen imprinted it on their consciousness indelibly and unequivocally. There was no dispute that this happened. No one could question the ferocity of the physical abuse, or the duration of the brutality. The police may have habitually defended themselves by citing the resistance of civilians, yet there was none in evidence. King was defenseless as the four officers attacked.

In itself, the footage of the battering was a powerful vignette about the conflict that still ripped through America. When coupled with an acquittal that few believed to be justified, it exposed a jarring truth: that the fault line of race continued to destabilize the social structure of the nation.

If middle America had felt relieved of the burden of race in the wake of the 1960s riots, it must have sensed its return after the Rodney King incident and its fallout. How were Americans to make sense of this devastation? The fortieth anniversary of civil rights legislation within sight, a bewildering number of programs, policies, and initiatives had been in motion, all designed in some way to address America's longest and most agonizing problem. And yet it remained, seemingly intractable. Why? This was the question to which there were no ready answers, save for the one most people did not want to hear.

Six years after the King incident, David Patterson wrote of a "strategy of distraction" that he detected was gaining in currency. "It denies the existence of racism itself and takes no responsibility," wrote Patterson in his 1997 article for the *New York Amsterdam News*. "It is manifested by the attempt to dehumanize victims and coerce some measure of responsibility on their part, rather than the predators." While Patterson wasn't referring to the King episode, he might well have included it in his assessment. After Rodney King, the need for such a strategy became felt perhaps more urgently than ever before.

There are few images in the popular imagination more terrifying to whites than that of the minatory black male. African American men's access to mainstream America is conditional: as a talented entertainer who performs in front of white audiences, or as a servant, neither of whom threaten the order of things. Or as a minister, scholar or similar de-sexualized character. Gunnar Myrdal, in his epic analysis of *An American Dilemma*, which was first published in 1944, wrote of a "close link between lynching and repressed sexual drives." Jan Nederveen Pieterse picks up his point in his *White on Black*: "Jealousy and fear of the black man's sexuality, and the inability or unwillingness to accept the masculinity, the virility of black men, play a key part in the American racial psycho-drama" (p. 177).

Nederveen Pieterse argues that there are various ways of emasculating black men, lynching and castration being only the obvious ones. Humiliation is another. Not just making someone a laughing stock, but obliging them to work in unrewarding and undistinguished jobs or denying them status and privilege. Or by withholding their right to participate in the political process. All these methods have been practiced historically. The mixture of brute strength and sexual prowess produces a figure whose virility approaches, or actually is, bestial. His presence or just the apprehension of his presence has induced panic, fear, and dread among whites.

Black men are no longer lynched in America, nor are they castrated. They are, however, tied to trucks and dragged until they die, shot in cold blood and, sometimes, beaten ruthlessly by police officers.

The specter of the menacing black male haunts American history. Perhaps, the most vivid embodiment is Nat Turner, leader of a slave insurrection in 1831. Inspired by visions, Turner and a group of slaves slaughtered over 50 whites in Virginia before being captured by the military. Turner was hanged and skinned.

As if to underscore the abiding potency of the image, George Bush, in his 1988 presidential campaign, all but exhumed the corpse of Turner, making use of a black convicted murderer, Willie Horton, to spook the electorate. Horton was serving a life sentence without parole in Massachusetts for a 1974 homicide. While out on a weekend furlough, he went on a rapacious spree. In an effort to dismantle his opponent Michael Dukakis, Bush accused him of being "soft on crime" and used Horton in television and newspaper advertisements to illustrate what happens when policies get too liberal. In Bush's hands, Horton became a metaphor for racial hatred. The campaign illustrated how terrifying the prospect of a dangerous black male remained: Bush's approval ratings rose sharply and he won the election. It was the same "racial psycho-drama," just a different act.

Other scenes of the same drama featured Jack Johnson, Marion Barry, Clarence Thomas, O. J. Simpson, Reverend Benjamin Chavis; all, in their own ways, black males who constituted, or, more precisely, appeared to have constituted, a threat of some kind. In all cases, the presence, perhaps even suspicion, of sexual transgression added appreciably to the impression of menace. In each case, the plot took the same turn: the dark figure was emasculated. Yet Tyson remained at large: middle America might have suspected he deserved the same kind of treatment as the others, but it came to realize that Tyson's real value lay in his uncontrollable nature. America eventually lost interest in taming, less still emasculating, Tyson. It wanted, perhaps needed, him unleashed and dangerous. Like this, he was living proof.

Black men don't get beaten up or refused work or get overlooked for promotion because of an image, even one so alarming as this. Yet there's no denying its enduring contribution to race relations in America. It informs and defines racist tensions, yet is turned around to defuse them. If the bestial dark menace remains, then he must be castrated, destroyed, domesticated, broken or tamed. In the process, a reminder is issued. Back in the days of Turner, it was something like: this is a glimpse of what will happen if ever slavery is abolished. Today, its content is different, but the significance essentially the same.

———

"I can't wait for you to kiss me with those big lips of yours," Tyson taunted his opponent, Donovan Ruddock, better known as "Razor." "I know you really like me." It was an interesting put-down. Much more original than "I'm gonna kill him" or "He won't last [whatever] rounds." For some reason, Tyson had decided to introduce a homoerotic element into the pre-fight hype, describing Ruddock as a "transvestite" and promising "I'm gonna make you my girlfriend." Quite why Tyson got this into his head isn't clear. Was this going to be a fight or a seduction?

Tyson had beaten Ruddock three months earlier, but the ending was inconclusive. Ruddock had held his own until the seventh round, when he ran into a solid, though not, it appeared, damaging, shot. The referee saw otherwise and intervened amid protest from Ruddock and his corner. The stoppage seemed premature. As Tyson himself had announced before the fight: "if I don't kill him, it don't count," it didn't count. So they would need to try again.

Tyson's two opponents before had lasted only a round each. Henry Tillman, who had beaten Tyson twice as an amateur and kept him out of the 1984 Olympic team, was crumpled like a paper cup in June, 1990. Tyson threw only one serious punch in the fight; but that was enough. Alex Stewart offered scarcely more resistance: he did, at least, land a decent shot; though it had no noticeable effect on a rampant Tyson, who almost threw himself to the canvas in his zeal to finish the fight quickly.

There was an interesting short film commissioned by HBO and directed by Spike Lee, then about to embark on his movie *Malcolm X*. It was part of the Tyson marketing, but there were revealing moments. "We're two black guys from the ghetto," said Tyson to Lee. "And they don't like what we're saying. We're not like prejudiced, antiwhite. We're just pro-black." The "they" presumably referred to white society. It was a political observation, not a new one, but certainly new from Tyson. As if to underline this awakening, Tyson entered the ring for the Stewart fight with Public Enemy's black power anthem "Welcome to the Terrordome" blasting from the speakers.

Around this time, Tyson was interviewed for ESPN by Charlie Steiner, who asked: "How do you think America perceives you?" Tyson's answer was both perceptive and prophetic: "They want to see me as a nigga in handcuffs in the back of a police cruiser" (quoted by Phil Berger in his article "Split decision").

This was an innovation on one of Don King's stock themes about America's not tolerating successful blacks. King, with whom Tyson had by then grown close, was promoting Tyson in a string of nontitle fights, though Tyson's eyes were on the bigger prize: the heavyweight title he had lost in February, 1990. King was guiding him toward a title shot, though, of course, it would not materialize until 1996.

Tyson was the central part of King's promotional operations. In 1990, King launched KingVision. This was a vehicle through which he would promote shows to be screened by Showtime cable television. The smaller shows would be available to regular subscribers of Showtime; but they would have to pay a premium for the very big shows. The pay-per-view platform was known as Showtime Event Television, or just SET. Tyson was promised that he would fight on the first two of the KingVision/SET shows.

Exactly how much Tyson stood to earn from these two fights remains unclear. At the outset, King boasted that Tyson would earn a staggering $120 million. This was in 1990, remember. Showtime agreed that $120 million was potentially available, though the tv company provided only $1 million to cover front-end costs of each promotion and up to $3 million extra for broadcast rights. In return it received a share of the ppv profits (not income, but net profits). Tyson's money would come out of the gross ppv receipts, though he would have been guaranteed a minimum amount.

The KingVision/SET initiative was in response to major changes in global media communications industries. Rupert Murdoch's arrival as a major player was not detected in 1983, when he bought a loss-making satellite operation called Inter-American. But, two years later, he bought a stake in Fox and proceeded to build his interest in what was then an insignificant television channel. Murdoch turned it into the fourth major US network, largely through the acquisition of key sports and in particular through acquiring the rights to Sunday National Football League games from CBS. At the same time, Murdoch was buying interests in a perplexing number of other sports media, stadiums, and franchises, not just in the US but all over Europe and Asia. His global reach ensured that, by the end of the twentieth century, he was the single most powerful person in sports.

Murdoch, more than any other media entrepreneur, showed how sports could be used as an instrument with which to make consumers part with their money; or, as he memorably put it, a "battering ram" – presumably to smash his way into people's homes. His dictum was something like: if people want to watch sports so much – and they do – make 'em pay and pay dearly for it.

There had been experiments with pay-per-view in the 1980s, though there were inhibitions, not least of which was the prospect of a backlash from consumers who had been reared on getting their sports free-to-air. There were also physical problems: not everyone had cable television facilities and, without them, they had no access, even if they were prepared to pay. In 1980, the fight between Sugar Ray Leonard and Roberto Duran became the first pay-per-view event, attracting 170,000 buyers who paid $15 each. Rock concerts, operas and other occasional theatrical events followed, though it was not until 1991 that Time Warner, which owned HBO, decided the time was right to establish a separate division specifically for ppv boxing events. TVKO, as it was called, was a response to the vision of Seth Abraham, who, in August, 1990, proclaimed: "I can look on the horizon and see what's coming."

About a quarter of the 60 million US households hooked up to cable could receive TVKO feed. Abraham, who was an HBO executive, estimated that, even if only a twentieth of those households bought a promotion for, say, $40, that would yield a gross of $30 million. This was a leap of faith from 170,000 to 750,000 viewers and from $15 to $40, all in ten years. But, in the interim, closed circuit television had been the main outlet and, quite apart from the awkwardness of collecting revenues it posed, it was simply not congruent with the times. With so many homes wired up for pay-per-view, it made more sense to take the shows to the viewers rather than expecting them to get to a movie theater.

Abraham's idea was to draw King and his deadliest rival pro-moter, Bob Arum, into the TVKO net. For a while, this looked like happening. King, at this point, had Tyson's confidence, and, though he wasn't the heavyweight champion, he remained the drawcard. King knew this and asked Abraham for $20 million for pledging Tyson to the venture. This was a signing-on fee, a kind of sweetener to procure Tyson's services. Further fees were to be negotiated. Abraham countered with a staggering $85 million, but for ten fights. Tyson had fought only ten times since May 1987. As it was then October, 1990, it might have taken Tyson a further three-and-a-half years to complete the deal – that is till about April, 1994. In fact, it took Tyson until January, 1999, to complete ten more fights; but even a sage like Abraham couldn't foresee the supervening events that were to disrupt Tyson's life.

King would emerge from the deal about $30 million richer by the time he had collected site fees and a percentage of foreign television rights. For this, he had to make the matches and ensure Tyson turned up for them. While these things can't exactly be contracted, it was assumed that Tyson would win the ten fights.

The deal went sour ostensibly because Tyson objected to HBO's ringside summarizer and interviewer, Larry Merchant. King conveyed this to Abraham, who wanted Merchant on board for TVKO. As interviewers go, Merchant is no pitbull, but he's no lapdog either and earns his dues with relevant probing that sometimes approaches an agreeable cynicism – agreeable for the viewer, that is. Tyson may not have liked his style, but whether he would wreck an $85 million deal because of it is doubtful. But that was the official version of why the contract never materialized. King had worked with HBO for the preceding eleven years, so it strains credulity to accept that the whole package disintegrated because of a Tyson whim. On the other hand, Tyson had been known for his fanciful decisions and an indifference or inattention to financial affairs. So his pulling out of a deal like this because of a petty personal dislike is just about believable. Just about.

Abraham constructed deals with Arum and other promoters and managers, such as Shelly Finkel and Dan Duva, none of whom had any connections with Tyson at that stage. While Tyson continued to command centerstage, there were other co-stars who made up the boxing bill in 1990. The renascent George Foreman had surprised the boxing world and delighted the rest of the world. Previously best known for losing an epic fight with Muhammad Ali in 1974 in Zaire, Foreman had staged an extraordinary, improbable comeback and fought his way back into title contention. Evander Holyfield had always been a dependable rather than spectacular fighter and was earning the respect, though perhaps not affection, of sports fans. He made easy work of Tyson's conqueror James "Buster" Douglas to become the world heavyweight champion. A title fight between Foreman and Holyfield made sense in every way.

Holyfield won the fight with his usual workmanlike efficiency, though Foreman extended him and walked away with credit. The promotion at Trump Plaza in Atlantic City was a TVKO triumph. Coming in April, only a month after Tyson's first fight against Ruddock, did little to harm its appeal. It was one of those fights that had an appeal that went way beyond sports. The idea that avuncular "Big George," famed for his outrageous appetite and his one-punch knockout power, could pull off a win was a tempting one. The fact that he couldn't didn't diminish the occasion.

Although it was far from his most demanding fight, it served a useful purpose for Holyfield: it introduced him to a new market. Before the fight, it was likely that you could ask 20 people in the street, "Who is the heavyweight champion of the world?" and maybe four or five of them would know Holyfield. The others would be "don't know" or "Tyson, isn't it?" After beating Foreman in a hugely publicized and well-viewed event, Holyfield could finally claim widespread name recognition. He may not have been in Tyson's league, but he was still the champion and, if Tyson wanted the title back, he would have to go through him.

Tyson's unfinished business with Ruddock was completed in June, 1991. It was a disappointing fight, Tyson seeming to struggle with a taller and heavier opponent who had learned enough lessons from the first fight to keep him out of harm's way. Ruddock had put on extra pounds since their first fight. Boxers do this on the assumption that the weight will give their punches more solidity and improve their resilience. But it also tends to slow them down. Tyson was the aggressor throughout and won a decision.

This was the first time Tyson had been taken the distance by an opponent for four years. He was still only two days away from his 25th birthday, but already evidence of decline seemed to be appearing. Occasional off-days are part of any professional athlete's career, of course. But, in the previous couple of years, changes in Tyson's approach signaled a departure from his earlier domineering approach in which he would push forward remorselessly, his head bobbing, knees bending, never allowing his opponent a stationary target. His was an approach that demanded an ardent work ethic. It was not an approach that permitted respite: every round had to be fought at the same level of intensity; continual movement was fundamental.

Two first round knockouts disclosed no changes in Tyson's technique; they were over too quickly to notice. The first Ruddock fight disclosed no noticeable change either. But the distance fight revealed a rather more pedestrian Tyson who appeared to be thinking about his fight, rather than just fighting it. Top athletes, when they have mastered their technique, can often execute it without concentration, focusing instead on other aspects of their performance, such as tactics or their opponent's intentions. They kind of surrender the skill to memory and think not about what they're doing, but why they're doing it. It's called automaticity. A pitcher, for example, does not need to think about the mechanics of pitching, though he might want to make a conscious adjustment to style in order to accommodate different batters, or changing weather conditions. Golfers are discouraged from thinking about their swing once they've acquired the basic technique. When skills decay, automaticity gradually disappears and retiring athletes often rue that they have to think about what they once did automatically.

Could Tyson have been edging past his peak before his 25th birthday? Boxers, like many other types of athletes, typically peak in their mid-to-late twenties and, with improved knowledge of how best to maintain a healthy mind and body, can often perform at their highest level into their thirties. While he was anomalous, Foreman presents quite an example: a world heavyweight champion at the age of 23, he won another, after a ten-year "retirement," at 45 and had his last fight at 49. Wilfred Benitez had a much more condensed career, having his first professional fight two months after his 15th birthday and winning the first of three world titles at the age of 17. At 23, he lost to Thomas Hearns and slid into obscurity thereafter.

Tyson was never likely to have a career span anything like Foreman's. A combination of his attritional fighting approach and turbulent lifestyle suggested a short, explosive reign ending some time before he reached 30. But tangible proof of decline appeared in the second Ruddock fight. Or was this just one of those fights? Tyson had been known to have them before. If his head wasn't in it, or his training wasn't quite right, or something just didn't feel right, the equilibrium so necessary to Tyson's effectiveness was upset.

In retrospect, the first interpretation was nearer the truth. Tyson's preparations may not have gone smoothly, and his state of mind may not have been quite right. But the reality only became apparent in subsequent fights. The early onset of decline was evident in Ruddock II. The head that once bobbed as elusively as an apple in a barrel had become a relatively motionless target. The punches didn't flow over opponents like an incapacitating cascade. The feet didn't advance in an unstoppable motion. The organic cadence of Tyson's boxing was replaced by a discontinuous, mechanical approach. Perhaps for the first time in his career, Tyson really did seem to be thinking out loud: "How can I get rid of this guy? My punches are having no effect and he keeps firing back."

At the end of twelve rounds, Tyson looked relieved to have his hand raised. Even more relieved was King, who must have feared at times that his prize asset – and Tyson was being treated as that – was being embarrassed by a big but technically limited foe. The win was all that mattered. A poor performance could be explained away, discounted and made to seem irrelevant: the important letter was the "W" at the end of the line. Coupled with the same letter at the end of the line reading "Foreman" on Holyfield's record, it meant the negotiations for the most expensive and most lucrative fight in history could begin.

——— nine ———

THEY BELIEVE WHITE MEN HAVE
HAD TO PAY FOR BLACK SUCCESS

A moment of humor Tyson-style leavened the otherwise somber atmosphere of the weigh-in for the fight against a visibly apprehensive Frank Bruno. Tyson, then undefeated and, many suspected, unbeatable, sought to establish his usual domination by eyeballing Bruno. It was difficult for opponents to avoid Tyson's fearful intimidation: he had successfully defended his world title seven times in under twenty-nine months, giving him a perfect 35–0 record overall. He'd recently elucidated his approach to boxing: "I just have this thing inside me that I want to eat and conquer . . . I want to conquer people and their souls."

Bruno wanted no part of the eyeballing, so he fidgeted and stared downwards away from Tyson's gaze, rather like a guilty schoolboy being admonished by a teacher. After a while, Tyson grew tired of Bruno's evasion of what he considered a manly conveyance, so pulled down his undershorts. Bruno found himself staring at Tyson's genitals. As if for emphasis, Tyson grabbed his crotch.

"I'm back," Tyson had declared when announcing the fight. "I'm glad to be back." He hadn't been seen in a boxing ring for six months, the longest absence in his professional career. It was December, 1988. By the time of the fight, Bruno would have been out of action longer than Tyson: in an effort to protect his challenger status, he remained inactive for sixteen months.

Now single again, Tyson told the media that he was "very happy at this particular moment in my life," adding "and Don King put a big hand on it." King, who was sitting next to him, smiled beatifically and thanked Tyson. They were a team.

"Inseparable," is how King himself described himself and Tyson. "No one is going to split us up."

"I ask for no sympathy. I despise sympathy. I hear people say, 'poor Mike Tyson.' There is nothing poor about me," Tyson reminded the press corps, just in case they felt sympathy coming on. It wasn't an emotion typically aroused by Tyson. One wonders whom he had heard expressing it.

No heavyweight since Ali had drawn the kind of acclaim Tyson had. He was talked about as the greatest since The Greatest. His celebrity status was also approaching that of Ali in the 1960s and 1970s. The likes of Sugar Ray Leonard, Thomas Hearns, Roberto Duran, Marvin Hagler, and Larry Holmes had been stars in boxing's firmament since the fall of Ali. Formidable athletes as they were, none strayed beyond the boundaries of sports as Ali had. But, in his own completely different way, Tyson had managed it.

At this stage, another point of comparison with Ali was emerging. After winning the heavyweight title by beating Sonny Liston in 1964, the then Cassius Clay proclaimed that he would from this time on be known as Muhammad Ali, the name given to him by the Nation of Islam. Ali had converted to the Nation of Islam, which was led by Elijah Muhammad and had as its most famous follower Malcolm X. Ali and Malcolm were close companions before Malcolm's assassination in February, 1965.

Among the Nation of Islam's principles were (and are) that whites were "blue-eyed devils" who were intent on keeping black people in a state of subjugation and that integration was not only impossible, but undesirable. Blacks and whites should live separately, the Nation of Islam argued, preferably in different states. The image was in stark contrast to the melting pot, which was America's popular ideal of the 1960s.

Ali's camp had only one white man, Angelo Dundee. Cassius Clay Sr was violently opposed to Ali's affiliation, not on religious grounds, but because he believed the retinue of Black Muslims he attracted was sucking money from his son. Ali's commitment deepened, causing the media, which had earlier warmed to his flamboyance, to turn against him. A rift occurred between Ali and Joe Louis, the former heavyweight champion, who was described as "a credit to his race." This presaged several other conflicts with black boxers whom Ali believed had allowed themselves to become assimilated into white America and had failed to face themselves as true African Americans.

Ali saved his most ardent criticism for Floyd Patterson, whom he called an "Uncle Tom" and "the rabbit" after Patterson refused to address him by his Islamic name. He seemed to delight in punishing Patterson in their 1965 fights. The almost malicious performance brought censure from sections of America, black and white. At the nadir of his popularity, Ali fought Ernie Terrell, who, like Patterson, insisted on referring to him as Clay. The fight had a grim subtext, with Ali constantly taunting Terrell. "What's my name, Uncle Tom?" Ali kept asking Terrell as he administered a callous beating.

Media reaction to the fight was wholly negative. Ali's biographer, Thomas Hauser, quotes the boxing journalist Jimmy Cannon: "It was a bad fight, nasty with the evil of religious fanaticism. This wasn't an athletic contest. It was a kind of lynching." We can't tell how widely Cannon's interpretation was shared. His conclusion that Ali was "a vicious propagandist for a spiteful mob that works the religious underground" would certainly not have elicited the approval of some. Ali was admired and revered by a great many whites and blacks who may have disagreed with his religious commitments, but stood squarely behind his stance on many racial issues and the Vietnam War.

Tyson underwent no epiphany, though, by the time of the Bruno fight, he had discarded most white members of his management and coaching team and installed African American replacements. In fact, for the Bruno fight, Tyson used three black cornermen for the first time in his career. King claimed that Tyson (and he) had made history in doing so. Preferential hiring can have its downside. The three African Americans, Aaron Snowell, John Horne, and Rory Holloway, had little experience of cornerwork and had appeared somewhat out of their depth in a world title fight. Michael Katz's description of Tyson during the Bruno fight for the *New York Daily News* could have been lifted from Cannon. He wrote that Tyson was "filled with arrogance, pumped up with poison."

Bruno posed little threat. In fact, he was on the canvas only eleven seconds into the fight when Tyson caught him with a right delivered with less than full power. But, after that ominous start, Bruno held and rabbit-punched till his head cleared and actually managed to connect with a shot that might have hurt Tyson. Bruno clinched, mauled, and grasped until Tyson extricated himself sufficiently to unload ten unanswered punches that left Bruno bereft of his senses. Tyson closed in, prompting the ref to call a halt in the fifth round. Bruno left the Vegas Hilton stunned, but $3.5 million richer.

Tyson's conscription into the King brotherhood effectively ended his relationship with Bill Cayton, who tried strenuously to retain his managership of Tyson, at first by working with King and, later, by filing a suit against him. King's official capacity as "advisor and counsel" to Tyson meant, in real terms, that Tyson had vouchsafed him responsibility for guiding him. Not just in professional terms either: King seemed to have gained Tyson's trust and confidence. So much so that Tyson was prepared to antagonize Cayton, his manager of record, and ignore whatever plans he had made for him. Cayton had designed a series of fights for 1989 that would have taken Tyson to Brazil and Italy, but Tyson chose to disregard them, announcing that he wanted King to handle his affairs. Cayton, whose managerial contract ran until February, 1992, would continue to take his percentage of Tyson's earnings, even though he had little, if any, say in Tyson's career. It wasn't an amicable settlement, but Cayton realized that Tyson had changed so much that, by taking legal action against King, he was practically closing off any opportunity he had of salvaging his relationship with Tyson.

Legal wrangling with Cayton was only one of the distractions that must have affected Tyson's concentration in the build-up to the Bruno fight. Another was a million-dollar lawsuit filed by a Long Island woman who said Tyson had grabbed her buttocks in a Manhattan club. These kind of accusations were to become more frequent and more serious in the years ahead.

Another distraction was the publication of a biography by José Torres, a former light-heavyweight champion who had known Tyson since the 1970s and was chairman of the New York State Athletic Commission. *Fire and Fear: The inside story of Mike Tyson* was published by Warner Books in June, 1989. Tyson co-operated with Torres for most of the book's development, though withdrew this after detecting Torres' sympathies with Cayton. As Torres himself wrote in the book: "My publisher, Warner Books, received a letter from [lawyer, Michael] Winston indicating that Tyson no longer wanted me to write his biography" (p. 208).

Torres went ahead and completed his book, which veered toward the salacious in chronicling Tyson's sexual proclivities. Tyson didn't deny that the tales were true, though he did express the feeling that he'd had his throat cut by Torres. Without doubt, the most repeated quote from the book is the one about "I like to hurt women when I make love to them . . . I like to hear them scream with pain, to see them bleed . . . it gives me pleasure."

This, in itself, would have been mortifying for Tyson, though Torres' response, which is usually overlooked, would have probably been enough to earn him a slap from Tyson: "Some men who dislike women at an unconscious level . . . could be considered latent homosexuals." Torres recounts how they explore this possibility. "I may imagine something," he says to Tyson. "Like, you are a homosexual" (p. 109). Tyson laughed, gave him a "brotherly punch in the chest," then kissed Torres on the cheek.

Tyson had posed with Torres only two weeks prior to the Bruno fight, so presumably could not have anticipated that the book would portray him as a man berserk with conflicting sexual drives, struggling to keep a lid on his natural urges toward violence. "José, I am that way and I don't know why," says Tyson as if in resignation. This was an image of Tyson as an unapologetic, misogynistic, brutal despoiler of women who was at the mercy of his lust for pleasure. It's possible that many agreed with this kind of analysis; maybe it gained more converts in the years that followed. It wasn't welcomed by Tyson, though; he felt that Torres' homicidal prose made him "worse than a murderer."

There was something a little too sanctimonious about Tyson's reaction to the book. After all, public perceptions of him were changing, albeit slowly. Stories of his infelicities were circulating. In 1989, an accusation that he struck a parking lot attendant outside an LA nightclub was later dropped, though the "no smoke without fire" principle suggested that something untoward might have occurred. A couple of weeks later, Tyson was arrested in Albany, New York, after doing 71 mph in a 30-mph zone in his new Lamborghini. While training for the Bruno fight, he angrily grabbed and smashed two cameras belonging to media workers. Individually, these incidents may have been meaningless, but, together, they were adding up.

Maybe the heavyweight champion of the world had too much, too soon. At 23, he had already earned approaching $70 million. Any young man with that kind of money might veer out of control. The difference was that, for Tyson, there was a media waiting to record the consequences of every lapse. The Torres book served to rubberstamp suspicions that Tyson was either heading or already out of control. He may well have been stung by Torres' account, but it was hardly full of shocking and new revelations.

In its summer, 1989 edition, the magazine *Boxing Illustrated* ran a cover story with the title "IS MIKE TYSON BECOMING THE MOST UNPOPULAR HEAVYWEIGHT CHAMPION IN HISTORY?" In retrospect, some might be tempted to conclude that Tyson himself read the story and contrived, over the next several years, to answer it – affirmatively.

Despite the growing feeling that Tyson was becoming, or had become, destabilized, King and his associates maintained exactly the opposite. John Horne, an associate of King and aide to Tyson, assured the media that: "This camp is much more at ease for Mike." Illingworth quotes Horne from 1989, when Tyson was preparing for a defense against Carl "The Truth" Williams: "We give him more stability . . . He's happier as a person all around, not just in the ring" (*Mike Tyson: Money, myth and betrayal*, p. 325).

Tyson was being wrapped tighter and tighter by King. There were no complaints from the boxer. This gave, at least some, the impression that he was being beguiled and used. It was a source of some encouragement to Williams' manager, who rather brashly said of Tyson: "He can be manipulated outside the ring. Why not inside?"

As Williams was to discover, there were eminently logical reasons why not. Once inside the ring, Tyson seemed to regress toward a primal state in which he experienced no pain, withstood punishment and recognized no apparent restraint. He simply stomped forward and, in his own words, conquered both the physical person and his soul. Of course, much of Tyson's fighting disguised a subtlety in his approach, a subtlety hewn out of months and years of steadfast routines. Every feint, every block, every duck, jab, hook, cross, uppercut, bodyshot; every little movement had been practiced over and over and over until it was perfect, then practiced some more. So that when Tyson went to work in the competitive ring, it looked natural. It was anything but. A supercilious Tyson alluded to this when reflecting on Bruno and his predecessors: "How dare they challenge me with their primitive skills?"

On the night of July 21, 1989, the essential Tyson was in town, the town being Atlantic City. Public Enemy's defiant anthem "Fight the Power," which was featured in Spike Lee's then-current movie *Do the Right Thing*, accompanied Tyson's entrance. When the first bell sounded, Tyson looked as he was supposed to: at one with his fighting self. Fluid, effortless, smooth; just as if he didn't have to think what to do. Williams jabbed, Tyson reacted as if instinctively, bending his knees, dipping his head under the extended arm of Williams, thrusting upward and forward, his left leg becoming a fulcrum, the entire force of his body converted with a spontaneous switch of the left hip, so that his left arm drove at Williams' head in a short arc, the glove connecting at the requisite angle, knuckles facing the ceiling. Natural.

Williams' contribution to the fight was over before it had begun. He went down, struggled to his feet, but was in no fit state to continue and Tyson had retained his title in under a round. Barely 23 years old and still undefeated, there didn't seem a man on earth capable of even giving Tyson a competitive fight, let alone beating him. He looked, for all intents and purposes, a force of nature.

———

Tyson grew up in a world in which race was an unacknowledged constituent of life. The civil unrest of the 1960s may have subsided, civil rights legislation may have introduced a new era of equal opportunity, but there were obdurate facts of life. More African American males were in prison, on probation or on parole than in college. Black families were about three times more likely to live in poverty than the rest of the population. There was a persistent pattern of educational underachievement among black children. A growing number of black children were raised by single parents (now, more are raised by single parents than in nuclear families). Race may not have been the organizing principle of life, as it had been before the 1960s, but it defined a line either side of which there were two distinct spheres.

Race remained an emotional as well as statistical reality. A quarter of a century after the 1964 Civil Rights Act, it retained the power to arouse passions, to stir deep, latent sentiments and rile people to action. Tyson's severance of his ties with white associates was, at one level, a business decision. If he felt he could get improved deals, better assistance with his preparations and more valuable support from elsewhere, it made sense. At another level, it suggested a change in arrangements that, from his vantage point, seemed liberating. Time after time, he would scatter allusions to black brotherhood and Jews, as if striking a blow for his new values. As he became audibly "blacker," so America began to understand him anew. Terrifying as the prodigious fighter was, there was always the comforting thought that he was under control; the control of whites, that is. As he swung away from those who had guided his career and toward new colleagues whose agenda was never clear, re-evaluations began.

Was the newly acquired swagger a sign of the kind of confidence that comes through being the undefeated champion of the world, or an arrogant reminder of his release from white guardians? In another context, the change in Tyson might have elicited a different response, but 1989 was a singular year. It was the year of the Central Park jogger.

The jogger in question was a white woman who, on an April evening, went on her usual run in New York's Central Park. She was attacked, raped, and left for dead. At 1.30 a.m., she was found unconscious, her body temperature at 84 degrees, having lost 75 percent of her blood. After twelve days in a coma, the woman, who worked on Wall Street, recovered consciousness, but had no memory of the events.

A group of black and Latino teenagers from Harlem had been assaulting strollers and cyclists in the park earlier in the evening. When the victim was discovered, police already had five youths in custody, being questioned about the muggings. Over the next few days, police questioned thirty-seven youths, before five confessed. Four of the youths did so on videotape, providing gruesome details of what were described as "wilding" episodes. They described how they beat, then held down the woman while the others took turns to rape her. Each sought to minimize his own role.

The confessions provoked an almost hysterical reaction, which, some argued, militated against a fair trial. Even so, the jury deliberated for twelve days. Some of the youths were taken back to the crime scene before they were taped, raising questions about the details they discussed on camera. It also emerged that most of the interrogations were not recorded until the youths had admitted to the rape.

A fusion of sex, race, and violence recalled centuries-old panics over black rapists. Myths about blacks' virility and sexual propensities lay not too far beneath the surface of the trial. It became another episode in the American racial psychodrama. Despite doubts about the testimonies, the jury returned a guilty verdict. The graphic, if unsupported, confessions of the young men effectively sent them to prison.

It was a case that helped create a climate of fear, not only in New York but across the USA. A sense of vulnerability among the citizenry grew: the prospect of parks, subways and streets becoming beset with marauding gangs of ethnic minority youths unsettled the nation. Under pressure to secure a conviction for a crime that made international news, the police produced a result that palliated rather than resolved.

Thirteen years later, Matias Reyes, a convicted rapist and murderer, confessed, providing credible evidence that he was the sole attacker and rapist. DNA tests established, to a factor of 1 : 6 billion, that Reyes was the source of the DNA on the jogger's socks and in her cervix. The convictions of the five youths were thrown out and the men, then in their late twenties, were released, having served their sentences of between seven and thirteen years for the other attacks in the park.

The action was a once unimaginable volte-face in a case that had wiped away any hopes that the race issue had reached some sort of settlement in the post-civil rights era. The jogger case was like one of those spam email messages: you want to delete it, but you suspect it may be something worth opening. Americans wanted to disregard the race issue, but when the jogger incident arrived, they knew they had to take notice. It was as if they ignored it at their peril.

The term racial profiling did not come into popular currency till the 1990s, though the practice had been going on for years before. Black suspects have for long been picked up by the police for the sole reason that they're black. After the Central Park rape, African Americans and Latinos would have been under particular surveillance. Still edgy, a nation gave its silent approval to a tactic that, at other times, has been condemned as sabotaging civil liberties. So, when Willie Bennett, a 39-year-old resident of Mission Hill, Massachusetts, was picked out of a police lineup on December 28, there was no protest and, if anything, a sense of relief. Another black assailant had been dragged off the streets.

Bennett's alleged crime: he had, it was said, shot a pregnant woman named Carol Stuart in the head, killing her and her unborn child. Bennett had form: he had served prison sentences for, among other things, shooting a police officer and robbery, and had assault and battery charges filed against him by the mother of one of his children, charges that were later dropped. Carol Stuart's husband, Charles, was, on his own account, also shot by Bennett during a botched robbery in Boston.

In fact, what happened was that, on October 23, Stuart, an affluent white suburbanite, fatally shot his wife in the head, then himself in the gut. He then called 911 on his carphone. Carol Stuart was heavily insured and her husband would be the beneficiary.

In a description to the police, Charles Stuart described a fictitious all-purpose African American male in terms vague enough for the police to justify "a search that was broad, intrusive, and oppressive," as Christopher Edley put it in *Manhattan Lawyer*, in March, 1990. Edley reported on how, almost immediately, Republican politicians demanded the reinstatement of the death penalty in Massachusetts. "The media's sensationalism provided fuel and bellows for the burning suspicion and public furor," wrote Edley.

Only after Stuart committed suicide by jumping off the Tobin Bridge, did the full picture emerge. Stuart's stomach wound was serious enough to convince even doubters that it was the work of an attacker (he damaged his bowels, gall bladder and liver, spent two days in intensive care and needed two operations). Yet his version of events was full of inconsistencies that might have alerted a more vigilant police. In the climate of 1989, in a city where African Americans, though making up only a quarter of the population, are prosecuted for most of the violent crime, in a country still raw after the Central Park rape, a rapid and expansive search for a black suspect made more sense. In describing the killer as a raspy-voiced black man in a tracksuit, Stuart opened up a racist Pandora's box. All the ills let loose when its lid was lifted simply overwhelmed the skepticism that might otherwise have prevailed.

Had Stuart not committed suicide, where would the inquiry have gone? It's possible that, in time, his story would have been exposed. Stuart's brother knew the truth and may have broken down. There again, Stuart was a respectable white man, who tended his rhododendrons and cleared the snow off his elderly neighbor's drive. Bennett was an unemployed African American who had spent a total of thirteen years in the joint. Although the media depicted him as the prime suspect, in fact, he was initially picked up for a motoring violation. While in custody, he was arraigned for robbing a video store, an offense for which he drew twelve to twenty-five years. (He was released on parole in 1998.)

The Boston mayor Raymond Flynn had worked to promote integration in a city that had been sundered by the bussing issue. In the 1970s, whites opposed attempts to desegregate schools, prompting widespread violence. Yet Flynn himself was criticized, at first, for not intervening in the police's handling of the crime, and, later, for failing to apologize to the city's black population. He simply asserted that everyone had been "victims of a sinister hoax." He might have pointed out that not all victims suffer equally.

Hoax it may have been, but, at a different time, in a different place, Stuart would probably have been "made," as the cop shows say. That he wasn't says something about the mood of 1989. The willingness to make gargantuan leaps of faith in an effort to secure the conviction of a black subject was surely one of the many indirect effects of the Central Park jogger case. Reverberations were still felt throughout the US. Responses to any incident that bore a resemblance, no matter how vague, had to be rapid and definite. The reappearance of the race question in public discourse was hardly welcome, but there was no denying its power to transform social life; not after 1989.

Yet there was one more case which added to the transformation and it was barely noticed amid the tumult of the more dramatic events. It had its origins in a legal action brought by Randy Pech, a white construction contractor, whose bid for a contract to build guard rails on a Colorado freeway was rejected. Instead, the contract was awarded to the more expensive Latino-owned Gonzalez Construction Company.

Congress required that at least 10 percent of all federal money spent on road building should go to businesses run by "disadvantaged business enterprises." Pech sued in 1989. It took another six years before he finally won the case of *Adarand Constructors, Inc. vs. Peña*. From that point, affirmative action programs, which had operated since 1965 and which encouraged the hiring and awarding of government contracts to minority groups, would be modified. In ruling on the case in 1995, the Supreme Court emphasized that federal affirmative action programs would be subject to "strict scrutiny by the courts," meaning that they would be "narrowly tailored" measures to advance a compelling governmental interest.

One implication of this decision was that an individual's personal rights to equal protection under the law were sacrosanct: affirmative action programs should not infringe them. The effects of Pech's actions would unfold over subsequent years as state after state either repealed or fiercely debated affirmative action. Had the tide turned? they asked. After more than two decades of favoring minority groups, was it time to examine the plight of the long-suffering, forgotten minority, the white male? These kind of emotional, if doubtful, appeals reached receptive ears and the roll-back began.

———

Tyson was a model of success. Along with Michael Jordan, Michael Jackson, Whitney Houston, Oprah Winfrey, Clarence Thomas, and a few others, he was an African American multi-millionaire who had defied the odds. In fact, he was privileged. Many whites would look at themselves, their family and friends as reminders of how badly off they were compared to the elite corps of black American athletes and entertainers. A deceptive calculus helped them understand this. As Aaron Gresson concluded in his book *The Recovery of Race in America*: "Because they see many of their own family and friends suffering, they believe white men have had to pay for Black success."

Gresson was writing his book around the same time as the Central Park jogger and Charles Stuart cases, and, while he doesn't mention them, they seem to complement his thesis. It is that, by the end of the 1980s, racism had become a defunct topos, that is, a once common theme that had lost its purpose. This didn't mean that behavior that might be described as racist ceased to exist: only that its meaning became what Gresson calls "renegotiable." What might have been considered a straightforward instance of racism in the 1960s or 1970s would, in the late 1980s, be subject to debate and discussion.

The moral force of a traditional idea of racism grew weaker as the older remnants of segregation were swept away and the more obvious practices of discrimination penalized. So, for example, opposing a black person's appointment to a job wouldn't necessarily be motivated by racism, but maybe by a recognition that preferential hiring policies had gone far enough and, as a result of them, whites were missing out. What Gresson called "a new racial story" began to circulate. Many whites inverted the traditional racism of yore. "They now experience and believe the story that Blacks and others are *privileged*" (p. 211).

The calculus behind this may have been flawed. That didn't make its consequences any less real. The logic of racism provided a rationale for turning yesterday's villains into today's victims. Whites' project became the recovery of what was being or had been lost. As the concept of race, or, as it became, "race" – to denote its doubtful status – grew less plausible and less effective as an explanation of why things were the way they were, so its value dropped off. The search for some support for the concept was in progress by the end of the 1980s.

This may explain the collective *schadenfreude* that followed Tyson's unexpected defeat by James "Buster" Douglas. Tyson's popularity was already sliding: his ostentation was becoming tiresome and his demeanor was that of an uncouth and even uncivil brute. You don't have to like someone to be fascinated by them. Watching them meet their nemesis can be deliciously engaging.

None of Tyson's previous six opponents had gone beyond the seventh round. James "Buster" Douglas wouldn't either. A boxer of only mediocre caliber with an unimpressive record and a defeat in his only other world title challenge, Douglas looked grotesquely overmatched. The only interest centered on how many rounds Tyson would take to complete the job. Given the chillingly efficient dismissal of Williams, a first-round win for Tyson seemed a rational bet.

Douglas appeared to be a softer touch than Tyson's original challenger, Donovan "Razor" Ruddock, who was fresh from a seventh-round win over James "Bonecrusher" Smith. The same fighter had taken Tyson the full twelve rounds. Tyson pulled out of that fight complaining of chest pains, later diagnosed as pleurisy. The whole promotion was canceled. Some suspected that Tyson, perhaps complacent after a succession of relatively easy wins, had slackened off his training, causing alarm in his camp. Coupled with the positive vibes coming from Ruddock's training camp and his 23–1 record, it may have prompted enough hesitation among Team Tyson to opt out. Whatever the reason, Tyson proceeded to what seemed a simpler assignment.

Simple tasks can become complicated by all sorts of contingencies. Objectively, Douglas was not in the same class as Tyson. His previous venture to wrest a world title ended in defeat when he was beaten by Tony Tucker. In victory, Tucker took the International Boxing Federation (IBF) title, which Tyson duly took from him. There was nothing, absolutely nothing in his record to suggest Douglas could pose even the remotest threat to Tyson. Not even he could have entertained the possibility of winning. Presumably, his motive for taking the fight was a career's best payday of $3.5 million.

Douglas had faith. In mid-1989, he underwent a religious conversion and became a born again Christian. Religion has inspired countless athletes. Count how many who acknowledge the role of God in post-competition interviews. Evander Holyfield never missed the opportunity to thank God for guiding him safely through his fights. Goran Ivanisevic entered Wimbledon 2001 as a wild card and emerged as champion, pronouncing throughout that his progress was destined by God. Some rivals of Ayrton Senna, a Roman Catholic, maintained that his belief in an afterlife influenced his devil-may-care style, which won him four world motor racing Formula One championships, and might also have contributed to his death in 1994. Whether or not deities intervene in the earthly matters of sports can't be known, of course. What can be known is the motivating power of believing that God is "in your corner," so to speak. Douglas may have believed exactly that on the night of February 11, 1990.

Things had not gone well for him of late. His wife had left him. Then the mother of his 11-year-old son discovered she was terminally ill. But the event that may have convinced him that he wouldn't be alone in the ring fighting Tyson was the death of his mother in the weeks before the fight. This contributed to a potent motivational mix.

Much was made of Tyson's seeming lethargy. He wasn't up for the fight. He didn't want to win it badly enough. It wasn't the real Tyson in there. He didn't train like he should have (though Tyson's weight, $220\frac{1}{2}$ lbs, suggested that he'd trained as normal). These were all aired as possible reasons for his demise. There is another way of looking at it: the way Douglas fought that night in Tokyo, no fighter in the world would have stood a chance.

One of the popular and, indeed, plausible explanations for Tyson's hitherto unqualified success was that opponents were intimidated by his aura. They were beaten before they got in the ring, boxing pundits would remind their audiences. Sport psychologists would call this a form of self-handicapping: in other words, they'd have their excuse for failure prepared before they started. "Iron Mike," as everyone knew, was indestructible. Hit him with police batons, lengths of timber, even steel bars, and he'd still keep coming. What chance did mortals possessed of two good hands and nothing more stand? Tyson's presence alone was enough to strike fear into the hearts of opponents.

Douglas, on the other hand, was fearless. Driven perhaps by the belief that God was with him, he fought without inhibition. There was no wavering at all. Unfazed by the prospect of being hurt, Douglas dictated rather than responded to Tyson. His shoulders were loose and limber – always a good sign of a relaxed athlete – enabling him to discharge hard shots in rapid-fire action. Tyson just kept walking onto them.

This was a Douglas never seen before: determined, purposeful, unafraid, it was as if a new fighting cyborg like those in the *Universal Soldier* series was being unveiled. The savagely efficient advance of Douglas was interrupted only once by Tyson, late in the eighth round. Lottery winners probably pause for a moment hours after they've been given the news that they've won and think to themselves: "I must be dreaming." We'll never know if similar thoughts flashed across Douglas' mind as he lay on the canvas, his challenge looking as if it was about to end, gloriously but inevitably like all the others. Benefiting from an unusually slow count from the referee, Douglas was able to find his feet and survive the round. After the fight, King protested futilely that the ref's count was out of sync with the timekeeper's and that this invalidated the eventual result of the fight.

Having felt the full impact of a Tyson uppercut, Douglas might have been expected to introduce more caution into his approach. He didn't. If anything, he fought with more abandon, bouncing right crosses off Tyson's head with jarring regularity. A swelling over Tyson's left eye had impeded his vision for most of the fight, but, from the ninth, it was large enough to affect his depth perception. In other words, he probably couldn't gauge the incoming punches accurately enough to evade them. He didn't evade a volley that came his way in the tenth. Tyson dropped, then lifted himself to his haunches and groped for his displaced mouthpiece. It was a peculiar moment: Tyson could have used the ten seconds more valuably trying to get to his feet rather than searching for his mouthpiece. The image of his confused attempt to lodge the accessory in his mouth is an abiding one and furnished newspapers, magazines and books for long after the fight. Tyson's title had gone, his reputed invincibility exposed, his supposedly unstoppable march toward greatness halted.

It may have been the biggest upset in sports history. Douglas was such an underdog that most Vegas bookies didn't open a book. Those that did offered about 40–1 against Douglas.

Even in the aftermath of the fight, there was a question about whether Douglas would actually hold on to the title, or whether the fight would be declared no-contest, or even whether Tyson could be reinstated. King's howls echoed his desperation. He had ensconced Tyson in his self-styled "family" only to see his commercial value plummet. His rather pathetic argument was that Douglas received the benefit of a "long count" and that, if it had been correctly observed, he would have been counted out in the eighth; in which case, the rest of the fight would have been rendered irrelevant. The boxing federations actually listened to King and even considered his argument before dismissing it and confirming that Douglas was the rightful champion.

While King had options on Douglas' future fights, the official number one contender was Evander Holyfield. Douglas' manager opted to make the mandatory defense rather than grant Tyson a rematch. It probably wouldn't have made much difference either way. Every dog has its day. Douglas, a ferocious underdog against Tyson, was an overweight bitch against Holy-field. At 246 lbs, he was 15 lbs heavier than he was against Tyson, a sure sign that he hadn't trained adequately. Slothful, unmotivated, and free of any semblance of resolve, Douglas accepted defeat with the resignation of someone slumped in a dentist's chair. The particular set of circumstances that had facilitated his extraordinary performance could not be replicated.

Douglas' apparent lack of eagerness in his first and only defense is made more understandable when the size of his purse is considered. He received a jaw-dropping $25 million from hotel-owner Steve Wynn, at that stage making what turned out to be a short foray into promoting. With that kind of money guaranteed, Douglas could hardly describe himself as a hungry fighter. It showed. Had he won, he would have earned a further $35 million to meet Tyson again. His lack of effort suggested that he felt able to limp by for the rest of his life on the 25 mill.

Tyson had already earned twice as much as this, though how much he still had in his bank accounts is not known. The probable answer is: not as much as he thought.

Some of what might be called the mythological elements of Tyson had been stripped away: like the Greek hero Achilles, who was also near-invulnerable, Tyson had a previously undetected weak spot. If Douglas could find it, maybe others would too. Still only 23, Tyson had been compromised though not entirely discredited. There was a future for him. But, even at this point, critics were pondering how much King's influence was affecting Tyson. In his *McIlvanney on Boxing*, British writer Hugh McIlvanney expressed the views of many arguing that, of all the contributory factors in his downfall, "Most damaging of all, perhaps, has been his alliance with Don King, who has precipitated decay in practically every fighter with whom he has been associated."

ten

TIME TO LEAVE THE WHITE MAN'S WORLD

Robin Givens was born in 1964. By that time, Don King was already one of the leading players in the Cleveland numbers racket. Thirty-three-year-old King lived large, always traveling by Cadillac and never without a roll thick enough to choke a racehorse. Givens was barely two when King was imprisoned for beating to death someone who owed him $350. A murder conviction was reduced to manslaughter, enabling an early release after just under four years. It was then 1971. Givens had moved with her mother and sister and was enrolled at the exclusive, private New Rochelle Academy. Her mother, while not well off, strove hard to provide both daughters with the kind of education that would equip them to climb rather than stay rooted.

Givens and King were separated by more than three decades. They came from different backgrounds. And they might never have met, had it not been for Tyson. Yet they were linked by more than him. It wasn't just one of life's capricious breezes that blew Tyson toward them both. Givens and King grew up and learned in the decades of release, when America was dismantling the constricting apparatus of segregation and freeing African Americans to pursue their own destinies. Both Givens and King were aspirational blacks, possessed of an achievement ethic that their forebears might have had, but couldn't use to any great effect. King was prospering by foul means rather than fair at the time of civil rights. By the time he came out of prison, racial discrimination was just like debris from a demolished building, at least in theory.

King pursued his own American dream in a New World liberated from the old restrictive bonds that had held back black people. Like so many other ambitious African Americans, he yearned to become a black bourgeois, a member of that small but elite group that had transcended race, or, more accurately, had enough money to make it irrelevant. Like King, Givens saw her blackness less as an obstacle to progress than as an instrument to be brought into use when necessary. Being black in the 1970s was not an impediment for those savvy enough to exploit the opportunities of a culture newly enlightened and eager to make up for the injustices of history.

Tyson was part of the same culture, though it's unlikely that he shared the same kinds of ambitions as Givens and King, certainly not until he met Givens. She seemed to ignite a newfound eagerness in him. Never a social climber, Tyson, shortly after meeting Givens, told *Life* magazine that she "exhibits so much class," adding "I hope it rubs off on me." It was an improbable remark from a man who had never displayed any desire to be anything other than a kid from Brownsville with lots of money and who had never tried to ingratiate himself with anyone.

Products of the same beckoning culture of ambition and opportunity Givens and King might have been, but they had different and conflicting interests in Tyson. Yet both influenced his life in ways even they could barely have imagined, and, while doing so, changed their own lives in ways they almost certainly did imagine.

Givens was well aware of the influence of others. She had been pushed by a status-seeking mother who sought to provide her children with the best of everything. Ruth Newby married on the day of her graduation in 1964. Her husband was Rueben Givens, a basketball player at the University of Kentucky. The marriage lasted three years, during which time she gave birth to Robin and sister Stephanie. Moving north with her daughters, Newby struggled initially in the Bronx, working for TWA. She picked up enough know-how about the travel business to set up her own agency. The business thrived sufficiently for Newby to move her family to the more upscale suburb of New Rochelle. A short-lived marriage to Phil Roper left her as Ruth Roper, a name she kept.

Robin and Stephanie were privately educated. They were inculcated with the need to be successful. Roper had moved them out of the Bronx to an environment where all their neighbors and school friends were white achievers. Stephanie was a good enough tennis player to make a living on the professional circuit. Robin had her sights set on being a doctor, then dreamed of going into show business. At a time when educational institutions were actively seeking minority admissions, she enrolled at the Sarah Lawrence College, where competition for places was intense. Robin was one of a small minority of African American students.

Roper made a minor impact in the media when she sued Dave Winfield, of the New York Yankees, for giving her a sexually transmitted disease. She settled out of court without an admission of guilt from Winfield.

Robin, having studied drama since the age of 10, landed roles as an extra in the movies *The Wiz* (1978) and *Fort Apache, the Bronx* (1981) as well as soaps. She had also modeled for the Ford Agency in New York. Like many aspiring actors, she headed west for Hollywood, mother Ruth accompanying her. At an audition for *The Cosby Show*, she was spotted by the show's star, Bill Cosby, who offered to pay for her graduate education should she not make it in show business. It was an offer that was, eventually, irrelevant: Givens was given a part in the ABC sitcom *Head of the Class*. Still only 19, she became a minor celebrity.

As well as being aspirational in her own right, she also appears to have been aspirational in her choice of partners. Eddie Murphy was the first of her celebrity courtesans: she went out with him in 1985 when she was still a student. It was far from a clandestine relationship: Murphy sent his car to collect her from campus on occasion. She talked openly about him. The relationship ended acrimoniously. Michael Jordan came into Givens' sights. Roper sounded out Jordan's parents in North Carolina while Givens sent a portfolio of photographs of herself to Jordan with a wish to meet him message. Jordan took the bait and the two had a relationship. Roper, by all accounts, acted as a kind of matchmaker in all Givens' affairs.

Tyson had seen Givens in her tv show role as Darlene Merriman, a brilliant, rather haughty student who spoke in modulated tones and radiated superiority. Tyson was not exactly abstinent when it came to women. He took full advantage of his status – as the complaints from women seemed to indicate.

Being one of the world's premier athletes, Tyson had ready access to sexually receptive groupies. Givens, though, must have seemed agreeably remote, unattainable even. Having discovered her phone number, Tyson met her on a dinner date in LA and, over the next few weeks, lavished presents on her. Apparently expert in the art of courting men, Givens maintained Tyson's interest by playing hard to get.

Tyson's next fight was to be in Vegas on May 30, 1987. He turned up with Givens at the New York press conference to announce the fight. While stories of his heroic sexual deeds had circulated for a while, Tyson had never invited a woman to accompany him to a public event such as this. The media rightly read this as holding some significance. Tyson, at this point, was known as an athlete, a boxer, the best heavyweight in the world. The rest of his life was of no great importance. In fact, the gossip, hearsay and full-on lies that appear in the magazines that fill the racks of any newsstand today were of only passing interest in the late 1980s. As for *paparazzi*, it was a word that you'd have to look up in an Italian dictionary. The dawn of what we now regard as the age of celebrity had yet to arrive. Things were about to change, of course. As was Tyson's life.

But, prior to the unveiling of Givens, Tyson was a boxer, the most famous boxer in the world and even one of the most recognizable figures in the world, yet someone known principally for his feats in the ring. He talked only sparingly, confining his comments to boxing. The media followed him, but as they would track any prized athlete.

Presumably hoping to capitalize on the publicity, ABC Television's press office sent out a résumé for Givens in which skeptics spotted a few anomalies, for example, her supposed training at Harvard Medical School. Givens, who had achieved some fame in her own right through the tv show, was thrust under a bigger and more revealing spotlight. It seems fair to suggest that she didn't shrink from it.

The pursuit continued after the Pinklon Thomas fight. Perhaps the *frisson* of conspicuously accessible women had disappeared and Tyson became excited by the prospect of someone who was tantalizingly out of reach. The extravagant gifts kept coming. Still confirmation of a Tyson–Givens item never came. In fact, by June, it looked to be over. Tyson turned up at a press conference without her. It seems that they had argued and Tyson had become morose, at one stage saying that he wanted to quit boxing.

The on–off cycle continued, until, in January, 1988. Roper called Tyson's co-manager, Jim Jacobs, to inform him that Givens was three-and-a-half months pregnant with Tyson's child. On February 7, Tyson and Givens went to an NBA All-Star game in Chicago, after which they attended a charity function. Here they met a reverend whom Tyson asked: "Do you have the power to marry us?" The answer was yes. All three went to the reverend's house, where a religious ceremony took place. In José Torres' 1989 book *Fire and Fear* the then commissioner of the New York State Athletic Commission recounts how Roper called Jacobs again, this time with a demand: "She said that if Jacobs didn't arrange for Tyson to marry her daughter legally in New York 'at once,' she'd take matters into her own hands" (p. 150).

The legalities were tied up within two days. There was no prenuptial agreement. Tyson charged Roper with responsibility to find a house where the three of them would live. They settled for an estate in Bernardsville, New Jersey, valued at $4.5 million. Torres documents a revealing phone conversation within weeks of the wedding. Givens called Cayton, who was then sick in a hospital bed. "I'm Mrs Mike Tyson," she announced herself. "And I'm taking over my husband's affairs."

At least one other person had the same idea.

———

Former heavyweight champion Larry Holmes summed up Don King: "He looks black, lives white and thinks green."

On his release from the Marion Correctional Institute, Ohio, in 1971, King befriended three people who were to prove crucial to his rise. Don Elbaum was a smalltime boxing promoter who operated in Pennsylvania and Ohio. Lloyd Price was a rock 'n' roll singer who had had a commercially successful version of his own "Lawdy Miss Claudy" before it was covered with even more success by Elvis Presley. Muhammad Ali was the premier boxer of the period and symbolic leader of countless blacks all over the world.

Price had known King for many years and met him from prison. He also knew Ali, who had been beaten by Joe Frazier some months before. King always had one eye on the main chance and, when he read of the impending closure of a Cleveland hospital that served a black neighborhood and had mostly black staff, he asked Price to solicit the help of Ali. It would be a service to the community: Ali would box a few exhibition rounds with local fighters and help raise funds. King knew nothing about booking referees, doctors, renting a ring, applying for licensing and so on. Elbaum did and was recruited for this purpose.

Eight and a half thousand people watched Ali spar with four men. Price used his influence to bring Marvin Gaye, Wilson Pickett, and other black singers to the show, and they performed a concert before the main attraction. The gross take was $81,000, an astonishing amount for an exhibition. Elbaum's recollection is: "Ali got ten thousand for expenses. I got paid one thousand instead of five thousand. The hospital got about fifteen hundred. And King pocketed the rest."

The portentous quote is on page 133 of Jack Newfield's 1995 book *Only in America: The life and crimes of Don King*, which chronicles the rise and rise of King up a greasy pole that was left even greasier after King had climbed it. Newfield charts how King incorporated himself into a standing business partnership between Elbaum and Joseph Gennaro, who were cultivating a number of promising fighters, including soon-to-be contender Earnie Shavers. By 1974, Elbaum was out of the picture and Gennaro was suing King for a share of the profits from boxing ventures. This was settled, with King paying $3,500. It was one of a great many boxing-related disputes to which King was party, but it didn't stop his progress.

King was perfectly positioned on the space–time curve. The new consciousness that had inspired riots in the streets had counterparts in sport. The memorable black power salute by Tommie Smith and John Carlos at the Mexico summer Olympics in 1968 signaled a newly politicized black athlete.

Ali's conversion to the Nation of Islam boded well for King. He presented himself as the embodiment of what black Muslims strove for: black economic independence. Acting as an agent of a company called Video Techniques, King was able to convince Ali to let him promote one of his fights. He reminded him that he would otherwise be making money for white capitalists rather than a brother.

Bob Arum was the promoter of many of Ali's fights. He was a white lawyer who enjoyed the confidence of Ali's manager, Herbert Muhammad. "Arum's a Jew who hates brothers," King told Ali, according to Jim Brady (*Boxing Confidential*, p. 327). "If you see a black man can do the job, ya got [to] give him the job before the white man."

When Ali eventually succumbed, King promised him money that he didn't have. He spun an elaborate, if fragile, web of financial arrangements to create the illusion that he was a bigtime promoter and had his braggadocio rewarded with one of the most momentous fights in history, perhaps the most commemorated sports event of the twentieth century. It was "The Rumble in the Jungle," in which Ali regained the world heavyweight title at the age of 32, knocking out George Foreman in Zaire in 1974. The fight became as much a showcase for King as it was for the protagonists. He presided over press conferences, gave interviews and made his presence felt at every opportunity. King cut an unforgettable image with his electric shock hairstyle.

King's next major venture was a $2 million boxing tournament televised by the ABC network. Allegations of kickbacks, fixing, and mob connections surrounded the show, though King became adept at neutralizing them, often by arguing that every successful black person is immediately suspected of misdeeds. Newfield's book includes the network of contacts he had with the underworld as well as his phenomenal resourcefulness in avoiding conviction. King emerged unscathed from an FBI operation codenamed Crown Royal, which attempted to link him with organized crime. One of the investigators, Joseph Spinelli, recorded details of this for the November 4, 1991 issue of *Sports Illustrated*. Even the old tax evasion standby wouldn't stick to King: he was acquitted of twenty-three counts in 1985.

King kept an interest in the heavyweight championship, either by promoting fights or managing champions. The World Boxing Council (WBC) was extraordinarily careful in its treatment of King, giving rise to rumors that its president, José Sulaiman, was unduly generous. For example, when Ali lost his title to Leon Spinks in 1978, the fight was promoted by rival Bob Arum, who held a contract giving him options on Spinks' first three title defenses. It worked greatly to King's advantage when the WBC stripped Spinks of the title and declared it vacant, allowing King to promote a title fight between boxers he effectively controlled. Spinks was penalized for giving Ali an immediate rematch. Yet, when Buster Douglas beat Tyson for the title, he tried to force Douglas into doing the same thing and meet Tyson instead of the number one contender. Sulaiman's decision to dispossess Spinks broke up the world heavyweight title into two different versions and King was later to capitalize on this, promoting a $16 million HBO television tournament to unify the title again.

Several of the boxers King had either managed or promoted turned against him. Larry Holmes, Tim Witherspoon, and Mike Dokes, for example, claimed that there were financial irregularities in their dealings with King. Coming from African American boxers, these were cutting criticisms. Witherspoon in particular complained strongly after defending his world heavyweight title against Frank Bruno in 1986. He agreed to fight for $550,000, but received only $90,094, while Bruno – the challenger, remember – made $900,000. King received revenue from HBO, BBC, Miller Lite, and the live gate, making him at least $2 million. Witherspoon's deductions included $275,000 to King's stepson, Carl King, who acted as the boxer's manager (as he did for many of the fighters promoted by his stepfather).

Unlike many of the fighters who griped, Witherspoon pressed his claims against King and, in 1992, received a million-dollar settlement. His verdict on King (quoted in Newfield's book) reads like a misanthropic epigram: "Don's specialty is black-on-black crime. I'm black and he robbed me" (p. 54).

King dismissed this and most of the other claims. But, as *Esquire* writer Mike Lupica asked in his 1991 article "The sporting life": "Are they *all* lying? Holmes and Witherspoon and Tony Tubbs and Pinklon Thomas? Or is King a hypocrite, screaming about racism on one hand and preying on black fighters himself?"

Certainly, King behaved hypocritically in regard to South Africa, upbraiding boxers and promoters who went there in defiance of the Gleneagles Agreement to sever sporting links with a country that enforced apartheid up till 1990. Yet Newfield points out that King had taken a million-dollar "under-the-table" payment from a South African promotion.

"King gives you this bro' stuff and tells you that the white man did this and we should stick together," former heavyweight Mitch Green reflected on King to Jim Brady (p. 334). "Then he starts cutting your purse. I was with him six years. You put your head in a noose when you sign with Don King."

Tyson had kept his head clear of King, though it was no secret that King had rope ready for him. King had managed to keep an interest in the world heavyweight title through Holmes, Witherspoon, Dokes, and others. But Tyson eluded his control. Until March 23, 1988.

On that day, Jim Jacobs died. Jacobs had been Tyson's co-manager and had, for nine years, suffered with leukemia. Although King wasn't a friend of Jacobs, nor invited to the funeral in Los Angeles, he went anyway, knowing that Tyson would be there. Recently married, Tyson was, according to all reports, as content as he'd ever been. He'd already defended his title twice earlier in 1988, tearing apart an aging Larry Holmes in four straightforward rounds and razing Tony Tubbs in two, the latter defense taking place in Tokyo.

King traveled on the same plane as the funeral party, which included Tyson, Jacobs' former partner and still co-manager, Bill Cayton, Tyson's trainers and other close friends of the deceased. "These people don't know how to deal with this kid," King said to Torres, who was also in the party. Torres was to hear the same message from Givens when he returned to New York. "These people" were all white.

———

John Dahl's *Rounders* opens with a voiceover from one of the professional poker players at the center of the film's plot: "The thing is this: if you haven't spotted the sucker within the first half-hour at the table, *you are* the sucker." Tyson might regret missing this movie.

As the mourners grieved on the west coast, Givens and Roper were busy on the east coast. Foregoing the niceties of making an appointment, they crash-landed at the office of James Brady, vice-president of Merrill Lynch at New York's Park Avenue, where Tyson had an account. Givens and Roper instructed Brady to transfer $1.9 million from Tyson's account to a joint account held by Tyson and Givens at Citibank. Their purpose, so they said, was to make a down payment on a New Jersey residence. The next day, Givens and Roper returned, this time with a document testifying that Tyson had given his wife six weeks' power of attorney for the purchase. Givens requested that the $1.9 million that was now in the joint account be moved to yet another account, this time at the European-American Bank. This was a newly proposed account in the name of Robin Givens.

Transferring funds from joint accounts to single-name accounts, while not unusual, typically needs specific authorization from one of the parties in the joint account. So Brady sought the approval of Tyson. Once contacted in LA, Tyson instructed Brady to comply with his wife's requests. Brady was the guardian of a $2 million annuity set up by Jacobs for Tyson the previous year. Jacobs had specifically told Brady never to let Tyson withdraw money without notifying either him or Cayton. Presumably Jacobs was mindful that hangers-on would besiege Tyson. When Givens dissolved Jacobs' arrangements to ensure Tyson's financial well-being, she signaled the arrival of a new order, though perhaps not exactly the one she had in mind.

Meanwhile, King was pitching other ideas on a new order. Dismissing the possibility of a conflict of interests, he suggested to Torres that, as well as being Tyson's promoter, he should become his manager too. A boxer's manager is duty bound to secure for his fighter the best possible deal and, to do so, he bargains with a promoter. A promoter's main interest lies in maximizing his profit rather than feathering the nests of boxers and their managers. With the increased involvement of television, promoters frequently work for a fixed sum. Even so, there remains at least the potential for a conflict of interests.

King was to be the undercard matchmaker on the promotion that featured Tyson's next fight. The main event was Tyson against Michael Spinks, whose business associate Butch Lewis took charge of the promotion. King had no direct interest in the big fight. The $3 million he received for handling the supporting contests wasn't compensation enough, it seems.

As Tyson had presented Givens with gifts, so King did the same with Tyson, sending him two Rolls-Royces with a value over $380,000. These were intended to replace his own $180,000 Bentley convertible, which he had given away. The circumstances in which he gave it away are the stuff of myth. Driving in lower Manhattan on May 8, his wife and mother-in-law the only passengers, Tyson quarreled with Givens and lost control of the car, causing a collision. No one was hurt, but two New York Port Authority police officers arrived at the scene. Tyson tossed them the keys and told them to keep the car.

Tyson had signed an extension contract with Jacobs and Cayton six weeks before Jacobs' death. Given the nature of Jacobs' terminal illness, the move seemed a logical way of ensuring that Tyson stayed with Cayton, who would continue to manage, with Jacobs' wife becoming a new assignee in the event of her husband's death. It was a legally valid contract, appropriately witnessed by Torres at the offices of the New York State Athletic Commission and freely signed by Tyson. The contract was a source of exasperation for both Givens and King. While it remained, neither could assert the measure of control over Tyson they wanted. It also served to set Givens and King against each other in, for want of a better phrase, a tug-of-love.

King's attempts to persuade Tyson that his future lay in a glorious and richly rewarding partnership were familiar. "The Jews want to control Tyson," he told Torres – and, we can safely assume, Tyson himself. Givens' approach appears to have changed slightly after the money transfer maneuver. On June 19, 1988, *New York Newsday* carried a story written by Wally Matthews in which Stephanie Givens was quoted on the subject of her sister's marriage, "a big mistake from the beginning," as she called it. According to Stephanie Givens, Tyson was prone to bouts of heavy drinking, temper tantrums and had hit her sister with his fist. She said that the rest of the family was afraid to leave Tyson alone with his wife. Both claims were to be elaborated over the following months. Matthews was the beneficiary of the "scoop" presumably because he had, through his column, been a consistent critic of Cayton.

Amid the swirl of accusations, Tyson pressed ahead with what many considered the most difficult fight of his career. The unbeaten Michael Spinks, brother of Leon, had moved up the weight divisions from light-heavyweight to heavy and twice beaten Larry Holmes, albeit closely and somewhat controversially. Taller than Tyson with a longer reach and an awkward, ungainly style, Spinks shaped up as a genuine test.

Tyson's locker room provided the scene for one of the best examples of a psyching that backfired. As is customary in world title matchups, a representative of the opponent is permitted to watch as a fighter bandages his hands. In his book *Tyson: In and out of the ring*, Peter Heller tells how Butch Lewis, on Spinks' behalf, noticed a lump in Tyson's bandage and insisted the whole hand be unwrapped and re-bandaged. It was a tactic Lewis believed would irritate Tyson and gain an advantage for Spinks. Instead, Tyson grew furious. After Lewis left the room, Tyson promised: "I'm gonna hurt this guy." He did: with barely controlled rage, Tyson shattered his opponent in ninety-one seconds of destructive action. For this, Tyson earned $20 million, $221,000 per second.

With his briskly emphatic win, Tyson became indisputably the best heavyweight in the world. All the disputes were about other facets of his life.

Torres tells of what on reflection might have been a crucial fifteen-minute meeting between Tyson and King at a party to celebrate the champion's 22nd birthday eight days after the Spinks win. King emerged with a smile and, referring to Torres, told Roper and her attorney: "We don't have to worry about him. He's with us . . . with Mike."

Within weeks, Tyson called a press conference at Trump Plaza at which he declared that he would manage himself and that Cayton "wants to control everything and everybody." Cayton was still his legal manager, a fact affirmed over and over in Torres' book. King's attempt to align himself with Tyson became manifest with his public condemnation of Cayton, whom he characterized as "Satan in disguise."

For a while, the "any enemy of my enemy is a friend" saying rang true and King found himself an uncomfortable ally of Givens/Roper, all of them questing to annul Tyson's contract with Cayton. "I support Ruth Roper," said King. "I support Robin Givens." All parties demanded transparency: contracts, tax returns, foreign rights agreements and so on. Cayton argued that, as his contract was with Tyson, only he was privy to the accounts. A manager is entitled to up to a third of a boxer's gross purse. Cayton was taking his slice. There was no issue about that. The question raised was: was he worth it?

In his 1989 book *Blood Season: Tyson and the world of boxing* Phil Berger quotes Tyson: "Look, if she [Givens] asked for every dollar in my account, I'd give it to her. No questions asked. Bill [Cayton] works for me. He's not in a position to say no" (p. 255).

It's an insight into both how the reference points in Tyson's world had changed. Berger's account, like many others (including Brady's, Heller's and Torres'), is sympathetic to Cayton. He suggests that Cayton well earned his $33\frac{1}{3}$ percent, negotiating high purses for relatively easy fights and lucrative endorsement deals, such as the $1.25 million contract with Pepsi. Illingworth, by contrast, believes that when Tyson, Givens, and Roper wanted Cayton to drop his commission to 20–25 percent, "Tyson was entitled to demand the reductions." The implication was that Cayton's value to Tyson had up to this time been inflated. Tyson was, we assume, receptive to this kind of argument. When augmented with King's diatribe, it became an effective chorus.

Tyson began to speak of being oppressed. "They'll slaughter me," he suspected, they being Cayton and his business associate Shelly Finkel. He was parroting the words of those around him, according to Berger: "Force-fed recriminations and allegations and shit-stirring innuendoes." Around this time, he began to use a phrase favored by, among others, King: "Jews in suits."

Another King stock-in-trade was the slaveowner metaphor. Cayton, he reckoned, "wants you to be a sycophant. Yes, massa, Mr Cayton. Yassah."

By demanding a renegotiation of his contract with Cayton and by investing his faith in African Americans, including his wife, mother-in-law, and King, Tyson must have felt Emancipation had arrived. People who undergo a mid-life religious conversion are said to make a retrospective interpretation of their lives. They scan back on their earlier years and apply a new type of understanding, sometimes concluding that they were harmed rather than loved by their parents, misled rather than educated by their teachers, deceived rather than enlightened by their spiritual advisors and, generally, prevented from realizing the truth. Tyson seems to have looked back on his life and arrived at similar conclusions.

Even the media that had served Tyson well and played a gigantic part in elevating him to one of the world's pre-eminent figures came in for criticism when gossipy rumors of Givens and Roper began to seep out. Were they conniving with King to pry Tyson away from Cayton, so that they could carve him up among themselves? Or were they gold-diggers, plain and simple, just out for what they could get? At one point, Roper actually took her attorney along to meet Wally Matthews and express how hurt she and her daughter were by the media's image of them. She raised the possibility that Cayton had orchestrated some sort of "smear-and-scare" campaign.

Givens miscarried, claiming the stress of the first six months of 1988 was a contributory factor. As Cayton was instrumental in the stress, he was blamed for this too. This no doubt deepened the rift between him and Tyson. When Cayton took legal action against King in retaliation against King's attempt to have his contract with Tyson voided, it was the end. Cayton himself accepted that, in that move, he virtually confirmed Tyson's conspiratorial suspicions. Tyson now regarded King as a confidant;

someone he could trust as implicitly as he could his wife and mother-in-law. He didn't want peace with Cayton, but he wanted him out of his life. They settled: Cayton continued to earn a reduced commission, though King would make his fights, negotiate his purses and, generally, decide his future.

There was Tyson, sitting at the table, looking at his fellow players, still trying to figure out which one of them was the sucker.

———

Tyson seemed a soul poised between self-realization and anguish. Heralded as a fighter like no other, yet tortured by an inability to confine his violence to the ring. The *New York Newsday* article had disclosed a facet of Tyson that some had suspected, but no one could confirm: he wasn't just violent in the ring. Givens, as both a tv actor and the wife of the world's best-known athlete, was the subject of buzz and, in mid-1988, the buzz was that she and Tyson were already estranged. Gossip about his beating her stayed just that: gossip. No one had come up with proof, not even a bruise or minor abrasion, less still testimony from Givens herself. But the rumor persisted.

Right on cue (as ever), Tyson provided something from which evidence could be inferred. On August 23, Tyson was out in New York. Around 4.30 a.m., he was approached by ex-boxer Mitch Green, whom he had beaten on a ten-round decision in 1986. Green had fallen foul of the law and was down on his luck. He berated Tyson, claiming he hadn't really beaten him and that King, who managed Green, had ripped him off. A scuffle broke out, which ended in Green's needing six stitches. Tyson didn't escape unscathed: he fractured his hand. (He was eventually ordered by a New York jury to pay Green $45,000, even though it was agreed that Green provoked him.) "Another blotch on Tyson's increasingly besmirched image," wrote Wally Matthews, as if in ignorance that he and other media personnel were the ones doing the smirching.

Witnesses to the event weren't forthcoming, but anyone who has ever seen a street fight can easily imagine what happened. Pro boxers are always targets for alcohol-fueled chumps. Green had taken Tyson the distance, then watched as Tyson soared while he plunged. In common with many other fighters handled by King, he was broke and felt aggrieved. Sensing an opportunity to exact a revenge of sorts, he tackled Tyson as he left a nightclub. Tyson got paid millions for fighting. Why would he want to do it for nothing? He defended himself, using minimal force. Tyson's version of minimal force meant a single punch that opened Green's cut and dumped him on the sidewalk. End of argument.

But, it was far from the end of a different argument. This one was about whether or not Tyson was a fit and proper champion. "So began a radical shift in perspective," wrote Illingworth. Having hailed and glorified Tyson in his ascendancy, the media "wiped away the rosy mist to see a monster." Illingworth interpreted the media's new angle: "What made him a great boxer proved his downfall as a human being" (*Mike Tyson: Money, myth and betrayal*, p. 285).

Pressured by Givens and Roper to seek advice, Tyson consulted Henry McCurtis, a psychiatrist, who prescribed Eskalith CR and Thorazine, a combination used typically to treat manic-depression. The former contains lithium carbonate. Tyson had a well-known aversion to any drugs, even aspirin. The very fact that he agreed to take a course of powerful medicaments suggests the extent to which he had submitted to his wife and her mother.

As if scripted by some malevolent screenwriter, Tyson's next misadventure delivered him to the bosom of gossip columnists and sports journalists. His Beamer stuck in mud in Catskill, he revved too forcefully, causing the car to surge forward into a chestnut tree. On impact, Tyson jolted forward, crashing his head against the steering wheel. He spent a few days in the hospital. An accident. Or was it? Not according to the New York *Daily News*, which reported a suicide attempt. Tyson later denied this, but, with the stories that were, by then, circulating, anything was believable – even the sight of a ferocious and untamable champion rendered sheepish and domesticated.

This is how viewers of ABC's *20/20* show saw him in September. Here was Tyson. Next to him was Givens. And here was Barbara Walters, asking questions about their marriage, by then a topic newsworthy enough to command discussion on a popular magazine program. This was the "pure hell" interview, in which Givens unexpectedly shared with millions her hitherto private suffering. "It's been torture," Givens revealed of her life with Tyson. "It's been pure hell. It's been worse than anything I could possibly imagine."

People have stormed off television sets for far less than this. In April, 1994 on ESPN2's *Talk2* show, Jim Everett, the former NFL player, famously attacked his interviewer, Jim Rome, for trying to humiliate him by calling him "Chris," in allusion to the female tennis player Chris Evert. Tyson just took his humiliation, meekly, gently, and submissively, while Givens detailed how he often veered out of control. "Michael is manic-depressive," she concluded.

Crediting Roper for being the "glue" that kept them together, she confirmed what many observers already knew: "I do come with the package." The package consisted of her, Roper, and her sister.

Tyson, looking drowsy with medication, offered no counter-punch. Instead, he acknowledged that he had made millions of dollars. "My wife would just have to ask for it and she has everything I have." Tyson was to discover that Givens took that quite literally.

Playing Iago to Tyson's Othello, King had alluded to Givens' friendship with Donald Trump, the flamboyant entrepreneur who had yearnings to become a bigtime boxing mogul. After Givens – to stay with the Shakespeare theme – had come on like Lady Macbeth, Tyson was beginning to listen. So when he received photographs of his wife aboard Trump's yacht, he reacted. Fearing the brunt of Tyson's fury, Givens and Roper flew to LA, while Tyson sought refuge, not with King, but with Cayton. One of Cayton's first actions was to gain an independent medical opinion on Tyson, to clear him of the stigma of being manic-depressive. Stigmas are not so easily removed.

King, who had ordered the detective report of which the photographs were part, was equally as quick thinking. He rushed Tyson to each of the banks where he had accounts and gave instructions to transfer funds into accounts bearing Tyson's name only and not to honor any future checks signed by either Givens or Roper. A total of $35 million (according to Newfield; $15 million by other accounts) was secured. A check for almost $600,000 signed by Givens and made out to "Robin Givens Promotions" was stopped.

King and Tyson also swung by the offices of Roper's company, which also housed an organization called Mike Tyson Enterprises, which she had set up to handle all Tyson's business affairs. They scooped up records, accounts, checkbooks and other documents.

Givens filed for divorce almost immediately, citing "irreconcilable differences." Filing in California, where everything divorcing couples own is considered community property, was obviously to Givens' advantage. Under King's guidance, Tyson filed for an annulment in New York, claiming he was misled into marriage by a pregnancy that never was. Givens' gynecologist confirmed that Givens had miscarried, but in June, that is four months after the wedding, casting doubts on whether she was pregnant at the time.

Tyson described Givens and Roper as "the slime of slime," Givens retorting with a $125 million libel and slander suit. She also argued that King was instrumental in turning her husband against her.

A year and a week after the wedding, the marriage was dissolved. The final decree was granted in the Dominican Republic. Raoul Felder, who represented Givens, used the term "minimal settlement," though no further details were disclosed. "Basically, she will keep what's hers and he will keep what's his," said Felder vaguely, appending an ominous rider "with a floor to what she receives."

Givens featured in Bill Dukes' film of the Chester Himes novel *A Rage in Harlem*, in 1991. The following year, she was reacquainted with Eddie Murphy in Reginald Hudlin's comedy *Boomerang*. She appeared as a host in the tv show *Forgive or Forget* and kept up her profile in several films, including *Head of State*, with comics Bernie Mack and Chris Rock, who also directed. In 2004, Givens, then aged 40, was in *Hollywood Wives: The new generation* directed by Joyle Chopra.

Figure 5 "She exhibits so much class," said Tyson of Robin Givens, whom he married in 1988. "I hope it rubs off on me." After their divorce in 1989, he reflected that she craved "to be white."

Despite her acting credentials, the name Robin Givens will always summon one thought: "Tyson's ex." She was never shy in discussing Tyson publicly, especially in front of cameras. The marriage may have been, in her words, pure hell, but it was made-in-show-business heaven. Her career may not have taken off on the same trajectory as, say, Helen Hunt, Will Smith, or Jennifer Aniston, all of whom broke out of sitcoms to become movie stars. But without the associations with Tyson she may have had a similar future to her *Head of the Class* co-stars, such as Jeanetta Arnette or Leslie Bega, both of whom continued to appear, though in nonstarring roles, in tv shows like *ER* and *CSI: Crime Scene Investigation*. Worse, she could have suffered the same fate as the countless other sitcom actors who sunk without trace after a few modestly successful seasons.

Before he met Givens, Tyson was acknowledged as an athlete of great prowess. The interest in him concerned his ability, his strength, even his place in history. He exhibited evidence of these every time he climbed into a boxing ring. There may have been passing interest in the vagaries of his character, but not in his intermittent emotional pain, or his vacillating moods. He was opened up for inspection only after his union with Givens. She may have unwittingly or, much more probably, intentionally cultivated interest in Tyson. As a show-business performer, her inclination was to attract publicity rather than repel it.

Even if she'd tried to shun publicity, the fact that she was part of a sports-showbiz liaison would have made the task impossible. From DiMaggio/Monroe onwards, these liaisons have been fuel for the media. But in the late 1980s, culture was changing. The media was no longer content to snap pictures of the happy couple and scribble down a few inane quotes. The new age of the celeb was beginning and with it came new curiosities. Public inquisitiveness ensured that Tyson's life would become, like the assets of a California marriage, community property.

This might have happened with or without Givens, of course. The prying eyes and ears to the wall would have still made anything resembling a private life impossible for the heavyweight champion of the world. The short-lived marriage (short-lived in the late 1980s, that is; not in the J-Lo'd 2000s) exposed some features of Tyson that were to become marks on a template: abusive, depressive, headstrong, and, perhaps, above all uncontrollable. The irony is that none of these were supported by the evidence of 1988. If anything, Tyson had shown that, while he could be capable of abuse, he could also be too gentle for his own good. His tendencies toward depression were perhaps not greater than anyone else's and were probably exaggerated by the medication he was prescribed. If he was so headstrong, he would not have so easily conceded to many of his wife's often inappropriate demands. And, if he was uncontrollable, how come his entire life seems to have been surrendered to others, whether Givens herself, Roper, King, or the many others who directed all the major moves in his life? If ever there was a man under control, it was Tyson.

———

In any period of change, there is superfluity: people and things considered to have outlived their usefulness have to be discarded in the interests of renewal. Of all the errors that Tyson made in 1988, boxing analysts consider his most serious was in dumping his trainer Kevin Rooney. Like Cayton, Rooney was white. With Tyson's newfound black consciousness, this didn't bode well.

Perhaps Tyson was waiting for a reason to fire Rooney. If so, he found it when Rooney was interviewed on tv shortly after Tyson and Givens had split up. Rooney was not a fan of Givens and Roper: he made no secret of the fact that he regarded them as destructive influences on Tyson. So it was curious when Rooney, when asked on tv about Tyson's future, answered that he wouldn't be surprised if Tyson got back together with Givens. After confronting him with this, Tyson dispensed with his services. Incredulous, Rooney couldn't accept that Tyson had made the decision and insisted that King lay behind it. So began a long and messy legal process that dragged on for eight years and culminated in Rooney's being awarded $4.4 million in compensation. Rooney was known to have gambling debts and unpaid tax bills that would have taken care of most of that amount.

King installed Aaron Snowell and Richie Giachetti as Tyson's trainers and Jay Bright as his chief second (cornerman). They were parts of what King called Team Tyson, a new assembly of handpicked people all answerable to him, rather than Tyson. Two key members were John Horne and Rory Holloway, and they were to be Tyson's aides-de-camp, each on $7,000 per week. It's easy to reflect on how gullible Tyson seems to have been, especially considering that he later sued King for $100 million and was forced to declare himself bankrupt. But King, for all his machiavellian guile, had appeared to have served Tyson expertly, first in destabilizing his marriage, then by shielding his money from Givens and Roper. Whatever King's motives, the results of his endeavors were to get Tyson out of a relationship that would almost certainly have left him deprived in many respects. Tyson must have approached the end of 1988 believing he had been extricated from a tangle. Othello must have had a similar feeling while being ensnared by Iago.

Part of King's induction – it seems an apt word – was to give Tyson a copy of Jawanza Kunjufu's *Countering the Conspiracy to Destroy Black Boys*, which was a sort of black self-help book. It shared with several other books the premise that black people were expendable and that the entire economic system was geared to their extermination (a postulate spoofed in Malcolm D. Lee's 2003 comedy *Undercover Brother*, in which an attempt to reassert white supremacy starts with a drug that makes an African American military hero not unlike Colin Powell change his mind about running for President and open a KFC-style restaurant instead).

Many of King's proclamations seemed to confirm that he subscribed to the conspiracy theory. Tyson too: as his immersion into King's subculture deepened, earlier criticisms of whites became criticisms of assimilating blacks. "They want to be white so bad," said Tyson, in this instance referring to Givens and Roper. "They were trying to take me from the people I grew up with and throw me into their kind of high-class world," he told the *Chicago Sun-Times*. Givens' status was, on his own account, one of the factors that attracted him in the first place.

Despite Tyson's caustic remarks about Givens, Rudy Gonzalez, his chauffeur and part of the newly constituted Team Tyson, believed she left a "gaping hole in Mike Tyson's existence." In his short memoir "From the inner ring" (written with Martin A. Feigenbaum), Gonzalez recalled how Horne and Holloway filled the hole. Like Givens, they drew him away from old associations, but while she had designs on moving up, Horne and Holloway moved Tyson "into 'the street' where crime and violence were glorified" (p. 121).

"Part of the plan orchestrated by Don King was to distance Tyson from long-standing friendships which included people from all races, nationalities and religions," according to Gonzalez and Feigenbaum, who believe it worked. Witnessing close-up, they observed a "transformation" in which Tyson became "submissive to the wishes of King and Horne": "It was as if they held some special power or control over him which could take away his will to resist whatever they wanted him to do" (pp. 127–8).

But, only "as if": King didn't literally have a special control over Tyson. The decision to leave Cayton, Rooney and the others, to split with Givens and Roper and to reorder the priorities in his life was Tyson's. He exercised free will and, while he did so within a framework of possibilities, he actually chose to pursue one course rather than another. King hadn't surreptitiously attached electrodes to Tyson so that he could jolt him with electric shocks. He hadn't hypnotized him or plied him with mind-altering drugs. Well, not the drugs part, anyway: in an interview with the *New York Beacon* in 2002, King revealed that he had hired a hypnotist for Tyson to help him "redirect his energy in a more productive and positive way."

If Tyson, as Gonzalez and Feigenbaum detected, turned submissive, he initially submitted himself to a regime he clearly believed was more comfortable than his old one, more compatible with his specific needs and more conducive to his progress as a boxer. Every writer on the subject presumes Tyson was wrong. Had he stayed with Cayton, he would have been richer for sure: Cayton had already penciled a six-fight scheme that would have grossed Tyson $50 million. Additionally, he would have continued to endorse the likes of Diet Pepsi, Nintendo, and Toyota. King secured Tyson only $29 million in his first seven fights and no new endorsement contracts. To which Tyson might have replied: so what?

Motivation is rarely straightforward: money was not high on Tyson's hierarchy of needs. By the end of 1988, he had already earned $48 million. Many athletes, having dedicated themselves to the pursuit of success in sports since their early teens, reflect on the self-denial necessary to achieve that success, compare their own abstinent life with those of their peers and feel deprived. They ache for the kind of gratification available to others. Maybe Tyson valued the new opportunities offered by King *et al.* Maybe he bought into the idea that black people are challenged by an institutional form of racism that threatens their survival. Many others did and still do.

What if the marriage had survived? Givens would surely have interpolated herself in his business activities and persuaded him to exercise more independence from Cayton. It's unlikely that she would have supported his transfer to King, though. Newfield documents a call from Givens to Cayton, in which she confessed she had been duped by King. Perhaps she would have devised a way of developing Tyson's career without either of the two competing managers. Later, boxers like Lennox Lewis and Naseem Hamed, in efforts to retain autonomy, set up their own promotional businesses and worked directly with tv companies. Promoters like King and Arum were employed and paid set fees for their services.

With her showbiz connections, Givens would have known how A-list entertainers often start their own production companies to run their own affairs. The fact that Givens and Roper were disliked by almost all of Tyson's boxing associates (and probably the entire boxing fraternity) might actually have worked in his favor. Roper, in particular, might not have known much about boxing; but she was a quick learner and a redoubtable businesswoman.

As when anybody arrives at a crossroads in their life, there are several routes, some leading to different destinations, others circling to the same destinations. Some of Tyson's destinations would have been different. He probably contributed somewhat to his downfall against Douglas, but, as I have argued, Douglas looked unstoppable on that night and fought like a man possessed. He would have beaten anybody that stood in front of him.

The question is: would another manager have even matched him with Douglas? It was a voluntary defense of the title in an unfamiliar environment (though he had fought once before in Tokyo) and the rationale behind making it wasn't clear. In other words, someone else might have steered Tyson toward a different challenger on safer terrain.

If he had stayed with Givens, would he have been the lothario that landed in trouble in Indianapolis? Unlikely. She might not have kept him under lock and key, but she would have curbed his philandering. The incident involving the presentation of the car to the New York police officers was, by Heller's account, precipitated by Givens' discovery of condoms in Tyson's jacket pocket. Even if marriage didn't turn Tyson into a reformed man, it made him think twice about getting involved in perilous situations. It's unlikely he would have been allowed to judge the beauty pageant at all and wouldn't have gone within 500 miles of Indianapolis otherwise.

Unlikely as these scenarios are, they could conceivably have changed Tyson. But would anything have stopped Tyson getting locked up in what bell hooks, in a May 1995 interview with Kevin Powell of *Vibe* magazine, called "the successful black people zoo?" Like other members of the black entertainment elite, Tyson's role was always going to be a tightly defined one, no matter what he did. Like the gangsta rap artists, he was an emasculated player in the white psychodrama. He might have earned more money, got into fewer scrapes with the law, abused women less. But, he was always going to serve as a kind of reminder of white superiority, a reminder to whites of what they were *not*.

Prior to 1988, Tyson's athleticism had been universally praised. He was a boxer of immense prowess. And for this he was, not exactly respected, but highly regarded. Maybe he didn't change, but, the context in which he operated changed drastically in barely a year; this, in turn, prompted new evaluations of him. As Illingworth put it: "Tyson had been mythologized for so long, and now it was time to demonize him" (p. 285).

In 1984, King promoted a concert tour for The Jacksons. Michael Jackson was the attraction, his brothers being no more than his backing singers. It was called the "Victory" tour. There was tension between Michael and King, the reason for which wasn't clear. At least, not until after the tour. "What Michael's to realize is that Michael's a nigger," said King in an interview featured in Randy Taraborelli's *Michael Jackson: The magic and the madness.* "It doesn't matter how great he can sing and dance . . . He's one of the megastars in the world, but he's still going to be a nigger megastar" (p. 377).

It was perfectly consistent with King's philosophy. For example, talking to Richard Regan, of *Interview* magazine in

1990, King suggested that he was the epitome of the American Dream: "But instead of getting plaudits and accolades, I get condemnation and vilifications." A predictable dividend for a successful African American entrepreneur? "Absolutely! As long as I stay black! And I don't see no change coming. I want to be black. You know the reason that I use 'nigger' is because it's consistent."

King's frustration is understandable. Business deals are done every day in sports and fighters leave managers and coaches all the time. When Tyson moved to King, the process elicited this description from James Dalrymple, a journalist writing for the respected British *Sunday Times*: "Like some dark crooning nemesis, he came to Tyson, when he was down and beaten and bewildered, took him in his arms and whispered to him that it was time finally to leave the white man's world for good and join the brothers" (Magazine section, September 18, 1994, p. 21).

It's difficult to imagine a white promoter's attempt to sign a boxer or a general manager's transactions with a football player being described in such disdainful and theatrical terms. Not that King himself would be surprised. "The media always twist anything where black success is concerned," he told Regan. "They always want to couple a black's success with a negative association – undesirable conditions, evilness, lewdness, depravity, anything demeaning in black ambition, because it's always got to be put in some kind of subordinate capacity in order to justify the superiority of the racist point of view" (p. 104).

Were the same point to be made by, say, the scholar Henry Louis Gates or an erudite actor like James Earl Jones, it would be accepted as a critical commentary of contemporary culture. From Don King, it's self-serving hypocrisy. Even if the charges of the IRS and FBI can be explained by reference to King's own theory of black success, the allegations of boxers he has managed, the majority of them black, tend to weaken his case.

Perhaps it was a genuine error, but Tim Witherspoon was angry about it, when he received an itemized bill of his training expenses, the total of which was deducted from his purse. For twenty-eight days of training camp, the tab should have been $2,800, but, on King's invoice a zero had somehow been added, making the figure $28,000. Witherspoon was one of the few who, instead of just bellyaching, went to court and won substantial damages. It took Tyson ten years to arrive at a similar realization. In 1998, he turned sharply against King, physically lashing out at him at one point, and then instigating a $100 million lawsuit against him.

Never known for his frugality, Tyson blew millions on his extravagances. Even so, with career earnings totaling more than $300 million, one might assume he would have something left after tax and other deductions to show for nearly two decades of boxing. So, when he declared bankruptcy in 2003, it cast a reflection on King's proprieties.

King's immediate riposte was: "I love him. He's my beloved brother," though, in 2002, he gave a particularly revealing interview to Bobby Ramos for his story "Don King on Mike Tyson – unplugged" printed in *New York Beacon*. It included this striking appraisal of Tyson: "He's a traitor, he acts like he's a poster boy for the Ku Klux Klan. He's the embodiment and personification of the stereotypical image that they level on us: lazy, lethargic, depraved, rapists and lascivious" (p. 39).

The argument is a potent one: that Tyson had become a living advertisement for racists, portraying all the base and amoral features associated with characterizations of blacks typically used to justify and rationalize racist beliefs and behavior. What King failed to notice was that he, in tandem with the media, had played a large part in that process. In fact, during the crucial period from 1988 onwards when, to repeat Illingworth, the demonization of Tyson began, King was the commander of Team Tyson. He oversaw and assisted a reconstruction of Tyson as "the personification of the stereotypical image."

After leaving King, Tyson's lurch toward self-parody might well have been his awkward attempt to assert more control over his own image. "He makes his own decisions," King confirmed in the same article. But they weren't always informed decisions and perhaps King had some role in restricting the flow of information to Tyson. He certainly had with Witherspoon.

King didn't fight too hard to keep Tyson, nor even persuade him not to sue. At the time of Tyson's departure in 1998, King

Figure 6 In the early 1990s, Tyson and Nelson Mandela were among the most famous men in the world. While the presence of Don King in Tyson's life was not yet fully visible, he was lurking in the background.

was busy fending off nine charges of insurance fraud that had been brought against him by the federal government. The charges related to a canceled fight featuring Julio Cesar Chavez, who should have appeared on the undercard of the promotion topped by Tyson's second fight with Razor Ruddock in 1991. King was acquitted. He claimed it was a victory, not for him, "not for black America and not white America, but all America."

It was a vintage King proclamation, hailing American unity and banishing suggestions of racial difference. King's brilliance was in sustaining this conception of a color-free America, while nurturing an alternative view of a country so divided that black people were perpetually challenged to achieve material success, only to be damned when they did so. It's testimony to King's acumen, insight, and ingenuity that he was able to maintain this Janus-like presence for so long. He repelled virtually every attempt to undermine his credibility. He hardly needed to play the race card: more often than not, he would bluff others into folding.

Tyson didn't exactly fold. He quit King's game, minus his money, but with a complaint about how fairly the game was played. Maybe he did realize who the sucker was. Trouble is: the realization came much too late.

———

Around the time of the Spinks fight, Tyson must have cultivated a sort of "another day, another fight, another twenty million bucks" attitude. Barely three years in the pros and he was the richest athlete in the world. Still only 23, he could reasonably look forward to another five or six years as champion and retire undefeated as the biggest earner in the history of sport. Gross career earnings of a billion dollars were not out of the question. So it was odd when he told writer Tom Callahan: "When I'm out of boxing, I'm going to tell everyone I'm bankrupt."

It was meant as a joke and, in his article "Iron Mike and the allure of the 'manly art'," Callahan recorded it as such. If Tyson wasn't kidding, it was one of the most extraordinarily prescient forecasts ever.

——— eleven ———

FACTS ARE LOST IN THE PRECONCEPTIONS OF RACIAL GRIEVANCE

The occasion was vintage Don King. A gaudy mock coronation to crown the new sovereign king of boxing. King smiled sublimely as he watched his friend the Reverend Al Sharpton, resplendent in a long, velvet robe and coaster-sized medallion, present Tyson with the International Boxing Federation (IBF) championship belt to confirm his status as the undisputed heavyweight champion of the world. Tyson was dressed in a crown and ermine-edged robes and held a scepter. A massive chain hung around his $19\frac{1}{2}$-inch neck. It was August, 1986, before Sharpton's immersion in a case that would establish him as a national figure. Less conspicuously, the case changed Tyson's life.

Everybody was moved by the case of Tawana Brawley, the 15-year-old highschool cheerleader from Wappinger Falls, New York, who disappeared for four days in November, 1987. She was discovered half-naked curled up in a plastic garbage bag near a dumpster. Later, she told of how she had been repeatedly raped and sodomized by police officers. Maybe it was a piece of opportunism. Maybe it was genuine concern. Whatever the motive, King paid a well-publicized visit to Brawley, taking with him the new heavyweight champion. Tyson and King spent almost seven hours consoling Brawley. They left her with $100,000 for a fund for abused children and enough money to put her through college. Tyson also gave her his gold Rolex wristwatch. Other prominent African Americans were also galvanized to act. Bill Cosby and the publisher of *Essence*, Edward Lewis, offered a $25,000 reward for information leading to the arrest of the perpetrators of the particularly hideous attack.

Brawley's body was found smeared in dog feces with "KKK" and "nigger" scrawled in charcoal across her chest. Burn marks were found on her lower body. She remembered how her assailants had bundled her into a police car, told her to shut up, smothered her in a towel and whisked her off to an unknown destination. Her screams for "police" were answered with: "Shut up, bitch, I am the police!" There were, as Brawley recalled, six white men, some in police uniform, at least one wearing a badge, who violated her.

Sharpton, who had earlier surfaced when he helped focus public attention on an incident in Howard Beach, Queens, where three black men were attacked, quickly became involved in the Brawley case. He emphasized the gruesome nature of the assault, reminding everyone that this was a black teenager who had been attacked not by a pillaging bunch of gangbangers, but by white law enforcement officers.

After her initial statement, Brawley became hysterical; understandably so, given the fearful attack. When asked for a description of her attackers, she wrote on a sheriff's notepad "white cop." Then, she fell silent. She and her family refused to discuss the incident with authorities on the advice of their attorney, Alton Maddox Jr. He argued that no local official could properly investigate the case. The Dutchess County district attorney bowed out after two months, citing an unspecified conflict of interest. The local prosecutor named in his place withdrew after less than a day. New York governor Mario Cuomo then appointed State Attorney General Robert Abrams as a special prosecutor. Maddox still refused to let Brawley talk unless Abrams agreed personally to present the case to the grand jury and conduct key parts of the trial. Abrams, who had no recent trial experience, refused to agree to the conditions, leading to a stalemate.

Meanwhile, the case spiraled upwards, becoming infamous nationally. Brawley claimed to be too physically and emotionally traumatized to talk, even if Maddox had allowed her. The meeting with Tyson and King was a rare exception, suggesting how special Tyson and, perhaps, King had become – either to the young black woman, or to the ambitious black lawyer. "She's going to need a lot of help, a lot of treatment and a lot of TLC," uttered King as he left their meeting.

A white part-time police officer roughly answering Brawley's description of one of her abductors killed himself days after she was found, adding to a deepening mystery. Brawley's family issued a statement to the effect that she had seen a newspaper's picture of him and identified him as one of her attackers. Steven Pagones, a lawyer and son of a local judge, called the police, explaining that there must have been a misidentification: he was out shopping with the suicide victim at the time he was meant to have been molesting Brawley. According to Pagones, he was depressed by the news that he had failed to get a job with the Highway Patrol.

Then Brawley was said to have recognized Pagones in another newspaper picture and identified him as another member of the gang of rapists. This emboldened Sharpton to fling allegations at Pagones. Drug dealing and links with the Mafia were thrown into the mix. Appearing in front of a bank of television cameras in New York, Sharpton challenged Pagones to respond with legal action. He did exactly that. Sharpton quickly became embroiled in the kind of cause for which he later became a national celebrity.

All the time, the trail went colder and the investigation began to founder for lack of evidence. No arrests were made. The furor over the lack of progress became inflected with race. Had a young white woman been brutalized in this way by a group of blacks, would there have been such a shortage of suspects and an absence of evidence? Black activists, including Sharpton, wondered aloud why investigators seemed to be centering on the Brawley family. It was one of those cases in which the complete lack of headway invited all manner of sometimes hysterical conjecture. Everyone had his or her own theories on who did what and who was covering up for whom.

"There is no question that the justice system works differently for blacks than it does for whites," argued Maddox, who had worked the Howard Beach trial the year before, when he successfully argued for a special prosecutor. Maybe he planned that the speculation would take on a racial dimension. But, he probably didn't anticipate the skepticism that began to take root, at first in the local press near Wappinger Falls.

Hospital reports indicated that Brawley had possibly been raped, but found no semen in the vaginal area. So there was no evidence of a sexual attack and no evidence of the kind of physical injury consistent with a struggle or an attempt to restrain her. When recovered, her underwear was singed, suggesting that someone had tried to destroy evidence. Searches of the areas surrounding the place where she was found unearthed nothing.

A local paper, the *Hudson Valley Hornet*, began to question the reliability of Brawley's version of events. On the day of the abduction, she had skipped school and visited a friend held in a nearby prison. The friend who took her there was later apprehended driving a stolen car, which he claimed he'd bought from a drug dealer. Brawley's family had only weeks before left an apartment complex adjacent to where she was eventually found. After the discovery, police were called to deal with a heated quarrel at the Brawley home. The police questioned Brawley's stepfather, who had served time in prison for the slaying of his first wife. None of the events individually meant much; but, cumulatively, they added up.

An alternative version of events to that offered by Brawley began to take shape: she made up the whole story, perhaps afraid of what would happen if her father found out she'd missed school. In other words, Brawley had constructed an elaborate fabrication. This is how the case is best remembered: as an outrageous hoax. Fraud or not, Brawley remained at the center of the kind of case that, as Charles Lawrence of the *Ottawa Citizen* put it, when reflecting on events a decade on, "has the power to transform reality between the races. Facts are lost in the preconceptions of racial grievance" (January 1, 1998, p. F7).

While Lawrence didn't expand, we can suppose he meant that, more than twenty years after the removal of legal barriers to full participation of black people in society, barriers still remained. It took only one case involving race to remind the nation of those barriers. In issuing that reminder, the Brawley case changed, perhaps "transformed," as Lawrence believed, relations. Brawley lived in lowrent public housing, just like millions of other poor black people. She hadn't enough money to pay for her college education, until Tyson provided it. She appeared, at first, to have been a helpless African American teenager tortured by rapacious white guardians of law and order. Even when her story began to unravel, Sharpton and his colleagues issued powerful, challenging polemics about how the entire justice system was biased against blacks.

America's melting pot began to resemble a wormwood-laced witch's cauldron, spitting as it came to the boil. The Brawley case proved more divisive than it at first appeared, many factions maintaining the validity of Tawana's story for many years after – even to the present day.

The case dragged on, new twists adding to its fascination. In a legal sense, Pagones was exonerated from blame in 1988. A grand jury convened to investigate Brawley's allegations and ruled that she had left home for a few days of partying, then made up the story to avoid the wrath of her stepfather.

Sharpton repeatedly used the phrase "white justice" to describe how the Brawley case had been filed under "hoax" and conveniently ignored. Neither he nor Maddox retracted their claim against Pagones. If anything, Sharpton became more vociferous. He, along with Maddox, a colleague, Vernon Mason, and the whole Brawley family, refused to co-operate with the grand jury.

Sharpton's hellfire-and-brimstone oratory had been heard before, though never as loudly and as suasively. He'd been on the fringes of New York politics for years. At one point, he became involved in an FBI undercover operation as an intermediary to set up a meeting with King, whom he knew through their common interest in the record industry. Bizarrely, he was involved with the staunch Republican segregationist Strom Thurmond and, at one point, induced his friend James Brown – *the* James Brown – to do a radio commercial supporting Thurmond.

Sporting a coiffured hairdo, flashy enough to rival even that of King, and with a trademark chunky gold necklace, Sharpton cut a startling figure, especially when he let fly with his bombast, again King-like. Tawana Brawley disappeared not long after the incident, leaving Sharpton and, to a slightly lesser degree, Maddox to drive the case into the 1990s.

After being exonerated, Pagones filed a $395 million defamation suit against Brawley, Sharpton, Maddox, and Mason. When Brawley failed to respond, a judge ruled that Pagones had won his case against her by default. That was in 1991; in 1998, a jury found that Pagones had been defamed and awarded him $345,000 in damages, $65,000 of it to come from Sharpton. While Maddox and Mason kept a relatively low profile, Sharpton loudly maintained his belief that Brawley had told the truth all along.

By this time, Sharpton had become a well-known figure, sure to show up and have an opinion in any civil rights dispute. When Tyson was released from prison in 1995 after serving his sentence for rape, many women's groups stringently opposed the intended "Welcome Home" celebration in New York. Sharpton defied them, working with the project co-ordinators to organize a hero's salutation. "Is it all right for white men to rape black women?" Sharpton asked in allusion to the Brawley case. Sharpton stuck to his guns, siding with King, at one point invoking the Bible. "The point of religion is to redeem people, especially in a community where you have a high percentage of people who have had brushes with the law," he told the *Baltimore Afro-American* for its story "Harlem welcomes back 'Iron Mike'" (June 24, 1995). "If we kill the idea of redemption, we will have thrown a large percentage of our community away" (p. A1).

Two years later, Sharpton was running hard and strong for the office of the mayor of New York City, but took time out to sit in on an event honoring Tyson and King. Mounting a robust defense of Tyson, who was then between the two Holyfield fights (and so nine months away from the earbiting incident), Sharpton declared: "If there were people here making false accusations against Mike Tyson, you would see it on the front pages of every newspaper."

His point was that good news of Tyson rarely seeped out, while bad news, even falsehoods, was an automatic contender for the front page. "It's not every day people who have made it turn around and help those they've left behind," said Sharpton, looking at Tyson.

The novelist Tom Wolfe must have had Sharpton in mind when he wrote *The Bonfire of the Vanities*: his character Reverend Bacon is a ringer for Sharpton. In danger of being sidelined by the Brawley case, Sharpton staged something of a comeback through his National Action Network and, in 2000, emerged with credit from the citywide protest over the shooting of Amadou Diallo. A regular on late-night talk shows, Sharpton, in 2002, announced his intention to run in the 2004 Presidency race.

Derided as a huckster, an opportunist, and a kind of racial ambulance chaser, he was also praised as a champion of the black underclass. "Sharpton is a plague," pronounced Don Feder in his 2000 article for *Human Events*, an article colorfully entitled "Rev. Al Sharpton is part buffoon, part brownshirt" (March 10). "But to the black Americans who back him, Sharpton is the unwavering champion of the black underclass, the focal point for an all-out assault on white privilege," wrote *The Weekly Journal*'s columnist Darrell Pawsey in his "The struggle is Al's stage" (March 18, 1993).

By the start of the twenty-first century, black America had extricated itself from the tangled politics of protest and victimhood. The faded relevance of Jesse Jackson suggested that African American politics was too manifold, too diverse, too tiered to warrant a single leader. There was no "voice of black America" and if Sharpton was still positioning himself (or being positioned) as the "champion of the black underclass" his appeal was to just one facet of a variegated African American population.

Editorializing about Sharpton in 2002, *The Economist* made the point: "Sharpton's greatest strength is not his ability to lead his own people. It is his ability to reinforce the prejudices of the white majority" (January 19).

Perhaps this is why the media continued to afford Sharpton such generous coverage. He was guaranteed to mobilize blacks (one way or another) and infuriate whites. Sharpton had an unfailing ability to get under everyone's skin. Buffoon? Neo-Nazi? Demagogue extraordinaire? There were many, many more lurid descriptions of Sharpton. While more practical and refined, multi-issue politicians of African American backgrounds were overlooked, Sharpton stayed in the headlines. It was as if he was wheeled out just to remind America that he was the only black politician worth following, the only one who would unfailingly get people's backs up.

———

Tyson needed to win three titles before he could claim to be undisputed king of the boxing world. At least in a technical sense: by late 1986, the abiding feeling was that there were few fighters capable of testing Tyson. In preceding years, the world title had divided into three different organizing federations recognizing different champions. Paradoxically, the boxer who had the strongest moral case for being recognized as world champion didn't have any kind of title. Michael Spinks, who had twice beaten the universally recognized champion Larry Holmes, had been stripped of his titles and opted to defend what was billed as the "People's Title."

Tony Tucker beat Buster Douglas for the vacant International Boxing Federation title and became that organization's world title-holder. Meanwhile, James "Bonecrusher" Smith erased Tim Witherspoon in less than a round to win the World Boxing Association (WBA) version of the championship. Trevor Berbick won the World Boxing Council (WBC) title with an upset win over Pinklon Thomas. To become the undisputed champion Tyson had to beat all three; he did so over a period of ten months.

Although Berbick was a champion, he was lightly regarded. A somewhat unathletic-looking Jamaican who had the uncertain distinction of handing Muhammad Ali his final defeat (in the Bahamas, in 1981, when Ali was 38), Berbick was one of those champions people figured had got lucky. Thomas was no great shakes, anyway; but, in boxing, a fighter who is pumped can occasionally surprise his opponent by foregoing the early feeling-out phase and leaping straight onto an all-out offensive. Berbick profited from the surprise tactic.

There was also something else to consider: the added confidence that comes of being a champion. OK, Tyson was a hot fighter, with twenty-seven straight wins, including fifteen first-round finishes, but he was still the challenger. A champion typically enjoys an edge in what psychologists call self-efficacy – a belief in their own capacity to produce the desired result. There was one other factor to consider: Berbick was trained by Angelo Dundee, who boasted Muhammad Ali and Sugar Ray Leonard among his glittering charges. Dundee talked openly about Tyson's power to intimidate opponents and how Berbick would negate it. He made no secret of the fight plan: to meet fire with fire. Berbick would go straight to war with Tyson. For all the talk, Tyson started the fight a 3–1 favorite. The fact that he was paid over double Berbick's career-high purse of $2.1 million indicates that he rather than the champion was the drawcard.

Berbick was certainly an intrepid champion, dispensing with the respect, or fear, that Tyson's previous opponents had afforded him, as he sought to assert his own authority. But, as all of Tyson's opponents had discovered, fight plans that look good on paper can be rendered useless in a single moment. Berbick's plan began to go haywire as soon as he felt the impact of Tyson's shots. Try as he might – and Berbick grimly strove to stay in the fight – he could simply not withstand the might of Tyson's punches. It became almost painful to watch as Berbick valiantly rose from the canvas, his pride impelling him to carry on fighting, but his legs failing to answer orders from his central nervous system. The fight was stopped in the second round. Tyson completed the fight in typically businesslike fashion and had the first of three world title belts strapped around his waist. Don King, who promoted the contest, rushed to the ring and hoisted him aloft, hailing him as the youngest boxer ever to win a world heavyweight title.

He was 20. A relatively rich young man. His earnings for the Berbick fight alone were $1.5 million. Even allowing for all the deductions, he would have taken home over $830,000. His quest was now to grab all three versions of the world title. The route he took requires a little context.

Tyson's win over Berbick was part of what was called a unification tournament, which was spread over several months and shown on HBO television. King had orchestrated it and maintained a hand in promoting the fights. Three weeks after Tyson had taken the WBC title, Tim Witherspoon, managed by King's stepson, Carl, defended his WBA title against James

Figure 7 "A popular and respected champion, who appeared genuinely modest and more interested in boxing than in fame and fortune." This is how Mihir Bose of the London *Times* described the image of Tyson at the time of his coronation as heavyweight king in 1986.

"Bonecrusher" Smith, who was a late substitute for the injured Tony Tubbs. Smith had been training for a matchup with Mitch Green for which he would have earned $35,000. He jumped at the chance to fight for the title for a purse of $230,000. But, there was a price: he had to sign over 50 percent of his managerial contract to Carl King.

With a viciousness he had never before shown, the 33-year-old Smith went after the title. Witherspoon was completely overwhelmed in under a round. Smith, who held a college degree and boasted of being the only world heavyweight champion to do so, earned his nickname with his pulverizing right hands. He used these to great effect against Witherspoon. Now, he promised to use them on Tyson in another King-promoted fight.

Meanwhile, the third variant of the world title was the subject of some discussion. Michael Spinks was the IBF champion, having defeated the former champion Larry Holmes twice. He was due to defend against the IBF's mandatory contender, Tony Tucker, as part of the unification tournament. This never materialized. All the remaining boxers in the tournament were African Americans; only Tyson had the presence that set him apart from the rest, none of whom were especially media-friendly. Competent though they were, the likes of Spinks, Smith, and Tucker were not well known outside boxing circles. None had been able to reach beyond sports in the way that Ali had and Tyson would. People might have been vaguely interested in, but they didn't really care who won the tournament.

So, when a white fighter announced he intended to come out of retirement and attempt to get into the world title picture, the context of the unification tournament changed. In strictly boxing terms, Gerry Cooney had no right to climb straight into a world championship ring. But, he was white. This qualification alone made him interesting and immediately guaranteed massive public interest. Spinks could defend against Tucker for a few hundred thousand, or drop out of the tournament and fight Cooney for $4 million. Their fight would not have the formal imprimatur of a world title, but it had the fascination that title fights featuring black and white rivals always have.

Cooney was a useful fighter who had exploited his whiteness. His ring earnings reflected his color as much as his punching power. He retired initially a multi-millionaire following a defeat against Larry Holmes. But the lure of more millions against a fighter who appeared a little short on power for a heavyweight was too much to resist. Spinks had started his professional career as a light-heavyweight and had trained-up to heavyweight. He used his speed and unconventional, sometimes rather clumsy, technique among the heavier fighters.

Spinks vs. Cooney, though a nontitle fight, had much wider appeal than anything the tournament could offer, even though it now had Tyson in the fold. The IBF title was devalued considerably by Spinks' departure. Two nondescript fighters, Tony Tucker and Buster Douglas, contested the vacant title, Tucker emerging triumphant over a man who would return in an almost unrecognizable guise three years later. With Tucker as champion, the IBF title had no cachet at all. Nor did the WBA title, held by Smith. So there was some relief when Tyson beat Smith in March, 1987, to bring two of the three titles together.

Smith, like Tucker, was an anonymous champion. The son of sharecroppers in Magnolia, North Carolina, he had studied business administration and began boxing in the military. He didn't have his first pro fight until he was 28 and could claim only a mediocre nineteen wins against five defeats in five professional years. He'd already lost to Holmes in his first bid to become heavyweight champion, but the lightning-fast win over Witherspoon brought him credibility in the autumn of his career.

His intelligence outside the ring carried into the ring for his fight against Tyson. Cognizant of the cost Berbick paid for his pell-mell approach, Smith boxed cautiously and protectively, showing no obvious ambition besides staying clear of Tyson's punches. He lasted the distance, though Tyson was a decisive winner on all three judges' cards.

While waiting for the IBF to discover a new champion, Tyson squeezed a defense into his vigorous schedule. Nineteen eighty-seven was to be the last year Tyson had four fights. Three was his most in any one year from then. Pinklon Thomas, like Berbick, had a plan worked out for him by Angelo Dundee. It was no more effective, enabling Thomas to last until the sixth, which was longer than Berbick, but exposing him to a further four rounds of punishment.

Spinks' manager, Butch Lewis, insisted his fighter was the true champion, having won the title from the then undisputed champ, Larry Holmes, and never having lost in the ring. In terms of lineal descent, he was right. But, no one seriously questioned Tyson's claim to be the best heavyweight in the world. Tyson himself talked as if this was predestined: "I knew I was going to win the championship as soon as I stepped in the ring."

Tucker emerged as the IBF champion and automatically gained the right to fight Tyson for the unified titles. Set for August 1, the fight would create a once-and-for-all world champion.

––––––

Even allowing for taxes and other deductions, Tyson had banked at least $3 million in the nine months leading to June, 1987. With the prospect of doubling that from fight revenue alone before the end of the year, it must have seemed as if there was no limit. Tyson, who had spent his formative years stealing his money, was suddenly a rich young man. He was one of the richest 21-year-olds in the world. All this had come about in just over two years boxing professionally.

Sudden wealth often brings with it unexpected consequences, not all of them favorable. One of them is an absence of the usual signposts and standards that serve to guide us in our conduct and give us a sense of how we should behave. Social scientists have a word for it: *anomie* or *anomy*, which derives from the Greek *anomos*, meaning lawless. Entire cultures can be in a state of anomie during times of crisis, such as war. Or it can affect communities and families as well as individuals. Typically, it occurs after momentous changes. Investors who take a bath after a heavy stock exchange crash sometimes find themselves in an anomic condition. Their life circumstances change so radically that they become confused and lose track of the basic patterns and rules that not so much governed their lives, but inclined them to act according to certain codes. Their lives are thrown into disarray and their behavior becomes irregular and unpredictable. Lottery winners and beneficiaries of unexpected windfalls can also be affected. Some call it "sudden wealth syndrome" and find evidence of it in a combination of unusual behavior, opinions, and other characteristics.

Jeff Benedict describes how bigtime athletes are prone to this: "Stardom, by nature, dulls adherence to social norms, luring athletes to overindulge in illicit temptations." In his *Public Heroes, Private Felons*, Benedict has a passage that could have been intended for Tyson: "The enticements available to rich, famous athletes can prove particularly irresistible to the growing number of players who come from socially and economically deprived environments" (p. 215).

Whether Tyson's steep ascent through the tax brackets also shot him into a state of anomie, we'll never know. But there was certainly speculation that the money had gone to his head, especially after an incident at the Greek Theater in Los Angeles on the night of June 21. Tyson had gone to see a concert featuring Run DMC and the Beastie Boys.

Wandering through the parking lot after the concert, Tyson came across a security guard named Tabita Gonzalez. There are certain privileges accruing to a heavyweight champion, of course, though being able to caress any woman on demand isn't one of them. Tyson didn't understand this and approached Gonzalez, encircling her waist with his substantial arm as a prelude to what he presumed would be a kiss. Gonzalez didn't resist. She later reckoned that she'd mistaken him for another security guard, so played along – to a point. When Tyson asked her for a kiss, she declined and tried to wriggle free.

Another, this time male, security guard driving a cart witnessed part of the episode and, guessing Gonzalez might be in a predicament, went to lend his assistance. Tyson, on his account, was angered by his intervention and thrust the palm of his hand into his face, forcing him back into the cart. The guard later claimed that the blow had caused "a contusion and/or laceration [on] the inside of my mouth or lip." In other words, a cut lip. It was enough to convince him that he should file charges. So did Gonzalez. Tyson settled out of court. The guard received $75,000 and Gonzalez $30,000.

It was a small, but indicative, incident. What did it indicate? Either that Tyson's newfound position as one of sport's premier figures with money to match had disoriented him to the point where he couldn't observe the usual norms of conduct and felt the rules didn't apply to him. Or, that a relatively minor episode, possibly based on a genuine misunderstanding, had been exaggerated. Had some anonymous guy from the concert acted as Tyson had, would the security guards have sued? Possibly.

For Tyson, the incident was a portent. Whenever he became involved in a fracas or even a trivial wrangle or even tried to steer clear of trouble, someone would file a complaint. Obviously, being a high-profile athlete makes someone a target. People stare, ask for autographs, take photographs. Any kind of transgression, however small, is likely to make its way into the news. Police are more likely to treat complaints seriously, if only, as Benedict puts it, "to counter the growing perception that athletes receive preferential treatment" (p. 79). In fact, if Benedict is to be believed, law enforcement officials sometimes "overcompensate."

Perhaps Tyson's recognition of social norms was "dulled" by his rapid elevation and perhaps this, in part, explains the growing roster of complaints against him. But only in part. Also in the mix were: the inclination of others to examine Tyson's every misdemeanor, bring them to public attention and, wherever possible make them subject to official prosecution; plus the overcompensating efforts of the police and the courts to repudiate popular notions about their being soft on star athletes.

Strange as it may seem now, Tyson was then "a popular and respected champion, who appeared genuinely modest and more interested in boxing than fame and fortune." At least that was the view represented by Mihir Bose in his book *Sports Babylon* (p. 112). Whether Tyson liked it or not, the fame and fortune brought their own pitfalls – even for one who seemed "genuinely modest."

Earlier, Tyson might have gotten away with a few infractions here and there. Before he was a "name" athlete, nobody really cared if he uttered the occasional rude comment, or made a gesture. He might have upset a few bartenders or sales assistants, or even security guards. But he didn't find himself getting sued. Once he was recognizable as someone who had money, then the lawsuits started. And they didn't stop.

Tyson himself became anesthetized to most of them. He usually let his lawyers settle. The $105,000 he paid out to the LA security guards was the first installment. Of course, not every transgression could be settled, as Tyson was to discover.

Such are the vagaries of sport that the man who was to be the first conqueror of Tyson had folded limply in his initial effort to wrest a title against an opponent far less formidable than Tyson. Buster Douglas lasted until the tenth round of a contest with Tony Tucker for the IBF title that had been taken from Michael Spinks. Neither Douglas nor Tucker was in the premier league of heavyweights: they were respectable pros with solid rather than impressive credentials. With Douglas out of the way, Tucker marched toward Tyson in a showdown that would determine the only heavyweight champion of the world.

At 6 foot 5 inches and weighing about 220 lbs, the 28-year-old Tucker was big enough to cause Tyson problems. Admittedly, Tyson had never had serious problems against bigger men; but Smith, who was also tall, had taken him the distance and made him look ungainly for long periods. Tucker had an unblemished record of 35 straight wins, 30 of them achieved via knockout. None of his victims had been of high caliber, however.

Tucker began the fight confidently, but hurt his hand and, from the fifth, opted for a policy of damage limitation. It made for a featureless fight devoid of knockdowns or changes of fortune. Tyson won a clear, unanimous decision. It was an anticlimactic way of winning the third of his three titles, especially compared with some of the breathtaking exhibitions that came before. But it made Tyson $2.5 million richer (gross; Tucker earned rather less than $2 million) and conferred on him even greater earnings potential. It also established Tyson incontrovertibly as the world heavyweight champion.

The occupant of this status is usually a wanted man. Not just by autograph hunters, memorabilia collectors, and other fight fans. Becoming the heavyweight champ turns a fighter into a product. The process had started early with Tyson. A heavyweight division bereft of an Ali, a Frazier or a Foreman craved a fighter with the capacity to excite. Tyson had that capacity, of course.

An entire industry can develop around a figure like Tyson. Television companies thrive off advertising revenue and that revenue comes in thicker and faster when the viewers can be guaranteed. Few programs can deliver that guarantee. *Friends* and *ER* are exceptional. Big sports events, like the World Series and Super Bowl, are also surefire: television companies charge premium rates for the commercial slots in these telecasts. Tyson fights fell into the same category.

Then there are the venue owners. Casino owners in Vegas and Atlantic City, where gambling is legal, are always looking for attractions, these being acts or other kinds of events that draw people from far and wide. While they're in town for the attraction, the audiences spend money at the hotels and casino. All the casinos profit, but the hotel/casino staging the events profits most, both from room bookings and, more importantly, the amount spent on gambling, known as the pit drop. In its efforts to entice gamblers, Caesars Palace, in 2002, paid $98 million to Celine Dion for a three-year engagement. The same casino also signed Elton John for two years in a deal worth $50 million to the singer. So keen are casino owners to stage big fights that they regularly pay promoters millions for the privilege of playing host.

This was manna from heaven to promoters. As well as earning a fee from the tv network, they clawed in money from the casino owners. Their outgoings included the costs of promoting and marketing the fight, distributing tickets, legal fees, and other ancillaries. The biggest outgoing was the boxers' fees. Out of these came managers' and trainers' commissions. Sparring partners might earn upwards of $1,000 per week to assist in a boxer's preparations for a big fight.

The various boxing federations, such as the WBA and IBF, also take a cut. They ask for sanctioning fees, these being monies paid to the federation in return for officials, including referee, timekeeper, medical officers, and so on. And the rights to call the particular fight "a title fight."

While the IRS isn't a part of the industry itself, it draws vast sums of money from heavyweight title fights. Everyone and every business pays taxes on earnings. Or at least, they should.

An inspection of Tyson's accounts later showed that he had been seriously delinquent in paying his income tax.

These are the main interested parties in the heavyweight champion industry. Advertising agencies typically take notice if they number among their clients a company with products that have the right "fit" with the champion. Historically, boxers have not been as appealing to advertisers as baseball, basketball, or football players, the reason being that team players operate in controlled environments and are subject to more surveillance. Technically, this limits their chances of getting involved in the kind of deviant activities that will reflect poorly on products. Limits, but not eliminates: high-profile cases involving the likes of baseball's Barry Bonds and NFL player Michael Irvin have indicated that league players can be unreliable. On the other hand, George Foreman was one of the most effective endorsers ever, lending his name and image to a variety of products, including the world famous griller.

Tyson's contretemps in the LA parking lot may have introduced doubt into the minds of several prospective advertisers. But his name and image were so recognizable and his association with entertainment so strong that advertisers were prepared to take the risk. International brands like Toyota and Kodak were among the risk-takers.

Add the extra gambling money taken by the casinos, the slices taken by promoters, managers, trainers, and other personnel, the revenue absorbed from ad agencies by television, the added sales of products endorsed, the fees charged by the boxing organizations, and the taxes paid by everyone concerned and you arrive at a turnover of around $25 million per year. This is excluding the boxer's earnings of $12 million in 1987. Tyson might have regarded himself as a fighter plain and simple; but he was also the center of a medium-size industry just by becoming the heavyweight champion.

As such, he commanded the attention of several figures, all of whom sought to profit from him, some directly, others indirectly. Donald Trump was a member of the latter camp who wanted to become a member of the former. He was the son of a New York real estate developer who, in 1976, bought a decayed Manhattan hotel, restored it, sold a piece of it to Hyatt and relaunched it as the 1,300-room Grand Hyatt Hotel. In the process, he began building a property empire that included two hotel/casinos in Atlantic City and one in Las Vegas. Trump, more than anyone, was responsible for transforming AC from a cheap and seedy retreat for smalltime gamblers into a genuine rival to Vegas. One of the ways he engineered this was by attracting bigtime boxing.

There was no bigger attraction than Tyson. Having won all three heavyweight titles, Tyson was in demand, especially from the Vegas casinos, who had prospered from his previous five fights. Tyson had fought in Atlantic City nine times before, particularly in his early career. But as undisputed world champion he was a much more marketable and so more expensive commodity. It seemed unthinkable that he would make the first defense as unified champion anywhere apart from Las Vegas. Trump decided otherwise and persuaded him to fight Tyrell Biggs at the Atlantic City Convention Hall, which was linked by a walkway to Trump Plaza, one of Trump's prime properties.

Biggs' credibility as a challenger was helped by the fact that he had won an Olympic gold medal at the 1984 games, something that had evaded Tyson. He'd boxed competently, if uninspiringly, as a pro, winning fifteen consecutive fights. Tyson, though, was a much more complete professional and looked in little danger from the outset. The taller Biggs prodded away from long distance, but never seriously threatened Tyson, who brought matters to a close in the seventh. The referee stepped in with Biggs, groggy and bleeding from the eye, looking grateful for the intervention.

After the fight, Tyson claimed rancorously that he had it within his power to have ended the fight in the third round. "But, I did it very slowly," he explained. "I wanted him to remember it for a long time." In his 1989 book *Blood Season: Tyson and the world of boxing*, Phil Berger recounts how Tyson chilled a post-fight press conference with his creepy analogy: "When I was hitting him [Biggs] to the body, he was making noises . . . like a woman screaming" (p. 199).

Known for his phrase "the art of the deal," Trump rubbed his hands together at the prospect of a rewarding relationship with

Tyson, or, more specifically, his managers and the promoter Don King. A Tyson fight might cost him a site fee, as it's called, of anything up to $11 million (the price he paid for the privilege of hosting Tyson vs. Michael Spinks in mid-1988), but, if it meant more coins dropping in the slots and more chips pushed across the green baize, then it made sense. There's no evidence that Trump was a fight fan: his interest in Tyson was strictly business.

For a while, it looked like Trump's association with Tyson would help him become a player in boxing. He'd paid $3.5 million for Spinks' fight with Cooney earlier in 1987 and broken even on the gate money. His profit came through the increase in pit drop, which was about $5 million.

Of the other business interests that gravitated toward Tyson, those of HBO were central. Over the summer of 1987, Seth Abraham of the subscription cable tv company negotiated a seven-fight deal with Tyson's co-managers, Bill Cayton and Jim Jacobs. It was worth $26.5 million. From HBO's perspective, writing a promoter into the deal was important: it entrusted the important role of organizing the show to someone with the know-how and so provided stability and continuity. From Tyson's perspective, it meant committing himself to just one promoter.

But the business interests closest to Tyson were those of his co-managers. After the death of Cus D'Amato, Cayton and Jacobs had steered Tyson to the titles and the capital that came with them. The rough division of labor was: Cayton, the business affairs; Jacobs, the boxing affairs – though, in reality, they meshed. Jacobs had leukemia and his health had been in steady decline until the second half of 1987, when his condition began to decline markedly.

Shortly before his death, Jacobs signed a new contract with Tyson and Cayton. Under the agreement, Jacobs' wife would inherit his commission in the event of his death. She wouldn't take any active part in guiding Tyson, however: Cayton would assume full management responsibility.

The legality, indeed propriety, of the deal was never in question. Tyson entered into it voluntarily, presumably satisfied that the working relationship that had proved so productive and remunerative was worth extending. Tyson had signed his first contract when he was 18, as he approached his first professional fight. He'd extended it in October, 1986, for four years. The 1988 contract superseded this, effectively terminating the earlier contract. In the earlier contract, Jacobs, as manager, assigned to Cayton half of his interest. The standard arrangement on a boxer–manager contract is that the manager is entitled to a third of all of a boxer's purses. This was unexceptional. The unusual aspect of the 1988 contract was the provision for the transfer of duties and commissions. If Cayton died, his interest would transfer to his wife; if Jacobs died – and he was due to undergo chemotherapy – his interest would transfer to his wife.

While Tyson had no compunction about entering into the agreement in February, 1988, he effected a U-turn after Jacobs' death and sought to nullify the agreement, expressing his desire for King to guide his career – which, of course, he did, at least until Tyson sensed that his leap from Cayton's frying pan was only as far as King's inferno.

There are at least two ways of looking at Tyson's change of allegiance: he was either becoming more independent-minded, or he was being persuaded by King's rhetoric. Or possibly both. The circles in which Tyson was moving were certainly changing. Sharpton's continual haranguing of a society where whites dispense justice according to their own dictates must have made some sort of impression. King supplied simple but perhaps appealing theories about a conspiracy to disempower black men, especially the visibly successful ones.

Even if these dizzying ideas didn't reach an immediately receptive subject, they would have seemed that much more plausible when set in context. A black teenage girl was claiming that a gang of white police officers had raped her and investigators were making no headway. Was it an isolated case? Or was it characteristic of a culture that viewed blacks as the detritus of slavery?

Tyson expressed his desire to lend his weight to Brawley's case. He actually told Jacobs that he wanted to get involved and it was Jacobs who put him together with King. As a white man, Jacobs felt that his presence would be inappropriate. King was the ideal person to accompany Tyson when he met Brawley. What Jacobs didn't see was that Tyson had become a philosopher's stone – a substance that can turn other metals into gold. He had the rare commodity under contract, but there were many other covetous parties. King was one of them.

When Tyson decided he wanted to make a public pronouncement of his sympathy and support for Brawley, Jacobs sensed King's influence was enlarging and urged caution. A press conference was convened. Tyson made his pledges. On the same day, Jacobs checked in to Mount Sinai Hospital in Manhattan. Coincidentally, Cayton was also admitted to hospital and, while he recovered in days, Jacobs' condition deteriorated. He died on March 23, 1988.

"There is a world of difference between prejudiced individuals and a social system institutionally committed to prejudice," wrote Lerone Bennett Jr in the 1975 edition of his *The Shaping of Black America*. Sometime between late 1987 and early 1988, Tyson seems to have grasped that world of difference. Surrounded by white men he trusted and who, he believed, had counseled him wisely, Tyson was aware he lived in a nation populated by white racists. He would also have been aware that there were other whites to whom racism was an abhorrence. He regarded his immediate company as part of the latter.

Perhaps it was the Brawley case, perhaps it was the hectoring of Sharpton or the whispering of King. Most probably it was the combination of these that pushed Tyson to a new synthesis. The idea of a social system's being loaded against the interests of black people seems to have become more plausible for Tyson as he enjoyed the first fruits of his championship reign. He began to develop a new perception of himself as a black person. The relatively sudden reversal of faith in Cayton, the sniping remarks against Jews, the mockery of blacks who were prepared to assimilate into white culture and the unquestioning rush toward the welcoming arms of King all suggest a man in the midst of change.

—— twelve ——

GIVE HIM ENOUGH TIME AND THE NIGGER WILL COME OUT IN HIM AGAIN

White America's material and moral right to dominate all others was once beyond question – almost. Since the 1960s, those rights have disintegrated. In a context where racism is officially condemned and white supremacist beliefs are censured, a recovery is taking place. The recovery process involves creating myths that, in some way, justify the right to rule whites once had, but have now been lost.

In the mid-1980s, Tyson was the subject of a myth. There were three elements to it. Gerald Early summarizes the first in his article "Mike's brilliant career": "The sappy story of the black street orphan taken in by a crotchety but good-hearted white boxing trainer, whose only wish was to live long enough to see the kid become a champion."

According to *Bad Intentions: The Mike Tyson story* author Peter Heller, it told: "How the brilliant, aging guru had found this troubled but talented black youth; how they had developed a father and son relationship that rescued him [Tyson] from reform school; and how D'Amato [the trainer] had taken this rough diamond and not only developed him as a fighter on the verge of greatness, but had instilled in him a sense of values and loyalty as well."

And it ended happily, as Montieth Illingworth concludes in his *Mike Tyson: Money, myth and betrayal*: "Tyson, with the guidance and love of D'Amato, had fought his way out of poverty toward a certain future of wealth and fame."

Like all myths, Tyson's embodied popular ideas made fantastical. The myth of Tyson's early life symbolically and literally told of a paternalistic old white guy who plucked a young lost soul from the ghetto and transformed him into one of the most famous, wealthy, and celebrated figures in the world. With a combination of fatherly love, wise counsel and disciplined guidance, Cus D'Amato saved Tyson. Yes, saved. Without him Tyson would definitely have ended up either dead or in prison serving time.

The salvation seemed complete when Tyson ascended to the position of the world's premier heavyweight. His personal fortune assured, his status confirmed and even his place in history made certain, Tyson had, with D'Amato's helping hand, dragged himself away from what seemed his grim destiny and found deliverance. The parts that didn't fit the script were airbrushed out.

It was a myth to excite big ideas about how America's race problem could be addressed. Through benevolence, paternalism, and compassion. If only whites could extend the same kind of magnanimity as D'Amato, the prisons would be less crowded and the welfare lines would be shorter. The myth contained great values.

But, remember: it was a myth. Even D'Amato, its originator, knew that much. In *Bad Intentions,* Heller relates how "Cus had once confided to an intimate 'Give him [Tyson] enough time and the nigger will come out in him again'" (p. 111. The insight is omitted from the first edition of Heller's text).

Outwardly, D'Amato kept up appearances, spinning out his classic tale of poverty and redemption. It was a fiction eagerly conveyed by a media hungry for melodrama and consumed by a public willing to believe almost anything good about race. The myth even had a name, "Cus and the Kid." It was first spun during Tyson's amateur days and, later, became a saleable way of presenting Tyson, the ghetto child made good.

D'Amato himself was from the Bronx. Born in 1908, D'Amato didn't box competitively, though he was attracted to the culture surrounding boxing and opened a gym in Manhattan. Drafted in 1942, D'Amato remained a GI on American soil throughout the war. On his return to civilian life, he resumed the running of his gym. He cultivated his own philosophy of boxing based on fear. Contrary to common sense, fear, according to D'Amato, was a prerequisite of competitive success. Those who didn't experience fear were either unaware of the seriousness of competition or not motivated enough to succeed. The trick, for D'Amato, was not to let fear take a complete grip.

D'Amato gave every boxer the same illustration of a deer crossing an open field. "Suddenly, instinct tells him danger is there," D'Amato related, "and nature begins the survival process, which involves the body releasing adrenaline into the bloodstream, causing the heart to beat faster and enabling the deer to perform extraordinary feats of agility and strength." This was D'Amato's own version of the "flight or fight" syndrome: when the body's arousal system is fully activated, there are only two basic choices available – get running, or battle it out. His boxers were taught to take the latter choice, of course.

In 1949, D'Amato met Floyd Patterson, who was in a school for emotionally disturbed young people. Patterson supplied D'Amato with the raw material for a project. He openly admitted that Patterson, being completely receptive to his thoughts, gave him the kind of unquestioning dedication he needed to make his big idea work. And it did work: Patterson surfaced as a quality fighter, winning gold at the 1952 Olympics, at middleweight, then growing into an accomplished heavyweight. D'Amato instructed him to box in an unusual but effective style that became known as peekaboo: he carried his protective gloves high, peeping from behind them to throw punches.

Sport psychologists later took up some of the principles laid down by D'Amato. For example, he taught imaging, without actually calling it that. Boxers would silently imagine throwing a shot, or defending one, over and over again. He also encouraged his boxers to switch to a kind of autopilot once they were in the ring, so that they never really had to think about what they were doing. This is now called automaticity: highly skilled athletes perform without conscious control of their movements.

Patterson may never be remembered as one of the great champions, but he took advantage of the void left by Rocky Marciano's retirement and became an efficient heavyweight titleholder. His reign was interrupted by the Swedish Ingemar Johansson, whom Patterson beat twice in rematches, and was ended savagely by Sonny Liston.

Up to and perhaps beyond the mid-1960s, bigtime boxing in the US was virtually controlled by organized crime. D'Amato's strenuous efforts to avoid becoming mixed up led him toward a kind of paranoid lifestyle. He suspected everyone and insisted on having complete custody of his boxers. He was what became known as a "control freak," devising the means to dictate every facet of his boxers' lives. This is what eventually persuaded him to set up camp in a remote part of the Catskill Mountains, far away from the influences of the city, where he could keep all his charges under close surveillance. Here D'Amato, his trainers, boxers, and aides lived in a large Victorian house. The house's title was in the name of Camille Eward, whose sister had married D'Amato's older brother, Tony. The exact nature of the relationship between Camille Eward and Cus D'Amato is not clear: they cohabited at the house from 1968, though never married or had children.

D'Amato trained José Torres to the world light-heavyweight championship in 1965. Torres, who had won a silver medal at the 1956 Olympics, was born in Puerto Rico and relocated to the USA to submit himself to D'Amato's regime. His period as world champion was neither long nor distinguished, though it added to D'Amato's credentials. After retiring, Torres became the chair of the New York State Athletic Council and wrote a biography of Muhammad Ali. He continued to associate with the Catskill camp and befriended Tyson. The friendship yielded a book on Tyson, *Fire and Fear*, published in 1989.

After Torres, there were no potential world champions at the D'Amato camp. Teddy Atlas' career was shattered by injury and he became a trainer. His friend Kevin Rooney was a contender, but never managed to snare a title. He also became a trainer. Both were instrumental in shaping Tyson's boxing style.

This was most of the cast in the myth: a bunch of misfits, including a slightly eccentric but benevolent patriarch who favored the austere solitude of the mountains, a woman, who cooked, cleaned and generally kept the camp together, and an

assembly of young men, many using boxing as a kind of rehabilitation after an early life of crime. Tyson fell into this category.
When he was introduced to D'Amato, he had already compiled
a prodigious rap sheet and was on course to live what would, in
all statistical probability, be a short life, most of it spent behind
bars.

The link between Tyson and D'Amato was Bobby Stewart, a
former pro boxer, who was working as a supervisor at the Tryon
School for Boys, Johnstown in upstate New York. It was a security facility for young offenders. Tyson was only 13 when he was
sent there. For the previous two years, he'd been in and out of
juvenile detention centers, his offenses usually involving theft
and violence.

Stewart was in charge of Tryon's boxing program. Boxing was
thought to produce what might be called the *Angels with Dirty
Faces* effect. As in the classic Michael Curtiz movie of the 1930s,
youths were drawn away from their fatalistic resignation to a life
of crime and taught to assume charge of their own destinies. The
morally and socially uplifting power of sports is underlined by
the sense of purpose and achievement that seems to emerge from
even the most limited success in sports.

While watching Tyson, Stewart saw something out of the ordinary. At 13, he was already about 190 lbs, yet only 5 foot 8 inches
tall. The powerful mesomorph was untutored in boxing skills,
but his appetite for fighting and his immense strength made him
a formidable presence in the ring. Stewart was impressed
enough to take him to meet D'Amato, then 72 and aching to discover one more world champion.

Most early accounts of Tyson's life stress that he was abun-
dantly motivated and pestered Stewart to teach him boxing
skills. It could also have been straightforward opportunism: life
at the Catskill camp was no picnic, but it was better than at the
facility; and the food was good. Tyson impressed D'Amato sufficiently for him to offer him a residency at the Victorian center-
piece of the camp. All he had to do was fight. As this was
something he'd been doing since he was a bespectacled child
with a lisp who seemed ripe for bullying, it must have seemed
a good deal.

Neither were D'Amato's motivations as philanthropic as the popular myth was to suggest. Besides Patterson and Torres, D'Amato hadn't produced a world champion, or anyone who came close. In Tyson, he espied a young man who could fulfill his ambitions. There were also pecuniary advantages of having an above-average heavyweight – and such is the interest in heavyweights relative to lighter boxers that any big man who can fight decently is guaranteed several lucrative paydays. D'Amato doesn't appear to have been an acquisitive kind, but he had money problems: in 1971, he declared bankruptcy, owing hundreds of thousands of dollars in tax. His friends and associates, Jim Jacobs and Bill Cayton, provided funds for the upkeep of the camp, but they expected something for their money. Namely, a fighter who would furnish a return on their investment.

Whatever the various motivations of the principals in the myth, their interests converged on June 30, 1980, the date of Tyson's 14th birthday, when he was formally released into D'Amato's custody.

Tyson's biographers uncritically accept D'Amato's prescience. "The next heavyweight champion of the world," is how D'Amato is said to have described Tyson to anyone who would listen. Every account maintains that D'Amato was convinced that Tyson was on a predetermined path to the title. It makes for good romance, though a trainer in his seventies has usually had his fair share of false alarms. Young terriers, at 14, can be also-rans by the time they're 24. Injuries, demoralizing defeats, distractions: there are too many reasons to list why a promising young athlete might fail to fulfill potential. D'Amato had been involved in sports too long to be carried away by the sight of a stocky teenager, possessed of strength and punching power. Even if he mentioned that he thought Tyson would become a heavyweight champion, it's unlikely that it was anything other than wishful thinking. Or maybe a motivational device to keep Tyson himself focused. D'Amato was a trainer, not a visionary.

Tyson grew up according to a code, a code of the street. If you didn't wear the right kinds of footwear, or did well at school, you could expect to get beaten up; and, if you don't show "nerve" when it happens, then you could expect it to happen again and again. Young men lived by a code that prescribed their "maleness," and fighting – as well as getting women pregnant – was a potent signifier of this.

He came from a neighborhood where residents reacted to the sound of a driveby shooting as others might to a car alarm. Where they shrugged at mothers who spent welfare cheques on clothes in preference to food. They lived with every urban pathogen: compound-dysfunctional families, homelessness, crack babies, teenage pregnancies, and internecine conflicts. People from Brownsville tended to watch their backs.

At Catskill, Tyson needed to adapt to a different code, one in which discipline had the highest priority. The other boxers at the camp had either adopted the new code or left. D'Amato may not have been quite the martinet many thought him to be, though Atlas was. Atlas, as head trainer of the camp, was a disciple of D'Amato. He preached his principles and practiced his methods; he demanded absolute obedience from the boxers. This became a source of tension: Tyson, as D'Amato himself had privately suspected, could quickly revert to the code of the street if circumstances changed. Atlas accepted that argument and imposed a strict regimen on Tyson.

The problem, as Atlas saw it, was that D'Amato was relaxing his own strictures and extending more slack to Tyson. For instance, Atlas would punish Tyson for an infraction by banning him from the gym for a set period, only to discover that D'Amato brought Tyson to the gym after the training sessions had finished and put him through a private routine. Atlas sensed that D'Amato had watched the early development of Tyson and suspected that Tyson was his one last chance of a heavyweight champion. Even if D'Amato wasn't as won over as the myth later suggested, he must have known that Tyson had as good a chance as any of the other mediocre hopefuls in the division. So, he didn't want to drive Tyson away. While Atlas persevered in maintaining the discipline of the camp, D'Amato discriminately flouted his own rules.

Whether the favoritism derived from expediency or a particular empathy with Tyson's struggle to adapt to the new code isn't known. But, for sure, it incensed Atlas, who found his authority progressively undermined by D'Amato's lenience. Contrary to the popular myth, Tyson didn't submit himself to a Spartan regime and drop his old wayward habits. On several occasions, Atlas was forced to deal with troublesome situations in which Tyson had become offensive with locals. The single most difficult came with Atlas' discovery that Tyson had made unwelcome advances to his wife's 11-year-old sister. Atlas thrust a .38 revolver at Tyson's head and threatened to kill him if he repeated the behavior (the episode covered in the introduction of this book).

It effectively finished what had been a conflictual, but fruitful, relationship between Tyson and Atlas. Tyson won nineteen of twenty amateur fights and probably several other fights on unlicensed promotions. Tyson didn't forgive Atlas and never acknowledged him as a formative influence on his athletic career. Atlas left the camp and was replaced by his former friend, Rooney. "Former" because Atlas believed Rooney would support his stance in relation to Tyson, but Rooney remained loyal to D'Amato. Atlas went on to become an eminent boxing trainer and analyst based in New York City.

Rooney, like D'Amato, was white. This might not have been relevant to Tyson in 1982, but it became a source of discomfort to him in later years, especially as the other members of his backroom crew, Jacobs and Cayton, were also white. But, while Tyson was on an upward curve, it made no difference. The only significant reverse came in the Olympic trials, when Tyson was beaten twice by Henry Tillman, who justified his selection to the US team by winning the heavyweight gold medal. Tyson next met Tillman in 1990, when they were both pros: Tyson knocked him out in the first round.

The style of fighting Tyson had learned courtesy of D'Amato and Rooney was much more suited to the pros. Amateur boxing rewards clearly visible shots to the head. The force of the shots is less important than their cleanness; a clean punch is delivered to a target area, the prime one being the head, with the knuckle part of the glove only. Tyson specialized in overwhelming opponents with a cascade of several shots, all of them thrown with what he memorably described as "bad intentions."

Failure at the Olympic trials may have been a blessing for Tyson. He was able to proceed through his first year as a professional in peaceful obscurity. Olympic champions typically sign remunerative contracts that tie them to a specific promoter and television company. Every fight is a kind of showcase for them. By contrast, Tyson's transition into the pro ranks went relatively unnoticed. His application for a pro license was filed on November 5, 1984, when Tyson was 18. On the form, D'Amato was his trainer and his managers were Jim Jacobs and Bill Cayton.

Having two managers was irregular. Jacobs was a friend and confidant of D'Amato's. An all-round athlete himself, he had excelled at handball, though the Korean War interrupted his career. Still, he won multiple titles and was one of the finest players of the 1960s. He was also a collector of old fight films. It was this pastime – perhaps minor obsession would be more apt – that brought him into contact with Cayton, who advanced him the money to travel to Australia to procure a rare film of the Jess Willard vs. Jack Johnson fight of 1918, which took place in Havana.

Jacobs and Cayton formed a business partnership in 1960, specializing in old boxing film syndication. It proved to be a successful venture. Jacobs was known to have other sources of income, though he was secretive about them. Cayton's interest in sports was more straightforwardly commercial. The son of a New York stockbroker, Cayton graduated from the University of Maryland, then worked for the DuPont chemicals corporation before starting his own advertising agency.

In 1948, when domestic television was beginning its rise, he gained the rights to classic fights and presented them as "Greatest Fights of the Century." Basically, he wanted to use the program to showcase a men's hair care product. When he amalgamated his own collection of news reels with that of Jacobs, he had an unmatchable collection. (In 1998, Cayton sold the entire collection to ESPN for a reported $100 million.)

Cayton handled the commercial side of their operation, while Jacobs, already known as a top athlete, became the public face of the business. Together they branched into other endeavors, including boxing management. In the late 1970s, Jacobs and Cayton managed, among others, Esteban de Jesús, Wilfred Benitez, and Edwin Rosario, all of whom held world titles.

Jacobs met D'Amato while presenting a screening of some old fight films. Their friendship yielded a business arrangement. D'Amato supervised the training of boxers, Jacobs made the fights and Cayton tidied up the business end. Jacob and Cayton would send their fighters to Catskill for periods leading up to fights. After D'Amato had taken charge of Tyson, he approached Jacobs and Cayton, who provided the funds for his early development and agreed to steer his professional career.

Tyson had his first professional fight on March 6, 1985, against Hector Mercedes, thus conferring a recognizable if dubious status on Mercedes, who can claim to be the first man to step into a professional ring with Tyson. After three quick wins in fewer than three months, Bob Arum, the promoter, featured Tyson in his *Top Rank Boxing* show that aired regularly on ESPN. It was national television exposure, though without the fanfare that would have accompanied him had he won an Olympic medal. It was also a fight-by-fight arrangement. Cayton judiciously avoided signing Tyson to any longterm deal.

It was during this period that the Tyson myth loomed large. The tale of an African American youth who appeared on a fast track from the ghetto to the joint, yet was derailed by a kind-hearted white trainer and steered toward greatness, was a brilliant accompaniment to the images of the terrible Tyson wreaking destruction in the ring. Yet, it was cheesy, trite and insipid. So why did it work?

Illingworth had a plausible answer: because the myth incorporated messages, or motifs, that endorsed two postulates that are central to American culture. They are, as Illingworth expressed them: "Charity is better than fundamental social change, and love, combined with the human will, conquers all" (p. 84).

In other words, the myth of "Cus and the Kid," as it became known, was an exemplar of reform "of the most passive variety," as Illingworth put it. Two decades after civil rights legislation and still the seemingly intractable race problem troubled the nation. It was as if those problems were being solved right there on the tv screen: an urban black youth fighting like mad to escape the ghetto and, most importantly, winning. And he was winning thanks to the encouragement and assistance of do-gooder whites. This was social change lite.

To work, the myth had to involve a degree of typecasting, assigning characters to stock types with which people could identify; stereotypes, in other words. Illingworth argued that one of the consequences of the myth was that: "Tyson was made into a black stereotype of the post-civil rights era in which equal political and social rights had supposedly been obtained" (p. 84).

While it wasn't made explicit by the myth, the subtext, on this account, was that, no matter how unpromising their circumstances were, African Americans had the opportunity to leave them behind. They needed to cultivate ambitions, work hard, stay determined, and, above all, persevere. Tyson satisfied all these conditions. He did so with some assistance, but he stuck to his task. Herein lay a lesson for all those blacks who carped endlessly about how the system was stacked against them and how the Man would never allow blacks more than a modicum of success.

It was an appealing and potent stereotype. In her book *For Entertainment Purposes Only?* Reba L. Chaisson has observed: "Stereotypes are one way in which racial identities have been denigrated over the last century, and they have materialized under the auspices of entertainment" (pp. 7–8).

While Chaisson was writing about black representations in film, her point holds good for sports: "Entertainment provides both a sense of security during troubled times and escapism during periods of leisure." Her point is that the stereotypes seep into consciousness when our critical defenses are down, while we are being entertained. They provide the reassurance that comes through familiarity.

The Tyson story was marvelous entertainment and functional ideology rolled into one. Tyson was a recognizable stereotype thrust into a changing landscape, in which his chances were abundant. Older myths about the permanence of racism,

poverty, and the cycles of despair that affected the black population were replaced by something altogether more satisfying.
Civil rights had brought forth a new dawn for America.

Tyson, in his way, proved this. He was to become evidence of
fouler aspects of post-civil rights America. As the advances
brought by the 1960s legislation slowed, stopped or were even
reversed – during the Reagan years, in particular – the Tyson
stereotype mutated.

———

Apart from Illingworth, there were others who sensed bogus elements in the myth. Gerald Early, for example, in his account of
"Mike's brilliant career," questions whether D'Amato had such
a great boxing mind or peerless coaching techniques.
"Certainly Tyson would have become champion had he been
instructed by almost any of the first-rate boxing teachers," wrote
Early in *Transition* (fall, 1996). "D'Amato had no special knowledge or insight into Tyson's ability."

Early pointed out that neither of D'Amato's previous champions, Patterson or Torres, were "particularly notable fighters."
This is a harsh appraisal, though a legitimate one. It's possible
that any of the other eminent trainers of the day, including
Emanuel Steward, Eddie Futch, or Lou Duva, could have pol-
ished Tyson's technical proficiency and guided him to a world
title. Whether they would have had D'Amato's patience we'll
never know. And whether Tyson would have maintained his
resolve amid the distractions of downtown Philadelphia,
Steward's base, or Detroit, where Futch operated, again, we'll
never know.

During an address in which he criticized President George
Bush's decision to send federal troops to Los Angeles to quell
the Rodney King riots of 1992, Alton H. Maddox Jr, the attorney
who represented Tawana Brawley, rebuked D'Amato, saying he
"did not understand how he got custody of Mike Tyson in the
first place." Maddox went on to ask: "How did the state of New
York permit a racist white man, whose cultural [values] were different [from] Mike Tyson['s] to gain custody of him? How could
he go into a prison system, put a rope around Mike's neck, and
drag him back to the Catskill Mountains to teach him how to box

and entertain white people?" (quoted in *The Philadelphia Tribune*, vol. 109, May 22, 1992).

Illingworth offers a third argument when he compares the presentation of the early Tyson to that of former heavyweight champion Joe Louis. Louis was memorably described – with no irony intended – as a "credit to his race." In the context of the segregated 1930s, when Louis was active, this was a compliment. Civil rights were not an issue and African Americans were "expected to feel empowered by the myth of individual salvation," as Illingworth puts it. "And yet, blacks had to 'behave,' especially when they obtained a measure of success that placed them in the public spotlight" (p. 84).

Jacobs and Cayton, perhaps more so than D'Amato, had the Louis model in mind when they projected Tyson. He had to appear controllable. Wild, naturally. Fearsome, yes. Brutal, of course. But, ultimately, under the control of three whites. He was safe.

Together, the views of Early, Maddox, and Illingworth offer an alternative reading of the Tyson-D'Amato story. Early detects a significance in the way Tyson, in his early career, constantly alluded to the feats of great fighters of the past, especially white fighters, like Jack Dempsey and Rocky Marciano. On Early's account this "made him a mainstream figure . . . someone with whom whites could, on some level, identify."

The fortunes of black boxers have been followed avidly by African Americans over the years. Since the days of Jack Johnson, special interest has been paid to their successes, which were in many cases (especially those of Johnson and Louis) attributed with symbolic relevance. But the real market base of professional boxing is the white population. You don't earn $10 million a fight without appealing to a wider and more lucrative market than African Americans. White demand has always driven boxing, as it has all other forms of popular entertainment. In the 1930s, the demand was for a black person who was as formidable in the ring as he was servile outside it.

By the 1980s, the context had changed. Cultural changes, many ushered in by civil rights, had made a submissive, Louis-type champion anachronistic and implausible. Whites may have detested Ali in the 1960s, but in the 1970s, he seemed exactly right for the times. They wanted a champion who was more defiantly black, a figure representative of the times. Like Ali, Tyson was someone with whom whites could identify – "on some level," as Early was careful to qualify his statement.

While Early never explained what this level was, another writer, David Samuels, offered a parallel when writing for *New Republic* about the pre-eminent rap band of the 1980s, Public Enemy. We considered Samuels' argument earlier in the book, when discussing the appeal of rap: it is that Public Enemy and other rap artists became whites' emblems of black radicalism. It was like they offered whites an invitation to an alternative world, a dangerous world at which they could peer as if down a semiautomatic rifle sight. This is the kind of level on which whites would identify with Tyson; like inquisitive peeping toms wanting to know more about black culture but from the safety of distance. "People could watch the problems of the black urban underclass being solved for them in the comfort of their living rooms," wrote Illingworth (p. 84).

This enhanced Tyson's entertainment value in a way that maybe even Jacobs and Cayton didn't realize. But, as Maddox submitted, he was certainly employed to entertain whites. It was well-paid employment and, far from being dragged along with a rope around his neck as Maddox argued, Tyson assented to it.

The myth survived D'Amato. On November 4, 1985, the trainer slipped into a coma and eventually died, aged 77. He had suffered from interstitial pulmonary fibrosis. Tyson had won his first 11 fights and, though there were stories of his bedside vow never to fight again, he was back in action within nine days. As with any athlete who loses his mentor, let alone surrogate parent and counselor-in-chief, there were doubts about Tyson's aptitude to progress further without D'Amato. Tyson responded to them with six straight knockout wins in little more than two months, four wins achieved within the first round. Following one of those wins (a one-round KO over David Jaco), Tyson told a local reporter from the *Times Union*, Albany, New York: "When you see me smash somebody's skull, you enjoy it." It was a soul-

226

less yet insightful commentary on the ghoulish appetites of fight fans and, perhaps, white America.

In February, 1986, Tyson began a five-fight deal with ABC television worth $1 million. Cayton had negotiated a flexible arrangement that permitted Tyson to appear on other tv channels while fulfilling the ABC contract. Tyson was approaching the end of his first year as a professional when he stopped Jesse Ferguson in six rounds. It was an impressive showing on national television, though Tyson's post-fight reflections made it something of a landmark: "I tried to punch him and drive the bone of his nose back into his brain."

It was a vicious comment and, once picked up by national media, it added a new feature to the myth. Tyson with D'Amato was a young black kid with a lot of talent and a benevolent tutor who knew how to make the most of that talent. Tyson without D'Amato might be a depraved, iniquitous, immoral, and vile degenerate who took pleasure in inflicting pain and suffering on others. The question was: which one of these was more entertaining?

Phil Berger, in his 1989 book *Blood Season: Tyson and the world of boxing*, wrote of Tyson (though he surely meant the *image* of Tyson): "He had the primeval passion for, and pleasure in his task" (p. 125). He points out that Tyson was not given to doling out clichés in the aftermath of a fight; nor was his expression a "slip of the tongue."

Tyson tried to wriggle out of accusations of sadism by insisting his remarks about Ferguson were made in jest, though subsequent declarations tended to weaken this. While few understood it at the time – and perhaps even now – Tyson had an intuitive understanding of the sources of his own attraction. "*You* enjoy it," he had advised the Albany journalist. Maybe he was having a kind of fun of his own in the ring, taking satisfaction from each win, trying to improve with each successive performance and accumulating gratification all the time. The nature of his sport meant that the source of his own fulfillment would be someone else's suffering.

It's unlikely that, after a year in the pro ranks, Tyson hadn't stumbled on an elemental truth: that boxing fans, while admiring the skill and artistry that are both parts of the "sweet science," also like to witness one human being inflict pain on another. It's perhaps the worst-kept secret about boxing, but one that has an ageless pertinence. Tyson was certainly not the first boxer to recognize the dark truth. But few others can have so forcefully reminded their audiences of it.

Seven months after Tyson had served notice of his intentions, he fought for the first of three world titles. In between he recorded nine consecutive wins, only one lasting the full ten rounds. That was against James "Quick" Tillis, whose nickname suggested his most prominent trait: his speed and evasion made Tyson chase, but the result was never in doubt. Perhaps his easiest fight was against Marvis Frazier, son of Joe Frazier, former foe of Ali. Frazier's purse was $300,000. "For Marvis to make the kind of money he was getting for Tyson, he'd have to fight five bouts against quality opponents," his manager was quoted by father Joe in his *Smoking Joe: The autobiography* (p. 193).

Despite being schooled in the famed Frazier crouch-and-hook style, Marvis simply didn't have his father's modus operandi and was consumed by Tyson in thirty warlike seconds. Reviving his son after the devastation, Joe looked across at the triumphant Tyson and asked anyone who was listening: "What is this guy? An animal?" The response was equivocal.

Just months before, in February, Tyson and a friend had been ejected from Filenes, a department store in an Albany shopping mall, after causing a disturbance. According to local reports, Tyson approached a saleswoman, who spurned his advances. Stung by the rebuff, Tyson started a commotion, using abusive language at the woman and scattering merchandise around the store. Coarse behavior is common among athletes, especially celebrities who are used to getting their own way. Tyson wasn't yet a celebrity, though he was known locally and the incident stirred enough interest for Jacobs and Rooney to respond with a damage limitation exercise.

Had Tyson been a football or basketball player, the behavior might have prompted some judgmental posturing and little else. Tyson, though, was a heavyweight boxer and the feral aggression he displayed in the ring complemented the wild demeanor outside. Complemented, that is, in the eyes of the media. The department store occurrence was a minor incident at the time; even the store's security officers described it as "very minor." Only later, when Tyson's fame had grown and his reputation had evolved, did the episode take on relevance: retrospectively, it was interpreted as the first instance of a pattern of unrestrained conduct.

Other boxers have fought with the kind of brutal disregard associated with savagery. In this respect, Tyson shared common ground with many of the greats, including Jake LaMotta, Rocky Marciano, and Roberto Duran. LaMotta's violent personal life paralleled his boxing career, as Martin Scorsese's 1980 biopic *Raging Bull* dramatically depicted. Tyson's out-of-ring transgressions in the 1980s were arguably no worse than LaMotta's or many other contemporary athletes and may have been a lot less serious. Yet in Tyson's case there was a coagulation of private and professional: you couldn't separate the primal creature that terrorized the boxing ring from the guy at the mall.

The emerging image of Tyson the boxer was that of an inhumanly combative and possibly indestructible force that recognized no obstacles. Build a brick wall in front of him and he would smash right through it. Human hindrance was ineffective. Even as early as July, 1986, when he all but dismembered Frazier, the word on Tyson was simple: he could not be stopped.

Yet, there was something else. As Berger wrote: "The feeling grew that Tyson's 'moodiness' might harbor a darker side" (p. 128). This may have been connecting to the gloomy, morose expression Tyson carried with him to the ring. Wearing no socks and covered only by a towel across his back, Tyson would enter the ring, flexing his shoulders, his gloves clasped together, his face a mask of ill humor. It was a vision as exciting for fans as it must have been forbidding for opponents. Berger contends that, as Tyson's celebrity status built, inquisitive fans wanted to know more about the "real" Tyson as opposed to Tyson the destroyer. D'Amato, Jacobs and Cayton were intent on keeping Tyson's personal life smothered. In the absence of raw material, fans began to suspect that the shadowy character they saw in the ring was all there was.

Still, the myth was transcending. As Tyson marched onwards and upwards, the fable of the street kid and his benefactor surpassed the trifling doubts that at least some quarters were harboring. Even without D'Amato the combined stealth of Jacobs and Cayton was enough to sustain the convenient fiction for at least another eighteen months. Cayton, in particular, seems to have stayed mindful of its marketing value when negotiating with television.

But with D'Amato gone and Tyson already a millionaire and a certain champion, a different kind of narrative began to replace it. In this story, Tyson was no longer an unseasoned youth guided by an elderly sage, but an ungovernable bundle of barbaric impulses. This multiplied fascination with Tyson, though: even as a contender, his appeal was greater than any boxer since Ali and arguably greater than any other athlete in the world during the 1980s.

Some measure of Tyson's allure came when he was added to a bill headed by Michael Spinks. Sales for Spinks' IBF title defense at the Las Vegas Hilton were slow before Tyson was brought in. They stood at a modest $200,000. Within days of the announcement that Tyson would appear against the former world cruiserweight champion Alonzo Ratliff, sales shot to $1.1 million. The draw was clearly not Ratliff, who was 30 years old and, at 201 lbs, giving away 20 lbs to Tyson. The crowd saw less than two rounds of Tyson in full flow. It was his final appearance before fighting for a world title.

Tyson's potential to excite not only a moribund heavyweight division or even boxing, but perhaps the entire world of sports and possibly beyond, had been sensed by HBO, which signed him to a three-right deal worth $5.5 million. This was an exorbitant amount to pay for a boxer who hadn't yet won a title. It guaranteed him the majority of the total purse when he fought for the title. This in itself was exceptional. But, HBO had its finger on the pulse. In late 1986, as Tyson approached the first of his world titles, there were few figures in or out of sports who commanded comparable interest.

———— thirteen ————

THE DEBT OF THE
GHETTO BOUND

On August 11, 1965, a white patrolman pulled over a black motorist in South Central Los Angeles. It seemed a routine stop for a traffic violation, though the exchange between the cop and the driver grew so heated that a crowd soon congregated, at first to watch the event, then to join in the wrangling. Police reinforcements were sent in and five arrests were made before the officers withdrew under a hail of stones from a throng of African Americans.

Instead of dispersing, the crowd grew and began assailing whites. Over the next few hours, rocks and Molotov cocktails were hurled, seemingly without targets. Then came a lull: police called in the National Guard and the situation seemed under control. This tactic, however, served to aggravate matters and the rioting escalated: buildings were burned and looting was rife. "Burn, baby, burn," chanted the incendiary crowd as it moved through the city.

"One of the most ravaging outbursts of Blacks in the history of this nation," is how Douglas G. Glasgow described the event in his 1980 book *The Black Underclass*. "Their rage was directed at white society's structure, its repressive institutions, and their symbols of exploitation in the ghetto: the chain stores, the oligopolies that control the distribution of goods; the lenders, those who hold the indebtedness of the ghetto bound; the absentee landlords; and the agents who control the underclass while safeguarding the rights of those who exploit it" (p. 106).

Clearly, the rage was not confined to LA. It affected African Americans everywhere. Over the next two years, there were

231

similar outbursts at other American cities. They reached a climax in the midst of the "long hot summer" of 1967, when a Detroit vice squad conducted raids on gambling dens frequented by blacks. Again, an apparently minor incident sparked a major uprising. In that year alone, police reported 150 "race riots" across the US.

The mid-1960s were a period of severe black discontent. Rioting may not have been an effective method for overthrowing the social order, but it certainly enlisted the attention of the American population and forced the problems unique to blacks into public visibility. In this sense, the riots were spectacularly successful. Reporters and cameramen rushed into the ghettos; elected and appointed officials followed behind. Academics analyzed the deep causes. A commission headed by Otto Kerner was established to identify the key issues. It concluded that the seeds of the riots were racism and the resulting poverty suffered by blacks, leading to their being undernourished, underpaid, badly clothed, and poorly housed. The USA was, according to the Kerner Report, "moving toward two societies, one black, one white – separate and unequal."

The civil rights movement had complained about precisely these features of blacks' lives, but frustration at the discrepancy between what the movement seemed to promise and what it actually delivered seems to have built.

Unemployment among African Americans had decreased since the formation of Martin Luther King's Southern Christian Leadership Conference in 1957, though it was still double that of whites. The proportion of blacks who lived in poverty remained stable at around 29 percent through the civil rights years, leading to the coining of the term *underclass* to describe the permanently poor section of the black population.

"It is not necessarily culturally deprived, lacking in aspirations, or unmotivated to achieve," wrote Glasgow of the black underclass, members of which "try to keep body and soul together and maintain a job" though without ever approaching any level of comfort, less still affluence.

Glasgow was raised in the northeastern ghetto of Bedford-Stuyvesant in Brooklyn, an area much like Watts, or Chicago's

South Side, or any other of the "war zones," as Alphonso Pinkney calls them in his *Black Americans*, "places where poverty and neglect have bred frustration that has generated widespread crime" (p. 88).

Tyson was also raised in Bed-Stuy. His mother, Lorna Smith, had joined the great migration north after the second world war and settled in Brooklyn, where she married Percel Tyson. They divorced, but Lorna kept the name Tyson. Jimmy Kirkpatrick came into her life with serious baggage: he had sixteen children, all living with their various mothers. He sired another three with Lorna: Rodney was born in 1961, Denise in 1964, and Michael in 1966. By the time Michael was born on June 30, Kirkpatrick had moved on.

Lorna worked on and off as a nurse's aide, but, with three children, relied mainly on welfare. She lived briefly with another man, Eddie Gillison, but, even with his income, the struggle rarely abated. Besides, homelife with Gillison was hardly paradisiacal; Lorna often wore the battle scars to prove it. The children would sometimes gang up on Gillison to protect their mother. Gillison died after being hit by a police car in 1987, aged 56.

The family had moved four times, each move a descent into poorer housing, before Mike Tyson's eighth birthday. Tyson's final home with his mother was in one of Brooklyn's most deprived areas, Brownsville. The family epitomized the underclass.

As a female-headed single parent family, the Tysons shared the same set-up as one in four African American families in the late 1960s. The proportion was to grow to about half of all black families by the 1990s. Brownsville was one of those forbidding areas in which the majority of young black men meet their deaths through homicide, 90 percent of them slain by other black men.

All the signs were that the young Tyson would become either one of the slain, one of the slayers and/or one of the one in three black men in their twenties who were in prison, on probation or on parole. From the 1960s, the USA's prisons filled up with black men to the point that, by the early twenty-first century, they collectively constituted half the prison population.

Taunted by his elders and called "fairy boy" on account of his lisp, Tyson retreated from the streets to care for his pigeons. He built a coop at the apartment block. His interest in birds and animals continued throughout his life. Returning to the apartment one day after school, he found that the coop had been smashed and the pigeons released. On discovering the identity of the perpetrator, Tyson plucked up enough courage to confront him. The confrontation turned violent and the young Tyson managed to overwhelm the older and bigger boy. This is an apocryphal story that became part of the Tyson myth. The tale of a plucky youngster righting wrongs by administering street justice to a vandal and, in the process, outfighting a stronger foe fitted nicely.

Tyson's aptitude for fighting probably had more mundane beginnings. He would have become accustomed to fighting just by living in places like Brownsville, where noncombatants typically become sacrificial offerings to predatory young men. Tyson became one of the latter. He earned the respect of his peers by running with gangs, snatching purses, pickpocketing, beating up and robbing drunks and any of the other petty crimes that are endemic in places like Brownsville. The police were considered almost like an enemy of occupation. "I have never feared cops," Tyson told José Torres for his *Fear and Fire*. "What pissed me off was being caught by them." His feelings were no doubt shared by his peers. "To be grabbed by these motherfuckers was to be stupid" (p. 21).

By the age of 11, he was drinking and smoking and effectively beyond parental control. The gangs became a surrogate family for him. His role models were pimps, drug dealers, and successful thieves, and his aspirations extended no further than any other ghetto resident: good jewelry, decent clothes and enough money to buy liquor. This was his version of keeping "body and soul together."

By his own estimates, Tyson was arrested 40 times by the time he was 12. He became familiar with phrases like "assault with a deadly weapon," "grand theft," and "receipt of stolen goods" and became a frequent visitor of Brooklyn's juvenile detention centers. Doing the crimes and enduring the punishments confer a certain respect in the ghetto. Even greater respect accrues to those who carry a gun. Tyson began carrying a piece. His status grew. The crimes became more serious. So did the punishments.

At 12, he found himself doing time at the Spofford Detention Center in the Bronx following an abortive attempt to snatch a roll of money from a prostitute. It was the first of several stays in the detention center, often considered a training ground for Riker's Island. At Spofford, Tyson learned that the hierarchy was based on much the same criteria as in the slums. Fighting earned respect. Once word went round that Tyson could fight, life became easier, "like a country club," he once reflected.

Tyson once mockingly pled to a judge to send him to Spofford. "All my friends are there," he joked. Or maybe he was only half-joking. Many of Tyson's friends truly were locked up and the secure, structured environment the center afforded him must have contrasted sharply with the disordered, dysfunctional world he experienced whenever he was free.

It was at Spofford that Tyson first saw Muhammad Ali. It's a somewhat romantic and idealized version of how Tyson became interested in boxing. Like most young men everywhere in the world in the 1970s, Tyson regarded Ali as a hero. Whether the sight of Ali actually triggered Tyson's interest in boxing is open to question. A much more likely inspiration was Bobby Stewart, whom Tyson met after he was sentenced to Tryon Reform School for Boys in upstate New York, 200 miles away from his family. From the day he left, he received no gifts or even birthday cards from his mother.

Historically, boxing has been a sport that attracts young black men. From the eighteenth century, when slaveowners selected their best slaves and turned them into prize fighters, boxing has been an escape route, a way off the plantations and then the ghettos. Tyson, not yet 13, had already compiled a formidable rap sheet. He had no chance of going to college and playing basketball or football. Among Tyson's peers, a baseball bat was more likely to be a weapon than a piece of sports equipment. Boxing, though, was a sport that needed little equipment. It obviously appealed to the young Tyson, who had learned the manly art of self-defense in places where Queensberry rules might just as well have been a gay speed dating operation. He approached Stewart, who had boxed professionally and was then working as a supervisor at the Tryon facility. Stewart watched Tyson, only 12 but with precocious strength. He saw in him a better-than-average fighter. In March, 1980, he took him to Catskill, where he asked Tyson to spar in the presence of his friend Cus D'Amato.

———

At 5 foot 6 inches, Tyson was unlikely to grow into a tall heavyweight (Larry Holmes, the WBC champion of the time, was 6 foot 3 inches; Tyson would eventually grow to 5 foot 11 inches). But, already 186 lbs, he would never be able to stay under the 190 lbs limit of the newly instituted cruiserweight class (which was introduced in 1979). For Kevin Rooney, Tyson looked too heavy and muscularly developed for his age; his first reaction to the sight of Tyson was to tell D'Amato to check his details. Stewart confirmed. He made no pretense about Tyson: he told D'Amato of his prodigious law-breaking, his broken family, and his reputation at Tryon. All D'Amato was interested in was whether or not he could fight.

Tyson himself was skeptical. For all Stewart's encouragement, he knew that his chances of making it to the professional boxing ranks were slim. He might not have known the statistical probabilities, but he intuitively knew that for every hundred thousand or so black kids from the ghettos who dreamed of becoming the next Ali, only a hundred or so would ever fight for good money; and, even then, for only a few years.

Stewart too was realistic. At Tryon, he might have initially harbored grandiose thoughts about rehabilitating the inmates with boxing, but he took a more pragmatic approach once in the job. He would cover up and absorb the youths' punches on his arms and gloves, letting them punch out all their anger. It was a rough-hewn therapy. When Tyson asked him to spar, he did the same. Tyson whaled away with the kind of crude, arcing shots that had won him many a street fight, but which failed to make an impact with Stewart who enclosed himself in a defensive shell. Tyson continued to flail away until Stewart let rip with a body shot which caused him to drop. Tyson climbed to his feet and resumed his tenacious, if futile pursuit. After, Tyson asked Stewart to teach him how to box.

The methods that had brought him respect in the ghettos and joints had brought only humiliation in the ring. Remember: Stewart was never more than a decent fighter, having compiled 13 wins and three defeats as a pro welterweight. If he could embarrass Tyson, what would a really good pro be able to do to him? This must have been a revelatory moment for Tyson, as if a magician had shown him a conjuring trick but not the secret of how to perform it. Stewart had the secret. But before he imparted it, he laid down a condition: improve academic grades.

Tyson could not read or write. At the time, the illiteracy rate among African Americans was 1.6 percent, compared to 0.4 percent among whites. Stewart discovered that, contrary to his own suspicions, Tyson had been classified as "borderline retarded." If Stewart had found Tyson reasonably intelligent, how could the school's psychiatrists arrive at such a contrary conclusion? The answer was that Tyson had been tested using conventional measuring instruments; as he could neither read nor write, he simply didn't understand them. Stewart then approached another black youth to help Tyson with his reading. The improvement was marked.

As Tyson's grades went up, so the time Stewart spent with him in the gym grew longer. And Tyson became a devoted, perhaps even zealous pupil. As Stewart told José Torres: "At three in the morning one could hear movement and the snorting from Mike's room, learning, perfecting what I'd taught him the day before" (p. 41).

Stewart sparred regularly with Tyson, though conceding about 30 lbs became something of a strain when Tyson's technical skills augmented his physical strength. Where he had once evaded Tyson's bull-like rushes and absorbed his unrefined slugs on his protective arms, he found himself being caught – and hurt. Stewart realized three things. First, that he couldn't carry on sparring with Tyson without ending up with cuts and bruises. Second, that he had taken Tyson as far as he could and any further improvement would come only with more experienced supervision. And, third, that Tyson had an abundance of raw power that, when allied to a proficient boxing technique, could make him a legitimate heavyweight threat.

A phonecall to his old boxing coach Matt Baransky, who was one of D'Amato's assistants, confirmed that D'Amato would take the time to watch Tyson (Baransky later worked in Tyson's corner). Most of the white people in Tyson's life up till this point had been law enforcement officers, judges, and guards. They were people who either punished or controlled him. On meeting a white guy who was supposed to be teaching him how to become a professional boxer, Tyson was suspicious. On the other hand, what were his other choices? To return to Tryon and accept that, on release, he would soon graduate to a higher-security prison? Or get shot? The alternatives must have looked very unfavorable.

D'Amato encouraged him with words of praise and a promise to turn him into tomorrow's champion if he was interested enough. Tyson was too streetwise to believe that this was anything more than a motivational tactic. But, again, his alternatives loomed. Tyson returned to Tryon determined to make a quick return to Catskill and to get started on turning himself into a pro boxer. Application was made to the New York State Corrections Department, which eventually granted Tyson permission to stay at the Catskill camp under D'Amato's supervision. Five years later, D'Amato became his legal guardian. Tyson's mother, with whom he had lost contact, died in 1982 and Tyson returned to Brooklyn for the funeral. She had known little of his boxing career, save for the occasional phonecall from Stewart. Tyson also called at one of the tenements his family had once called home. It was derelict.

At the moment Tyson moved to Catskill, one black youth had cheated fate. Avoiding the near-certain destiny that befalls denizens of the black underclass, Tyson surrendered himself to the custody of D'Amato and the Catskill team. Mythology aside, there was a bond of sorts between Tyson and his new ersatz family. It may not have been an exactly happy family, but it probably bore more resemblance to a conventional family unit than any of the centers where he had been detained and there was a semblance of stability that seems to have been absent from his own family.

Whatever D'Amato's motives – and they may not have unfurled further than adding another world champion to his résumé – the trainer pried Tyson away from correctional facilities, though, of course, not for ever. He also managed to fix Tyson's often wayward attention on a single goal, which had the effect of steering him away from the illicit activities that had kept landing him behind bars. Closeting him away in rural upstate New York may not have been an ideal rehabilitative approach, but it prevented Tyson from returning to the streets where criminality beckoned and where going straight would have been impossible for an untrained, unskilled, uneducated illiterate with an overwhelming criminal record. In other words, D'Amato's influence on Tyson lay less in what he did for Tyson, more in what he prevented Tyson doing.

Of the alternative scenarios, one is easy to surmise. For instance, in November, 1981, Tyson lost a close decision to Ernie Bennet. It was the first time he was forced to assimilate defeat and he was distraught. Still an amateur, Tyson had become accustomed to winning and his reaction to an unexpected reverse didn't manifest until eight months later, when he grew anxious and started to cry as he approached the final fight in a Junior Olympics tournament. The possibility of losing terrified him. Atlas comforted him and, eventually, psyched him back into a competitive frame of mind. So competitive, in fact, that he discovered a new level of intensity and overthrew his opponent within seconds of the first bell.

Had Atlas not been around to convert Tyson's negative anxiety into positive arousal, Tyson might not have entered the ring at all, or perhaps produced a lackluster performance and lost. Either way, it would have introduced serious doubts about Tyson's psychological makeup. Countless athletes with excellent technical skills and undoubted prowess have been known to choke on big occasions. Their confidence dissolves, their composure disintegrates and anxiety corrodes their competitive performance. Tyson won his Junior Olympics title and gathered momentum with every successive victory until the Douglas defeat in 1990, by which time both Atlas and Rooney had departed. It's arguable that Tyson never fully recovered from that loss. True, he won eight straight fights before he ran into Holyfield and lost twice back-to-back. But, once defeated, Tyson's link to his early self was always tenuous.

Had D'Amato suspected that Tyson was psychologically fragile and unlikely to fulfill his ambition of becoming a heavyweight champion, he would have been less accommodating. He might have sent Tyson packing as early as 1981, when Tyson was 15; in which case, he would never have become his legal guardian and Tyson would have been plunged back into the "war zone." In this case, we would never have heard of Mike Tyson. Or maybe Tyson would have been resourceful enough to avoid the deadfall of the ghetto.

Versed in the rudiments of boxing, Tyson might have drifted into another gym and, as Early suggested, could well have restored himself under the tutelage of one of several other experienced coaches, such as Emanuel Steward or Eddie Futch. While it's tempting to guess that history would have been very much the same had Tyson gone with one of these, it wouldn't. Both are African Americans. Don King would have found it tougher to woo Tyson away from either of these than he did Cayton, a white University of Maryland graduate whose associations with boxing began only when a client commissioned him to promote Vaseline hair tonic.

Steward, who managed world champions, such as Thomas Hearns and Dennis Andries, would have resisted King's attempts to take control of Tyson's career. It's also possible that he would have personally supervised Tyson's training in the unyielding atmosphere of the Kronk gym in Philadelphia in the crucial eight weeks prior to February 10, 1990, when Tyson suffered at the hands of Douglas. Someone like Steward might have kept Tyson as champion of the world, though whether he would have been able to prevent the calamity that ended with Tyson's imprisonment in 1992 is in doubt. The point is: there was more than one route available to Tyson in the event of a premature dismissal from Catskill. Not all roads led back to the ghetto.

———

When Atlas called D'Amato to report on how Tyson had conquered his anxiety and turned in one of his most effective performances to date, any residual doubts about Tyson's temperament must have dissipated. And a career of epic proportions began in earnest.

Within three years, Tyson opened his professional account in the obscurity of a small hall in Albany, New York. D'Amato's death in November 1985 cast Tyson adrift without his guardian, though the collectivity at Catskill continued to provide the matrix of Tyson's life. Never one to rule with a rod of iron, D'Amato had nevertheless functioned as an authority figure at the camp and, bereft of this, Tyson's errancy materialized. Thrown out of a department store, then accused of striking a parking lot attendant at an LA concert, Tyson disclosed another facet of himself that might have gone unnoticed had he not been a promising athlete.

D'Amato's influence lingered long enough for Tyson to win the first of his world titles in 1986 and seemed to evaporate by 1988, when Tyson groped at an independence of sorts by getting married to Robin Givens. Within weeks of the marriage, the death of Jimmy Jacobs left Tyson in limbo. Never quite trusting the remaining figure in the triumvirate, Tyson drifted, pulled toward King's rhetoric and his mother-in-law's persuasive, if unsound, reasoning. Hailed as the finest heavyweight since Ali and known throughout the world, Tyson was forcibly made to contend with his celebrity status: his every move was monitored by a gluttonous media ready to feast on any scraps he was wont to throw out. An auto accident when driving with his wife in 1988 made global news, especially when Tyson hamfistedly tried to resolve matters by giving away the car to the investigating police officers.

Dispatches on the turbulent and violent marriage escaped to the media via Givens' sister, though the most damning evidence came on national television, when Tyson's wife described life with him as "pure hell." A sedated Tyson, hardly recognizable as the self-styled "baddest man on the planet," just sat and listened, passivity written across his face.

Immediately prior to arguably the most impressive win of Tyson's career, a 91-second expulsion of Michael Spinks, Cayton was served a lawsuit notifying him that Tyson no longer wanted him. King moved in, encircling Tyson with an entourage that bore comparison with a secret police force. A street brawl with a former opponent followed by another auto incident and a frenetic scene at his home residence served notice that the wealth, the fame, and the other trappings of celebrity may have affected his judgement. "Is Mike Tyson out of control?" whispered the media. In one stormy month in late 1988, Givens filed a $125 million libel suit, Tyson fired his longtime trainer Kevin Rooney, Sandra Miller sued Tyson, claiming he fondled her in a nightclub, and Lori Davis filed a $1 million suit against Tyson, alleging he grabbed her buttocks. The whisper became a shout.

Tyson's miscellany of misdemeanors continued throughout 1989, a year in which he fought only twice. Returning to the ring in February, 1990, Tyson looked jaded and careless as he crumbled to his first professional defeat against 42–1 underdog Buster Douglas. And still the lawsuits continued to flow in: paternity suits, molestation allegations and, most damaging of all, a rape accusation. Convicted on four counts of rape, confinement and two counts of criminal deviate conduct, Tyson was sentenced to ten years in prison and fined $30,000. Unrepentant, Tyson refused to admit guilt, despite the possibility of early release. During his imprisonment, news of Tyson continued to fascinate: a conversion to Islam, a newfound zeal for the writings of Mao, Lenin, and Machiavelli, and a penchant for tattoos all stirred interest.

With four of his peak boxing years (when aged 25–29) relinquished to prison, Tyson came back with a sequence of quick wins (all inside three rounds), the fourth of which brought him the WBA title. Then, the two Holyfield defeats, the second of which brought Tyson even more infamy. Ordered to pay a $3 million fine, Tyson was prevented from boxing by the Nevada State Athletic Commission. The question of whether Tyson was out of control satisfactorily answered, another question over his sanity was raised.

While outsiders had often criticized King, Tyson himself stood by him until he had occasion to reflect on why he was not a rich man. Faced with a bill for unpaid taxes, Tyson broke with King and started legal proceedings against not only him, but his two confederates, Rory Holloway and John Horne. In 1999, when allowed to fight again, Tyson campaigned in Europe as well as in the USA, but without ever convincing anyone that he could muster the venom that he had in the late 1980s. A month shy of the tenth anniversary of the Douglas fight, he knocked out the nondescript English fighter Julius Francis in two rounds.

The world watched the decline of a once formidable fighter. But it watched avidly. So much so that his eventual title fight against Lennox Lewis became the richest fight in history, earning each boxer $17.5 million plus ancillary payments. Even that fight was laced with controversy, being postponed because of Tyson's erratic conduct at a press conference. The fight itself provided unequivocal evidence of Tyson's athletic bankruptcy. Within months of the fight, his financial bankruptcy also became evident. After a professional boxing career in which he had earned close on a half-billion dollars, Tyson was broke.

And still we are fascinated. Will he make more remarks about wanting to eat his opponents' babies or make them his girl-friends or needing to conquer their souls? Will he molest any more young women, father any more illegitimate children, strike anybody who interferes with his privacy? Will he acquire any more tattoos, pet tigers, mansions, cars, wives? Will he be remembered?

The answer to the final question is yes*. The * will carry the footnote that "remembered" when applied to athletes usually means that their heroic deeds and great accomplishments in, and in some circumstances out of, competition are brought back into people's thoughts long after their career or life is over. It carries the connotation of fondness and respect. Tyson will stay in the memory, but for different reasons. Long before the end of his ring career, writers and artists were reflecting on his status, impact and relevance. Director Uli Edel's HBO biopic *Tyson* was made in 1995, which was about the mid-point of his boxing career. José Torres' biography was published in 1989, before the crucial Douglas defeat. It was followed two years later by the more detailed and analytical account by Illingworth, a later edition of which included an epilogue on Tyson's rape trial.

These and the several other high-quality chronicles of Tyson's life will be followed, almost certainly, by reflective appraisals, such as the one you are now reading. Ali finished boxing in 1981, yet the most illuminating explorations of him did not arrive for years, with books by Thomas Hauser in 1997, David Remnick in 1998, Gerald Early in 1998, Mike Marqusee in 1999 and Charles Lemert in 2004. Tyson may not inspire a similar industry of publications, but he will probably be considered for years to come and he will surely be remembered. All of which leaves me with a final question: how?

––––––––– fourteen –––––––––

YOU'D STILL LOOK AT ME
AS A SCUMBAG

"Boxing is not an expression of ghetto criminality or primitive aggression or some innate human propensity for violence," wrote Mike Marqusee in his *Redemption Song: Muhammad Ali and the spirit of the sixties*. "Though when a Mike Tyson comes along, it is all too easy to paint it in those colors" (p. 15). Marqusee is far from the only writer to freight Tyson with responsibility for all manner of wrongdoing, in this case for defiling what the writer calls "the culture of boxing." Other commentators have pictured Tyson leaving behind a more expensive legacy.

"What the public career of Mike Tyson has cost black Americans is incalculable," adjudged John Hoberman in his book *Darwin's Athletes: How sport has damaged black America and preserved the myth of race*. "But, it is reasonable to assume that his well-publicized brutalities in and out of the ring have helped to preserve pseudo-evolutionary fantasies about black ferocity that are still of commercial value to fight promoters and their business partners in the media" (p. 209).

In common with other writers, Hoberman visualizes the development of American society as theater. "This Darwinian drama has been kept alive by black athleticism and by black prizefighters in particular." Charles Darwin's theory of natural selection explained evolution as a struggle for survival, those creatures best suited to adapt to the environment enduring, while the weakest perished. The theory has been used, perversely, to justify racism, whites flourishing because of their intelligence, blacks surviving on account of their physicality.

Hoberman believes that the idea of black "supermuscularity" is an old and sturdy one, dating back to slave times. Whites have imagined blacks as oversexed brutes possessed of great physical strength but little intellect. While the idea has mutated over the centuries, the essence of it remained well into the twentieth century. It was a convenient image that served to legitimize all manner of inequality, exploitation and downright oppression.

The presence, albeit an imaginary presence, of sexually promiscuous black men, their physical strength in inverse proportion to their mental strength, was a threatening one; and one that gave rise to violent responses. The wave of public lynching in the aftermath of slavery and the torture of African American men was one response to the image. More recent episodes revisited earlier in this book suggest that violence against black people has abated but not disappeared.

In Hoberman's view, there is a composite black masculine type that threatens, offends, disgusts, and continues to haunt white society – the bad nigga. The most aggressive or radical rappers brag about both their sexual prowess and violent proclivities and claim respect for both. Black athletes haven't been demonized like rap artists, though, in many ways, they've presented a comparable image based on physicality and aggression. They've been admired, occasionally revered for their physical abilities. But it's only a form of entrapment: glorifying black people for their physical deeds is tantamount to locking them in a gilded cage from where they can do nothing to affect the overall condition of blacks, which has improved only marginally since civil rights in the 1960s.

Stop reading for ten seconds and think of five African American men who have earned widespread social approval over the past fifty years. Martin Luther King will be on every reader's list, Colin Powell on most. Muhammad Ali will feature prominently with Michael Jordan, and possibly Arthur Ashe. Stretch back a little further and several readers might include Jackie Robinson, Jesse Owens, and Joe Louis. The sportsmen have ridden into our consciousness and they remain there not simply because of their indisputably great athletic achievements, but because they were and are dramatic and celebrated representatives of blackness. They were entertainers too. Whether running, jumping, volleying, left-hooking, or hitting homeruns, they were using their bodies to amuse onlookers.

Being impressed by someone's physical performances doesn't necessarily mean you change your overall perception of either that athlete or the ethnic collectivity with which he is associated. "The only difference between the black man shining shoes in the ghetto and the champion black sprinter is that the shoe shine man is a nigger, while the sprinter is a fast nigger," as Harry Edwards memorably observed in his *The Revolt of the Black Athlete* (p. 20).

In the 1930s, Joe Louis was famously described as being "a credit to his race," meaning that he had humility to burn. Deeply submissive, Louis was commended for knowing his rightful place in the order of things. But there was another reason he brought credit to his race. In separate biographical accounts, Richard Bak and Chris Mead recount how he was regarded as something of a specimen, a savage brute, "not quite human . . . out of the African jungle." Jay Coakley collects a few other choice descriptions of Louis in his *Sports in Society: Issue and controversies*: "a magnificent animal . . . all instinct" who "would never do a lick of work he could escape" (p. 290).

Perhaps the reason he's remembered so fondly is that Louis was a perfect living stereotype of the black man: animalistic in his physical capability, yet slavelike in his subservience. And for this, he was regarded as a good representative of African Americans.

Tyson has also been a good representative, or at least a serviceable one. Five decades after Louis, he issued a reminder that black people still harbored inhuman tendencies and retained the capability for acts of wanton savagery. No amount of social reform could alter that. Louis lived in an era when any sign of self-assurance was read as insolence and, as such, was subject to punishment. He was careful never to appear too satisfied with himself for fear of being called uppity. His survival depended on it. By Tyson's time, civil rights had swept away the restraints and, though he rarely issued direct political challenges, Tyson's entire life was a provocation. Maybe Louis would have been like this too – given the chance.

Tyson turned suspicions into self-evident facts. In this sense, Marqusee was right to visualize Tyson as someone who portrayed a "primitive aggression or some innate propensity for violence." As was Hoberman to argue that he sustained age-old ideas about black ferocity, ideas that were made flesh by any number of promoters, managers and tv executives who could exploit them. But was it Tyson or the *representations* of Tyson that supported and extended the ideas?

For more than a hundred years, boxing has, as Petrine Archer-Straw puts it, "provided an arena in which the myth of black savagery could be explored and confirmed and even supported" (p. 46). Archer-Straw's book *Negrophilia: Avant-garde Paris and black culture in the 1920s* explores the French's often uncomfortable embrace of black people: they loved them for their uninhibited primitiveness, their oneness with nature and their defiance of the rationalism that characterized Western Europe.

Blacks' position outside the moral boundaries of civilized society gave them access to a more natural order. As such, they enjoyed a special status, especially among the artistic innovators known as the avant-garde. Mythologizing blacks and the culture they were supposed to embody was questionable, if functional: it credited black culture for its primitivism, while creating a collective Other, a repository of inferior values that affirmed whites' superiority. This was an entirely one-sided process: it was, as Archer-Straw puts it, "a way for Europeans to project their fear of difference onto other races."

Black people, whether fighters, artists, musicians, artisans, or whatever, were always subject to scrutiny in the early twentieth century. Debates about race, evolution, slavery, intelligence, the Noble Savage, and Manifest Destiny ensured a scientific as well as popular preoccupation with black people. This was not just a case of observing the way blacks looked and behaved: the real issue was imagining *why* they were so strikingly different. This process of what Archer-Straw and other writers call "othering" operated through "the use of a powerful network of images and symbols that, by association, could conjure up deep-seated fears, the deepest of which were regression and loss of racial purity . . . Spurious symbolism continued to link 'blackness' with sin, death, ignorance, sexual deviancy, virility, fecundity – traits that at the same time validated 'whiteness' as pure, chastened and enlightened" (pp. 25–6).

Think about those traits again: sin, death, ignorance, sexual deviancy, virility, fecundity. Tyson embraced all six of them. A miscreant who talked of death and of inflicting pain, a man without formal education whose words sometimes betrayed this, a violator of sexual standards who committed the ultimate sexual transgression and who continually boasted of his own "penis-centeredness." Tyson would have fitted perfectly in the early twentieth century. As things were, there was another black heavyweight who was just right. Jack Johnson was born in 1878, fourteen years after the Emancipation, beginning his professional prize-fighting career in 1897.

In 1908, when Johnson challenged Tommy Burns for the heavyweight championship of the world, he carried to the ring far more than his gloves and gear: he carried the hopes of black America and the fears of white America. As Al-Tony Gillmore wrote in his 1975 book evocatively entitled *Bad Nigger! The national impact of Jack Johnson*: "When Johnson battered a white man to his knees, he was a symbolic black man taking out his revenge on all whites for a lifetime of indignities." Johnson did indeed batter Burns. So much so that the police had to enter the ring in the fourteenth round to rescue the outclassed champion. In a memorable description of the action, Jack London wrote: "Plucky but absolutely helpless, the white man seemed to be a victim of a playful Ethiopian who did just as he would."

The myths that grew around Johnson were much larger than the man himself. One of them concerned the protection he was afforded by the Almighty. In 1912, he tried to board the liner *Titanic*, but was stopped. No black passengers were allowed on the ill-fated voyage. Some believed the disaster was divine retribution. Others thought that Johnson had been specifically spared. Either way, Johnson's outrageous fortune seemed like evidence of his special status rather than of the more prosaic workings of racism.

———

From the word "go," Tyson was the subject of a myth and, in a way, the rest of his life was like a myth, an epic construction based on selective perception, expedience, well-filtered information combined with drama, folklore, and recrudescent ideas about race. None of this denies that Tyson did the deeds: he was the guy who groped, punched, and molested. Yet there is at least a chance that behavior that would have gone unpunished, perhaps unnoticed, were it performed by someone else became the raw material of scandal, infamy, and opprobrium when Tyson was involved.

Hoberman acknowledges that virtually everything Tyson did, whether in or out of competition, was well publicized. After a certain point, the publicity itself became self-perpetuating. Stories about Tyson circulated even when he was imprisoned. As the *Pittsburgh Courier* writer Barry Cooper wrote in his 1996 story "These days, Tyson's a marked man": "You can expect a lawsuit if Tyson as much as sneezes on the wrong person" (April 5, p. A9).

On the account I've presented, Tyson, having realized that his athletic powers were receding almost as quickly as his money, began to play up to the role reserved for him. He'd always fed the media in one way or another; he just began to feed them the victuals they craved. The symmetry was perfect. Here was Tyson, primal, crude, and unburdened by the requirements of civilized culture. Of course, Tyson was boorish, irresponsible, and perhaps unforgivably lecherous. But did he make us privy to his world, or did we just pry? Or, in a celebrity-obsessed age in which fame brings instant surveillance, is there much of a difference?

In his preview of the Lewis fight in 2002, *Sports Illustrated*'s Richard Hoffer mused about the colossal purse (a combined $35 million minimum): "Is there curiosity as to who the better heavyweight is? Some, but not enough to justify the magnitude of interest in the fight" (vol. 96, no. 21, May 20). The real curiosity centered on Tyson, more specifically what kind of deviant behavior he would serve up. It's impossible to imagine another athlete, at any time in history, who drew interest on the offchance that he or she would lose it. I'm not forgetting John McEnroe. Curiosity in Tyson was a kind of voyeuristic, peepshow inquisitiveness: the possibility of glimpsing or of sharing in something dark and forbidden.

Tyson himself felt manacled by expectations. His fitful outpourings, his abuse of interviewers and his coarseness owed more to role-playing than to disposition. As an example and a possible rationalization, Tyson offered his version of the time he saw Lewis in the Crustacean restaurant in Beverly Hills. At the behest of Monica, to whom he was married at the time, he approached Lewis' table and greeted him courteously, only to be met with silence. "He looked at me and stared me down like a damn dog," said Tyson. "Made me a punk. You see, I want to be a nice guy, but my wife, she hands him my nuts. Takes my balls away from me."

Asked by a female reporter in the lead-up to the Lewis fight whether he could ever "be a positive story," Tyson gave a surprisingly self-reflective, if idiomatic answer: "No, no way. Can't come across. That's why I won't talk, be nice to you and [I] talk about fornicating with you, then you to suck my dick. If I was to be eloquent with you, you'd still look at me as a scumbag. It won't work; you have your perception of me. You've lifted your perception of me from the cameras, from the news. So, I give you what you want." *I give you what you want.*

What we wanted was not a Tyson neutered, declawed, domesticated, or caged, but one whose very presence signaled danger. A Tyson so antithetical to the requirements of civilized society, so repugnant to cultivated tastes, so offensive to moral principles that there was no room for argument – he was outside the frontiers of normality. He was about as unlike us as it was possible to be. And he was black. And so were several million others.

Dwayne Redding argued that boxing represents "the utter core of man's violent nature and Americans' appetite for blood, sweat and tears" and that Tyson satisfied that appetite in the rawest, most unrefined way. In his 2002 *Michigan Citizen* story "Defending Mike Tyson," Redding issued a rebuttal to those who had attacked Tyson (April 18). Despite being boxing's dominant attraction, Tyson was never protected by the sport's governing federations, nor by Don King. When Ray Lewis, the NFL linebacker, was acquitted of two counts of murder, his club, the Baltimore Ravens, supported him. Tyson, in his moments of trouble, found himself dispossessed of friends or supporters. Redding discerned hypocrisy in boxing's "Oh my God, he's done it again!" reactions to Tyson's eruptions.

The gist of Redding's argument is that Tyson was attractive as a package. His tenacious style in the ring was the reason why everyone became mesmerized by him in the first place. To expect him to transform into someone else when he stepped out of the ring was like "Michael Jackson without the nose job, Mariah Carey without the hip-hop beats and George Bush without the ranch" (p. A7).

Redding closes his story with the reminder to his readership: "The only reason why Mike Tyson exists is because of you." And, while he doesn't expand on this, let's suppose. Everything Tyson said or did was an exploration: he took us to places we only suspected existed, made us parties to events we only ever imagined took place. Like uninvited guests, we were willing participants. As Teddy Atlas once told David Remnick of Tyson-watchers: "They want to see something dark . . . want to feel close to it and in on it, but, of course, only from the distance of their suburban homes" (in "Kid Dynamite blows up").

There was an urban fable on the 1990s that contrived to illustrate whites' fascination with black culture, its art, its music, its literature, and, by implication, Tyson. It bears resemblance to a scene in Barbet Shroeder's 1995 remake of the 1947 Victor Mature/Richard Widmark movie *Kiss of Death*. In the later version, Little Junior, played by Nicolas Cage, in preparing to beat an enemy to death, pulls on protective clothing to keep the blood off his white tracksuit. The scene offers a way of understanding the kind of fascination Tyson held. Imagine that, every time they see, read, or hear about another episode of the psychodrama, it's like whites donning the protective clothing. They can wander into the ghettos where they confront black people still angry at whites' historical sins. The residents then symbolically exact their revenge by urinating over the well-protected whites. Cowering under the cataracts, whites can see and smell the urine. After, they return to the safety of their homes, shed the wax clothes, shower and discuss the gruesome experience.

Tyson provided a way of sharing the black experience. He dramatized it in the kind of way that made it available, accessible, and safe. Middle America could venture into the perverse underside of black life without any compromise of their personal security. Watching Tyson – and I mean the whole double-decade narrative – allowed the observer to engage with a world that was at once touchably near yet as distant as another planet.

The most instructive part of this surveillance was the valuable insight that there was still a distance. It was irreducible. Tyson was the living evidence. And, while he never chose that status, it was thrust on him. On his own account, he became exhausted by the constant and eventually inescapable denunciations. He did nothing to disable them, of course. And, when the circumstances called for it, he actually pandered to the media. "I'm a monster," he claimed in 1996.

Tyson has been assailed on all sides, criticized for just about everything he did. Yet few, if any, have taken him to task for playing *Tyson*, a role that had independent origins. Reared in the backwaters of Catskill, the uneducated Tyson's tutors were trainers and boxers. A millionaire by his 21st birthday, Tyson never disguised the residual presence of the streets; it was still right there, every time he went near a camera or a mic.

After his release from prison in 1995, it seems Tyson became almost too comfortable with the bestial image that has been set aside for him. Maybe he could have resisted it more effectively than he did. The initial reason for playing up to it was almost surely the lucre that lay ahead; in which case the motivation was either greed or necessity or the persuasive reasoning of others whispering that play-acting had been a tradition in heavyweight boxing since the days of Jack Johnson.

Yet Tyson became less comfortable and eventually tormented. By this time, however, the case had hardened around him and he had little room to maneuver. Could he have rehabilitated himself, as Ali did? No. Could he have downplayed the monstrous part? Possibly. He would still have been remembered. But, as a champion who peaked too soon, he couldn't play the celebrity game, burned out by the time he was 24 and, like many other boxers, ended up in jail. Retrospectively, people would have regarded Tyson as a sad case. Sad, as in deserving of others' pity, compassion, or charity. It's still conceivable that, in the years ahead, Tyson will cut a sad figure; though his vilification of the media and anyone who believes it makes this doubtful.

———

One more scenario is worth considering. The one that introduced this book. 1982: Teddy Atlas, on discovering Tyson's misadventures with his sister-in-law, hunts down Tyson with the wrath of Achilles. He points a loaded .38 at Tyson's head. In reality, Tyson showed just enough contriteness to defuse Atlas' anger. If he hadn't, the world outside upstate New York would never have known of Tyson.

America might have created another beast, another psycho-celebrity, another creature about which it could tremble. Someone or something that would strip away the veneer of civility and reveal themselves as the true essence of black masculinity. In the event, it was Tyson who embodied primal African America, and it was he who took the plaudits and bore the burdens. In his absence, there would have been a variety of creatures surfacing from the black lagoon. Cold-eyed killers who terrorized and unsettled the innocent; feral kids who grew into gangstas and obeyed only their own laws of ruthless survival; rappers, with neither conscience nor scruples; unruly athletes who thought the world was theirs to do with as they pleased; wild Hollywood types with money to burn and no sense of value. All, in some way, threatened and comforted. The comfort was that they were different.

Tyson was absolutely, certainly, undeniably different. He was bestial, horrific, repugnant, savage, beyond every known pale. He was to be feared, loathed, and rejected. And, yet, for two decades, we – and I mean everyone – remained in his thrall. The source of the fascination was, of course, the very quality that repulsed us. He was an ever-present reminder of difference. Tyson was the embodiment of black America, a monumental physical force which, left unfettered, would wreak havoc, disregarding all known rules of civilization and reverting to some atavistic state that generations of white domination had managed to submerge. Tyson terrified America as he gave the real reasons why racial equality was only an ideal, never a reality. It never would be. Tyson showed this. And, in this sense, he provided the comfort. No amount of social engineering could ever put right what nature had intended to be wrong.

BIBLIOGRAPHY

Archer-Straw, Petrine (2000) *Negrophilia: Avant-garde Paris and black culture in the 1920s*. London: Thames & Hudson.

Bak, Richard (1998) *Joe Louis: The great black hope*. New York: Da Capo.

Benedict, Jeff (1997) *Public Heroes, Private Felons: Athletes and crimes against women*. Boston: Northeastern University Press.

Bennett, Lerone Jr (1975) *The Shaping of Black America: The struggles and triumphs of African Americans, 1619 to the 1990s*. New York: Penguin Books.

Berger, Phil (1989) *Blood Season: Tyson and the world of boxing*. New York: William Morrow & Co.

Berger, Phil (1999) "Split decision." *Sport*, vol. 90, no. 7 (July).

Bernard-Donals, M. (1994) "Jazz, rock'n'roll, rap and politics." *Journal of Popular Culture*, vol. 28, no. 2 (fall), pp. 4–16.

Bose, Mihir (1999) *Sports Babylon*. London: Carlton Books.

Brady, Jim (2002) *Boxing Confidential*. Lytham, England: Milo Books.

Callahan, Tom (1991) "Iron Mike and the allure of the 'manly art,'" pp. 233–41 in Bill Hughes and Patrick King (eds), *Come Out Writing: A boxing anthology*. London: Queen Anne Press.

Chaisson, Reba L. (2000) *For Entertainment Purposes Only? An analysis of the struggle to control filmic representations*. Lanham, MD: Lexington Books.

Coakley, Jay (2003) *Sports in Society: Issues and controversies*, 8th edition. Dubuque, IA: McGraw Hill.

Early, Gerald (1996) "Mike's brilliant career." *Transition*, vol. 71 (fall). Reprinted: pp. 197–208 in Daniel O'Connor (ed.) (2002), *Iron Mike: A Mike Tyson reader*. New York: Thunder's Mouth Press.

Early, Gerald (1998) *I'm a Little Special: A Muhammad Ali reader*. London: Yellow Jersey Press.

Bibliography

Edwards, Harry (1970) *The Revolt of the Black Athlete*. New York: Free Press.

Frazier, Joe with Berger, Phil (1996) *Smoking Joe: The autobiography*. London: Robson Books.

Gillmore, Al-Tony (1975) *Bad Nigger! The national impact of Jack Johnson*. New York: National University Press.

Glasgow, Douglas G. (1980) *The Black Underclass: Poverty, unemployment, and entrapment of ghetto youth*. San Francisco: Jossey-Bass.

Gonzalez, Rudy and Feigenbaum, Martin A. (2002) "From the inner ring," pp. 105–32 in Daniel O'Connor (ed.), *Iron Mike: A Mike Tyson reader*. New York: Thunder's Mouth Press.

Gorn, Elliott (1995) *Muhammad Ali: The people's champ*. Chicago: University of Illinois Press.

Gresson, Aaron David III (1995) *The Recovery of Race in America*. Minnesota, MN: University of Minneapolis Press.

Hauser, Thomas (1997) *Muhammad Ali: His life and times*. London: Pan Books.

Heller, Peter (1990) *Tyson: In and out of the ring*. London: Pan. 2nd edition published (1995) as *Bad Intentions: The Mike Tyson story*. New York: Da Capo.

Hoberman, John (1997) *Darwin's Athletes: How sport has damaged black America and preserved the myth of race*. New York: Houghton Mifflin.

Hoffer, Richard (1998) *A Savage Business: The comeback and comedown of Mike Tyson*. New York: Simon & Schuster.

Hoffer, Richard (2002) "All the rage." *Sports Illustrated*, vol. 96, no. 21 (May 20), pp. 34–41.

Illingworth, Montieth (1992) *Mike Tyson: Money, myth and betrayal*. London: Grafton.

Kerner, Otto (1968) *Report of the National Advisory Commission on Civil Disorders*. New York: Bantam Books.

Kunjufu, Jawanza (1990) *Countering the Conspiracy to Destroy Black Boys*. New York: African American Images.

Lemert, Charles (2004) *Muhammad Ali: Trickster in the culture of irony*. Oxford: Polity.

Lule, Jack (1995) "The rape of Mike Tyson: Race, the press and symbolic types." *Critical Studies in Mass Communication*, vol. 12, no. 2, pp. 176–94.

Lupica, Mike (1991) "The sporting life." *Esquire*, part 115 (March 3), pp. 52–4.

Marqusee, Mike (1999) *Redemption Song: Muhammad Ali and the spirit of the sixties*. London: Verso.

McIlvanney, Hugh (1996) *McIlvanney on Boxing.* Edinburgh: Mainstream.

McRae, Donald (1996) *Dark Trade: Lost in boxing.* Edinburgh: Mainstream.

Mead, Chris (1995) *Champion Joe Louis: A biography.* London: Robson Books.

Myrdal, Gunnar (1995) *An American Dilemma: The Negro problem and modern democracy.* New York: Transaction; originally Harper & Row, 1944.

Nederveen Pieterse, Jan (1992) *White on Black: Images of Africa and blacks in Western popular culture.* New Haven: Yale University Press.

Newfield, Jack (1995) *Only in America: The life and crimes of Don King.* New York: William Morrow & Co.

O'Connor, Daniel (ed.) (2002) *Iron Mike: A Mike Tyson reader.* New York: Thunder's Mouth Press.

Patterson, David (1997) "The errand of a fool: Father forgive them." *New York Amsterdam News,* vol. 88, no. 35, p. 12.

Philips, Chuck (2002) "Who killed Tupac Shakur?" *Los Angeles Times,* September 6, pp. A1–A27, and September 7, pp. A1–A15.

Pinkney, Alphonso (1993) *Black Americans,* 4th edition. Englewood Cliffs, NJ: Prentice Hall.

Ramos, Bobby (2002) "Don King on Mike Tyson – unplugged." *New York Beacon,* vol. 9, no. 24 (June 19).

Regen, Richard (1990) "Neither does King." *Interview,* vol. 20 (October 10), pp. 104, 115–18.

Remnick, David (1998) *King of the World: Muhammad Ali and the rise of an American hero.* London: Picador.

Remnick, David (1999) "Kid Dynamite blows up," pp. 283–96 in W. C. Heinz and Nathan Ward (eds), *The Book of Boxing.* Kingston, NY: Total/Sports Illustrated.

Remnick, David (2000) "Interview: Teddy Atlas – the man in the corner." *Independent,* November 19, pp. 33–41.

Roberts, Randy and Garrison, J. Gregory (2000) *Heavy Justice: The trial of Mike Tyson.* Fayetteville: University of Arkansas Press.

Samuels, David (1991) "The rap on rap." *The New Republic,* November 11, pp. 24–9.

Sherman, Len (1998) *Big League, Big Time: The birth of the Arizona Diamondbacks, the billion-dollar business of sports, and the power of the media in America.* New York: Pocket Books.

Sloop, John M. (1997) "Mike Tyson and the perils of discursive constraints: Boxing, race, and the assumption of guilt," pp. 102–22 in

Bibliography

Aaron Baker and Todd Boyd (eds), *Out of Bounds: Sports, media, and the politics of identity*. Bloomington: University of Indiana Press.

Steptoe, Sonja (1992) "A damnable defense." *Sports Illustrated*, vol. 76, no. 7 (February 24), p. 92.

Tapper, Jake (1998) "Neighborhood bully." *Washington City Paper*, December 11, pp. 1–29.

Taraborelli, Randy (1991) *Michael Jackson: The magic and the madness*. New York: Birch Lane Press.

Torres, José (1989) *Fire and Fear: The inside story of Mike Tyson*. New York: Warner Books.

Tosches, Nick (2000) *Night Train: The Sonny Liston story*. London: Hamish Hamilton.

White, Aaronette M. (1999) "Talking feminist, talking Black: Micromobilization processes in a collective protest against rape." *Gender and Society*, vol. 13, no. 1, pp. 77–100.

Williams, Juan (1987) *Eyes on the Prize: America's civil rights years, 1954–1965*. New York: Viking Penguin.

Wright, Robert (1995) "Tyson vs. Simpson." *The New Republic*, vol. 212 (April 17), p. 4.

INDEX

Note: page references in *italics* denote illustrations; MT indicates Mike Tyson

Bad Boy Entertainment 104
Baime, Albert 54–6, 59
Bak, Richard 247
Baltimore Afro-American 196
Baltimore Ravens 252
Baransky, Matt 238
Barry, Marion 124, 135
BBC 169
Bega, Leslie 180
Benedict, Jeff 57, 113, 121,
    203–4, 205
Benitez, Wilfred 142, 222
Bennet, Ernie 239
Bennett, Lerone, Jr 212
Bennett, Willie 153–4
Berbick, Trevor 198–9, 202
Berger, Phil 26, 137, 174, 175,
    209, 227, 229
Bernard-Donals, M. 106
Best Damn Sports Show Period
    (tv program) 16
bestiality: black people 68,
    80–1, 135, 248–9; boxers 229,
    247; *see also* Tyson, Mike
Biggs, Tyrell 209
black culture 80, 103, 105–6,
    226, 248, 252–3
Black Panther Party 102–3
black people 27, 151; ambition
    162–3 (*see also* Givens, Robin;
    King, Don); and black boxers
    68–9, 225; legacy of black
    athleticism for 245–8; MT's
    increasing alignment with
    137, 146, 151, 175, 182–4, 187,
    211–12; O. J. Simpson case
    88–90; opinion of MT's rape
    trial 124; Otherness 17–18,
    106, 248–9; reaction to MT's

punishment for ear-biting
    incident 83; response to
    MT's release from prison 94,
    196; white people's view of
    4–5, 16–17, 61, 68, 69–70,
    80–1, 88–9, 134–6, 156–7, 246,
    248–9, 254–5; *see also*
    bestiality; racial mythology;
    racial stereotypes
black success, attitudes to 4,
    124, 146, 156–7, 183, 186,
    189–90, 211
black underclass 11–12, 105,
    197, 226, 231–6
black women 124–6, 196; *see
    also* racial stereotypes
Blade Runner (movie) 13
Bloods gang 103–4, 105
Bonds, Barry 208
Boomerang (movie) 179
Borges, Ron 51
Bose, Mihir 205
Boston Globe 51
Boswell, Tom 128
Botha, Francois 44–6, 47, 58,
    98
Bowe, Riddick 62, 66, 92, 95–7
boxing 235, 245, 251–2;
    connection with organized
    crime 68, 168–9, 216; Don
    King's career as promoter
    166–71; heavyweight
    champion industry 206–12;
    methods 215; reaction to ear-
    biting incident 81–3; sadism
    227–8; *see also* International
    Boxing Federation; World
    Boxing Association; World
    Boxing Council

boxing career of MT 5, 24–8,
20; introduction to boxing
235–8; early training in
Catskill Mountains 1–3, 11,
103, 213–20, 236, 238–40, 241;
becomes professional boxer
221–26; (1986–1987) 11, 14,
165, 191, 198–203, 200, 205–6,
226–30, 241; (1988–1990) 10,
144–51, 170–6, 182;
(1990–1992) 10, 113, 116–17,
136–43, 157–61, 242; on
release from prison (1995)
91–2, 94–8; (1996–1998),
including ear-biting incident
and suspension from boxing
9, 26, 60–7, 70–86, 76, 100–1,
242–3; (1999–2001) 44–6, 48,
51– 4, 58–9, 243; (2002–2003),
including defeat by Lennox
Lewis 8–9, 13–16, 18–19, 27,
29–34, 41–2, 243; (2004) 6
Boxing Illustrated 149
Boyd, Angela 113
Boyz N the Hood (movie) 103
Brady, James 171
Brady, Jim 83, 168, 170, 174
Brawley, Tawana, case 11,
191–6, 224; MT's
involvement 191, 192–3, 195,
211–12
Bright, Jay 182
Brooke, Edward W. 24
Brown, James 37, 67, 195
Brown, Oliver 21–2
*Brown vs. Board of Education of
Topeka, Kansas* (1954) 21–2
Brownsville, Brooklyn, MT's
early life 29, 218–19, 233–5

Bruno, Frank 10, 95, 97, 98,
144, 146–7, 150, 169
Burns, Tommy 249
Bush, George 132, 135, 224,
252
Business Wire 126–7
Butts, Chevelle 43–4
Byrd, Eugene 36

Caesars Palace, Las Vegas 113,
207
Callahan, Tom 121, 190
Cannon, Jimmy 146, 147
Cantona, Eric 77
Carbo, Frankie, aka "The Gray"
68
Carey, Mariah 252
Carlos, John 168
Catskill Mountains boxers'
training camp 1–3, 11, 103,
213–20, 236, 238–40, 241
Cayton, Bill 147, 148, 166, 170,
171, 172, 173, 174, 175, 176,
178, 184, 185, 210–12, 218,
220, 221–2, 225, 226, 227, 229,
230, 240, 242
celebrities 91, 185; MT as 3–5,
6–7, 19, 25, 27, 92, 108–13,
145, 181, 229, 241, 250–5;
Robin Givens as 164
celebrity culture 7, 108–11, 130,
165, 181
Central Park jogger incident
10, 151–3, 154, 155, 156
Chaisson, Reba L. 223
Chavez, Julio Cesar 189
Chavis, Benjamin 135
Chicago Sun-Times 183
Citibank 171